Trent,

It was great having you in my group this week. I hope you will remember all you have learned here at EFY and most especially remember the spirit you have felt. Continue your commitments to read, pray and serve, and the Lord will bless you. Always remember who you are and to Choose the Right!

Enjoy these talks. The gospel is true!

Take Care

Love your counselor & friend,

Johnny Howard

SERVING WITH STRENGTH
THROUGHOUT THE WORLD

**FAVORITE TALKS FROM
ESPECIALLY FOR YOUTH**

Deseret Book Company
Salt Lake City, Utah

Chapter 4 "Feeling Great Every Day" by Diane Bills is taken from the talk tape "The Secret to Loving Yourself" by Diane Bills, produced and published by Covenant Communications, Inc. and is used by permission.

The Poem "Pretty Good" on pages 77–78 is used by permission of THE OSGOOD FILE, CBS Radio Network, Copyrighted by CBS Inc., all rights reserved.

© 1994 Deseret Book Company

Library of Congress Cataloging-in-Publication Data

Serving with strength throughout the world : favorite talks from
　　Especially for youth.
　　　　　p.　　cm.
　　Includes index.
　　ISBN 0–87579–836–5
　　1. Youth—Religious life. 2. Youth—Conduct of life. 3. Church
of Jesus Christ of Latter-day Saints—Doctrines—Juvenile
literature. 4. Mormon Church—Doctrines—Juvenile literature.
I. Deseret Book Company.
BX8643.Y6S47　1993
248.8'3—dc20　　　　　　　　　　　　　　　　　　93–50934
　　　　　　　　　　　　　　　　　　　　　　　　　　CIP
　　　　　　　　　　　　　　　　　　　　　　　　　　AC

Printed in the United States of America
10　9　　8　　7　　6　　5　　4　　3　　2　　1

CONTENTS

1

IS THERE LIFE BEFORE SIXTEEN?
ON YOUR MARK, GET READY, GET SET, DATE!

MICHAEL W. ALLRED

The temple was crowded with Saints who were anxiously performing their ancestral duties. My dad was trying to instill confidence in me by assuring me that everything would be okay. I kept wondering if I had made the right choice. Just think, within minutes, I will be sealed for time and all eternity. Will she always love me? Am I really ready to be married? I've always thought about this day. I THINK I am positive I have made the right decision, but how can I really be sure?

I could feel my heart beating in my chest, and then she walked in. Now my heart was pounding even harder. I'm sure everyone could hear, but I didn't care. For some reason, now all I cared about was her.

The temple sealing room was not elaborately decorated. But it was beautiful with its lights, mirrors, and chandelier all reflecting a soft white light. As we knelt across the altar, I gazed into her beautiful eyes. In fact, her eyes were far more beautiful than any of the man-made accessories decorating the holy temple. I finally knew I was in love (Mike!!), and that this love would never end (Mike!!). We were destined to be the happiest couple of (Mike, hellooh, would you please stop daydreaming and answer the question!!).

Many of us dream about that awesome day we hope will one day come. You know, the day when you will be sealed for eternity. I would like to share some ideas that might be helpful as you prepare for your wedding day. But before we can get to the wedding day, there has to be some serious dating. And, for many of you, before the dating can begin, there has to be some serious waiting. To help make the waiting easier and the dating more beneficial and satisfying, this chapter will focus on four major concepts:

1. Understanding the big picture.
2. Developing desirable qualities.
3. Commitment to standards.
4. Dating with purpose.

To make these concepts easier to remember, I will title them: On your mark, get ready, get set, date.

On Your Mark (Understanding the big picture)

After returning from my mission, I began looking up old friends that I had not seen for two years. I went to the house of a friend who was already married and met his wife. I also learned that his wife's younger sister was staying with them. She was just my age and was gorgeous. I remember thinking that she might be "the one." In fact, I went home that night and actually prayed: "Please, Heavenly Father, bless her to be the one." But even as I was saying the prayer, I felt uncomfortable. Something was not right.

Perhaps you believe, as I used to, that there is one person out there that we are meant to be with. But President Spencer W. Kimball said the notion of "soul mates" is an illusion. He taught that "while every young man and young woman will seek with all diligence and prayerfulness to find a mate with whom life can be most compatible and beautiful, yet it is certain that almost any good man and any good woman can have happiness and a successful marriage if both are willing to pay the price" ("Oneness in Marriage," *Ensign,* Mar. 1977, p. 4). Elder Boyd K. Packer made a similar statement when he said, "You must do the choosing, rather than to seek for some one-and-only so-called soul mate, chosen for you by someone else and waiting for you. You are to do the choosing. You must be wise beyond your years and humbly prayerful unless you choose amiss" (*Eternal Love* [Salt Lake City: Deseret Book Co., 1973], p. 11).

That means that within the next ten years, most of you teenaged readers will be making one of the biggest decisions of not only your mortal life, but of eternity. The decision has not already been made. We are not in a giant game of hide-and-go-seek, trying to locate the soul that we made promises to in our premortal life. Instead, we are to prepare ourselves to be compatible with the one we will choose in this life, one we will agree to share eternity with. In the scriptures the Lord teaches us how to make good choices (see Moroni 7:10–17). He has given us the ability to choose good from evil. Because we each are free to choose, we need to decide very clearly what we are looking for.

This being the case, is there life before age sixteen? You bet there is! Now that we understand that we are in the process of making the choice, we need to begin preparing to be "wise beyond our years."

Get Ready (Developing desirable qualities)

Some young people wonder why we develop the desire to date before we are old enough to date. Maybe an example from sports will help. Many coaches feel the purpose of practice is to drill so much that in a game a player will not have to decide what to do. He or she will have been conditioned to simply react, instinctively, to any situation. The time for preparation is over when the game begins. By requiring us to wait until we are sixteen to date, maybe the Lord has blessed us with a great opportunity to think through our dating experience before we are actually in the situations. David O. McKay said: "The seeds of a happy married life are sown in youth. Happiness does not begin at the altar; it begins during the period of youth" (*True to the Faith*, comp. Llewelyn R. McKay [Salt Lake City: Bookcraft, 1966], pp. 317–18). Happiness in marriage begins when we start to develop Christlike qualities (see Alma 37:35–37).

Take out a sheet of paper and write down the top five qualities that you would like in a future mate. If you can't think of any, here are a few that I've heard frequently: Good looking, smart, spiritual, genuine, and rich. After you have made your list, then prioritize the qualities from most important to least important. You may even evaluate your list and decide that some of the attributes you originally thought were important, are not. For instance, good looking may not be as important as some other character trait. To ensure you will be worthy of someone like that, begin today to develop those same qualities. In other words, become the type of person you want to marry (see D&C 88:40). "Success in marriage depends not so much on *finding* the right person as on *being* the right person" (Lowell L. Bennion, *Looking Towards Marriage* [Salt Lake City: Deseret Book Co., 1973], p. 47).

One important point to remember is that friendship plays a vital role in successful marriages. Having friends and being a good friend to lots of people before you begin dating is a good way to prepare for marriage. "The number of friends (both male and female) has been found to be significant in relation to success in marriage . . . the person who is able to get along well with friends has acquired the behavior patterns which are also important in getting along well in marriage. In many ways marriage is a friendship" (Rex A. Skidmore and Anthon S. Cannon, *Building Your Marriage* [Salt Lake City: Deseret Book Co., 1964], pp. 73–74).

With these qualities in mind, do you see any reason to wait to start developing them? Is there life before sixteen? Sure. And if you use those early teenaged years to develop your personality and learn to get along with people, instead of worrying about dating, you'll be better prepared to date when it's time. With the amount of work some of us need to do, turning sixteen may happen too quickly.

Get Set (Commitment to standards)

Let's do some reasoning. If Satan has been hanging around the earth for more than six thousand years, and we've been hanging around for fewer than twenty, who do you think knows the most about temptation? I think you can probably figure that one out. Satan probably knows all about temptation—what works best and what doesn't. One of his most successful strategies for getting youth to fall into transgression is to persuade them to date at an early age— before they have learned to exercise good judgment or control their emotions or recognize all the dangers. Satan has also been successful in destroying young couples who have begun to go steady in their teens. Therefore, the Lord has told us through his servants, the prophets, to not date until we are sixteen, and then to avoid going steady. "If Satan can bring about his purposes and win over a person before marriage, he has gone a long way toward putting the fate of at least one future family 'in the bag' . . . He will not wait until you have entered marriage to begin that challenge" (*Achieving a Celestial Marriage* [pamphlet, 1976], p. 10). Satan is the master of deception and sin, and you can be sure he will use his best tactics on us.

David O. McKay said that going steady limits our opportunities to become acquainted with a broad range of people, and it also creates a distorted sense of familiarity or ownership (*Youth of the Noble Birthright* [Salt Lake City: Deseret Book Co., 1960], pp. 21–22). There are many sad examples of young people who have ignored the counsel of our leaders and who have learned by bitter experience the wisdom of the advice we have been given. Our prophets have been right all along. But still sometimes we don't understand. In those circumstances we need to exercise faith and accept that the prophets of God understand more than we do (see Isaiah 55:8–9).

Because not everyone believes in the same dating standards that you do, it might be helpful to arm yourself with some great comebacks to use when the pressure is on. Imagine you are asked to go steady. What do you say? Here are a few comebacks that I've thought up or borrowed to help out while you are developing your own:

I didn't know you were an isolationist.

I have too many friends of the opposite sex, and you might get jealous.

I like you too well to tie you down.

Comparison makes the heart grow fonder.

It's against my "word of wisdom."

Would we have a joint checking account?

Sure, as long as we can date whomever we want.

My dad said I can't.

Can we just say that we "used" to go steady?

NO!!

Here is another exercise that really helps: Take a sheet of paper and make a large "T" (for temple) on the paper. On one side of the paper write down the standards you must keep if you are to be worthy and prepared for the temple. On the other side, write down the things you must not do if you are to be ready for the temple. Put the list somewhere

where you can see it often. There is something more you might put on this chart. Make a heading called "specifics" under each list of standards. Then write down the specific things you will need to do or to avoid in order to keep the standards. Look at those areas where you know you are weak or vulnerable. All of us have things we need to work on, so don't be afraid to identify the work you need to do. Be honest with yourself. Then review your lists frequently and evaluate yourself. Keeping such a set of goals in front of you will help you get to the place you want to go—the temple (see example on page 11).

Is there life before sixteen? Yes! And it is during those years before we are sixteen, when we prepare ourselves socially and spiritually for the great experience of dating.

Date (Dating with purpose)

In the early years of dating, we often fail to plan meaningful activities, so we end up driving around, asking each other what we want to do. I feel sorry for the girl who is asked out on a date where all the boy wants to do is go over to her house and watch television. Can you imagine how such a couple would spend their evenings together, should they actually end up married to each other? If you plan imaginative dates that provide for a variety of activities you will get to know your date's personality, their ability to have fun, to relate to other people. Watching television ought to be the last choice. There are too many fun things to do.

We need to understand the purpose of dating. "You are sent to this earth not merely to have a good time or to satisfy urges or passions or desires. You are sent to this earth, not to ride a merry-go-round, airplanes, automobiles, and have what the world calls fun. You are sent to this world with a serious purpose . . . the matter of marriage" (Spencer W.

Kimball, "The Matter of Marriage" [Address given at Salt Lake Institute of Religion, 22 Oct. 1976], p. 2). Dating becomes the prelude to marriage. Therefore, if marriage is a major purpose of life then so is dating. But does this mean we can't have fun? I hope not!

Here are some suggestions on how to have fun and still accomplish a more serious purpose on a date. First of all, we need to have the Young Women's values and colors in mind. For those male gender readers, let's review a little. The Young Women's values and related colors are:

Faith (white)
Divine Nature (blue)
Individual Worth (red)
Knowledge (green)
Choice and Accountability (orange)
Good Works (yellow)
Integrity (purple)

What if, each time you were getting ready for a date, you were to choose one of these values to focus on? While getting dressed, you were to choose some piece of clothing that reminds you of that value. For example, if I wanted to emphasize "Good Works" and find out my date's attitude on that value, I might wear a yellow shirt and plan a date where we would wash my parents' cars or something like that. By doing so, I would stay focused, and I would find out how my date feels about doing good to others. Plus, washing cars can get crazy if you're willing to get a little wet.

I would like to share a quote with you. I have added the words in the brackets to show how the values we are talking about relate. "Associating with others under wholesome circumstances helps develop friendships and permits you to learn about qualities and characteristics in others [integrity and good works], to get to know them [knowledge], to have fun together [individual worth], to widen areas of choice [choice and accountability], to achieve a wider and wiser vision of what one may seek in an eternal companion [divine nature], and to ultimately find someone who shares common convictions [values] and character traits and whom you can marry in the right way in the right place by the right authority [faith]" (Marion D. Hanks, *Now and Forever* [Salt Lake City: Bookcraft, 1974], p. 44.)

Think of all the crazy dating ideas you can and see if they can be made to relate in any way to these values. (See the examples on pages 12–13.) Using your imagination in planning dates can result in dates that are not only fun but productive. When you invite someone to go out or accept an invitation to date someone, it creates a situation where both of you can practice being courteous and thoughtful. Two young people on a date are usually trying to impress each other, and they are each on their best behavior. Developing these kinds of social skills is valuable and will help prepare you to be a better and more attractive candidate for serious dating and eventual marriage. You'll have a lot of fun on these kinds of dates, but you'll also get to learn something valuable from each of these relationships. That is one of the reasons why you'll want to date a variety of people during your teenage years—and not just one person. So, is there life before sixteen? Yes, but beyond sixteen, too. Make it count!

I testify that our Heavenly Father loves each of us. He knows what is best for us, and he is allowing us to work out our own salvation. The dating game is a major part of our future. If we are still in the pre-game warm-up stage—getting ready to play but not yet called into the game—we need to work on our friendship, our personal qualities, and our commitment to follow the standards of the Church, including our own specific rules. If we are already in the middle of the game, we need to find out all we can about the people we date, including their inner values. But if we are to succeed, we need to pay attention to what our leaders have taught us, live worthy lives, and follow the rules. Then we can use the dating experience to have fun, meet new people, and ultimately discover a partner with whom we can enter into a celestial marriage.

In summary I would like to share this poem with you.

On Your Mark, Get Ready, Get Set, Date!
by Mike Allred
They're off and running to get a date
To fill the void in their heart.
The girls are nervous, the boys all flirt;
The games are off to a start.
Some boys act cool, and tough, and mean
To show the amount of the man.
Some girls are ditsy; they're smarter than none;
When brighter the boys all ran.
When thinking of acting to get a date,
To fake yourself as some do,
Remember the goal of dating is clear;
To find someone just like you.
Some find a date and think they're in love,
Go steady; all friendships must end!
They fail to see that others around
Could help them become a true friend.
But friendships will always continue to grow;
A celestial value to earn.
Develop yourself to be a friend
By charity, love, and concern.
Dating with purpose, becoming as one,
In friendships and values and love.
Follow the counsel of our prophets and learn
The light from your father above.
The choice is coming to choose from them all,
Eternity, never to part.
On your mark, get ready, get set, date;
Take time in preparing your heart.
Is there life before sixteen? The answer is a powerful
    YES!

STANDARDS

Prepare now
Only double date
Keep Word of Wisdom
Keep Sabbath day holy

SPECIFICS

Do own school work
Be on time to work
Smile more often
Be more pleasant at home
Go to interviews when asked
Treat your date with respect
Set and then observe a curfew
Improve the way I speak

STANDARDS

No going steady
No dating until sixteen
No R-rated movies

SPECIFICS

Don't be alone with a date
Don't date the same person
twice in a row
No making out
Don't wear immodest clothes
No swearing
Don't gossip

VALUE DATING IDEAS

WHITE: FAITH
      1. Read the scriptures.
      2. Go to church.
      3. Go to a visitor's center.
      4. Do genealogy.
      5. Write in your journal.

BLUE: DIVINE NATURE
      1. Go to a crowded place, watch people, and try to discover if they know they have a divine nature (take notes). How can you help?
      2. Go to an airport and talk to people about their destinations and talk about missions.
      3. Borrow someone's kids (offer to tend) and play parents.

RED: INDIVIDUAL WORTH
      1. Make home videos.
      2. Look at old pictures and make up faith promoting rumors.
      3. Trade brothers and sisters.
      4. Cut out pictures from a magazine to tell your life story.
      5. Put headphones on and listen to music while singing; record your voice with another tape recorder.
      6. Watch TV with a shut-in.
      7. Take an instant camera picture of kids and give it to them.
      8. Have a goofy talent show.

GREEN: KNOWLEDGE
      1. Make up captions for pictures in your family albums.
      2. Do your own homework together.

3. Teach your date to cook.

4. Wash and fold or iron clothes.

5. Go grocery shopping for your family.

ORANGE: CHOICE AND ACCOUNTABILITY

1. Go shopping at a thrift store such as Deseret Industries and keep the items, give them to the needy, or re-donate.

2. Go house hunting or draw plans for a future home.

3. Listen to music and discuss feelings (rate the songs).

4. Go to a fair and pretend you're the judge.

YELLOW: GOOD WORKS

1. Change the oil in your dad's car.

2. Plant or weed someone's garden.

3. Shovel snow for a stranger.

4. Paint a house (with permission).

5. Buy some flowers; give them to people you see doing nice things for other people.

6. Visit a hospital or a nursing home.

7. Clean a garage or house, wash cars, mow someone's lawn.

PURPLE: INTEGRITY

1. Honestly evaluate your honesty.

Michael Allred teaches seminary at Bonneville High School in Ogden, Utah, and is a graduate of Weber State University and the University of Phoenix. Before becoming a teacher, he worked as a computer graphics artist and served in the Army National Guard as a counterintelligence agent and Japanese interpreter. Brother Allred teaches drum lessons and claims to love all sports "except synchronized swimming." He and his wife, Kathy, have four children, and he serves as a counselor in a bishopric.

2

THESE F'S ARE GREAT
ON YOUR ETERNAL REPORT CARD!

SUZANNE BALLARD

f you reported back to Heavenly Father after this life, having gotten only A's or B's on your Eternal Report Card, I think he'd be upset. That is, if A's and B's represented such things as Abortion, Adultery, Blasphemy, Belligerence, Antagonism, Anger, Boastfulness, and being an Atheist! You for sure can't make it into the celestial kingdom with those kinds of grades!

On the other hand, Heavenly Father would likely be pretty thrilled to have you study really hard and get F's here on earth! Let me explain what I mean.

F Equals Faith

"Faith is not to have a perfect knowledge of things; therefore if ye have faith ye hope for things which are not seen, which are true" (Alma 32:21).

My daughters and I traveled to Russia in the summer of 1993. I had the opportunity to give several speeches to teenagers from Russia and from the USA. Most of the American youth and some of the Russian teens were LDS. I was so impressed by the faith of the Russian Latter-day

Saints. They have been praying for years for the gospel. They have so much faith in Jesus Christ and the Church. Did you know that the Doctrine & Covenants is not even translated into Russian yet? They have been completely converted to the gospel by the Spirit and by reading the Book of Mormon. Their testimonies are so strong. It was such a moving experience to hear their testimonies in our church services and to listen to "I Am a Child of God" being sung in Russian and English at the same time.

After my speeches, these Russian youth came to us with their journals. They asked us for our birthdates and then made a notation on that date in their journals. Then they asked us to write our testimonies in their journals so that on our birthdates they would be able to read our testimonies and remember us! We were so touched that we cried.

How I wish that the youth of the Church in "richer" countries of the world might cultivate such faith.

F Equals Fasting and Fervent Prayer

"The children of God were commanded that they should gather themselves together oft, and join in fasting and mighty prayer in behalf of the welfare of the souls of those who knew not God" (Alma 6:6).

I know most teens look upon fasting as one of the harder commandments to live. After all, how can our going without food do anybody any good? Why not just donate money to the fast offering fund and eat too? We live in a land of plenty in North America. We don't really have to starve ourselves in order to help someone who is hungry, do we?

I had something happen to me several years ago that showed me just how important fasting and fervent prayer are. Maybe my story will help you understand too.

When I was pregnant with my last child, I went into a hypoglycemic coma for several hours. Since the coma happened very early in my pregnancy, when my baby was first developing, the doctors informed us that there was danger of giving birth to a brain damaged or severely handicapped child. They asked us to consider submitting to an abortion.

Being totally opposed to abortion, my husband, Russ, and I prayed fervently to Heavenly Father for guidance and comfort. As a result of our prayers, we felt the sweet assurance that all would be well with our child. Our faith was severely tried over the next few months, though, as I slipped briefly in and out of comas.

Six months into my pregnancy, I had lost over twenty pounds. I didn't look pregnant, and I hadn't felt the baby move. Russ and I were worried. I had been given several blessings, but Russ decided to also fast for our baby. Fasting helped him draw so much closer to Heavenly Father and to know His will. Russ was deeply impressed that he should give the baby a blessing. I will never forget the experience we had together as he anointed my belly with oil and used his priesthood to bless our baby to have a healthy mind and body.

In less than a week, I felt the baby move for the first time. What a joyous feeling! When Megan was born three months later, I had barely started wearing maternity clothes. But she weighed eight pounds and was healthy in every way. Megan is currently an 8th grader, and she does modeling and acting.

Russ had prepared himself spiritually to be able to act. He had practiced by fasting every Fast Sunday. He understood how fasting prepares a person to call upon Heavenly Father for guidance. So when our problem arose, fasting seemed a natural way for him to learn the will of Heavenly Father. (Remember, fasting does not change the will of God,

but it helps us *learn* His will.) Fasting is a terrific F to cultivate in your life!

F Equals Feasting on the Word

*"Wherefore, . . . feast upon the words of Christ; for behold,
the words of Christ will tell you all things what ye should do"
(2 Nephi 32:3).*

Everywhere we went in Russia, when we declined the
frequent offers of coffee, tea, or alcohol, we were immediately asked: "Are you MorMON?" When we replied that
we were, we were asked to tell them about the gospel. They
wanted to know so badly.

While we were there, we met for the first time our Russian pen pals with whom we'd corresponded for over five
years. After the fall of the communistic government in 1991,
we were finally able to send our pen pals copies of the Book
of Mormon and the book *Gospel Principles* translated into
Russian, and to tell them about the Church.

One of our pen pals is a young Jewish woman named
Paulina. She lives with her parents in a city 500 miles east
of Moscow. She is a concert pianist and performs all over
Russia. One week after receiving the Book of Mormon from
us, she wrote: "I have just received your parcel with books.
I read them with great interest and pleasure. The pictures
are delightful! Now I know who is Mormon, J. Smith, and
other[s]. My friends and all relatives wish to read these
books too. They will do it after me."

When we traveled to Russia, we met Paulina for the first
time (as well as two of our other pen pals). Paulina told us
that she and her parents have read the Book of Mormon
and believe it to be true. They had also read in *Gospel Principles* about the Word of Wisdom, and her family had vol-
untarily begun to live it. She said they all felt so much better

since giving up alcohol, coffee, tea, and cigarettes. She even bore testimony of that to one of our other pen pals who later wrote that she, too, was following the Word of Wisdom and telling others about it!

Feast on the Words of Christ. Think just how blessed you are to *have* the Book of Mormon and the other scriptures! Don't take them for granted. Take time every day to fill up on the messages that are written there for you.

F Equals Family

"Cultivate in our own family a sense that we belong together eternally" (President Spencer W. Kimball).

Is your family only a group of people who happen to live under the same roof—or is your family a *"forever family?"* Do you know that some families never do anything together, like eating, sitting in church, praying, or even vacationing? All of the latter-day prophets have urged us to work to make our families forever families.

You know, some families just seem to pull together and some seem to pull apart. Could you be the one to help your family, no matter what its size or makeup, be a "forever family?" Could you be a Nephi or Sam in your family, or are you a Laman or a Lemuel? If you have a brother or sister who is acting like a Laman or Lemuel, do you help your mom and dad to gently guide them back into the security of your family?

Remember the play *Saturday's Warrior?* Remember how the family pulled together to help the one son who was going astray? Who were his real friends? His family! Who cared about him more than themselves? His family. That's just what we all need to do in our families—be friends with our family members and help them see that being in our family is wonderful. I know you can be creative in helping your family (whether they are LDS or not) become more united. You can be the catalyst for change in your family!

While we were in Russia, we visited a village called Nova Okatova. It was a very poor town with no running water or indoor bathrooms. The people drank from, bathed in, and washed their clothes in the Volga River. We were able to visit inside some of the village homes. I visited with one young man who spoke very little English but who, by gesturing, introduced me to his wife and child and showed me his cow, chickens, pigs, garden, and his big Russian army truck! At the end of our visit, he put his arm around his young wife and baby and proudly patting his chest said, "I am a rich man!"

And he truly was. Though poor in terms of material possessions, he had a family that he loved and who loved him. How much more could he want? Perhaps someday he, his wife, and children will be a "forever family" with the help of our missionaries!

F Equals Fellowship

"Now therefore ye are no more strangers and foreigners, but fellowcitizens with the saints, and of the household of God" (Ephesians 2:19).

When we share the gospel with someone, that person becomes our friend. We shouldn't be God's Frozen Chosen! We should make them feel welcome in the Church.

When I joined the Church, I was seventeen years old. I had one friend in the Church. Her name was Alice. She was the one who had shared the gospel with me. I was also acquainted with other LDS youth—but they didn't fellowship me. They probably thought that I hadn't really been converted, and so they didn't want to befriend me. I lost nearly all of my non-LDS friends when I joined the Church because I wouldn't do the things they wanted to do, like party, drink, and such. I desperately needed the LDS youth to be my friends. But that didn't happen.

Later, when I went to college, the Institute of Religion students taught me a great lesson in fellowshipping. They all rallied around and helped me to *really* understand the gospel and the Church. They invited me to activities and told me they'd missed me when I didn't come. The Institute director gave me a calling as "Historian" so that I'd have to go to the activities to take photos for the scrap book! Everyone was friendly and concerned and cared for me.

Is there someone new in your ward? Have you helped them feel welcome? Have you looked past your own problems and concerns to see that they might need a friend? Could you be that friend? Don't wait for others to think of you—think of them first!

F Equals Forgiveness

"Forgive, and ye shall be forgiven" (Luke 6:37).

One beautiful spring day about fifteen years ago, my husband, Russ, went to our town's small shopping mall. He was wearing a new jacket he'd received for Christmas, but because the weather had turned rather warm, he left it in the car while he shopped. (Our town was so small that people usually didn't lock their cars.)

You can guess what happened! Russ's brand new coat was stolen from our car! I was so mad! I wanted to march right down to the police station and file a missing coat report! Russ, on the other hand, kept telling me that maybe someone else needed it more than he did. That just made me madder!

A few weeks later, we were back at the mall (you see, in a small town, that's about all the entertainment that's available)! I looked down the mall, and walking towards us was an older man, obviously homeless, and he was wearing Russ's ski jacket!

I started yanking on my husband's arm. I wanted Russ to confront the man right there and get the coat back! We just couldn't afford another new coat right then, and I hated seeing Russ in his old army jacket. I had jumped to the conclusion that the man wearing the coat was the thief.

Russ, on the other hand, assumed that the man had found the jacket after the thief had discarded it. All he saw was a man in need. He didn't judge him; he simply forgave as Christ would have us do. What a wonderful lesson in forgiveness my husband gave me and our children that day.

In the Pacific Northwest we have a slow-moving creature called a slug. Slugs here are just like snails only without shells. They are fat and slimy and revolting. And they can be very large—sometimes six or eight inches long.

When someone hurts your feelings or offends you, it could be compared to someone picking up one of our Pacific Northwest slugs and putting it in your hand. You would then have a choice to make. You could give it back to them ("Thank you very much, but I choose not to accept that offense from you")—you could throw it back at them ("Why you . . . take that!")—you could throw it away ("I choose not to be offended")—or you could swallow it! If you choose to swallow it, it sure can give you a big slug-ache! When you hold a grudge against someone or keep thinking about the offense, it's as though you've just swallowed that slug! Forgiveness could be compared to throwing it away.

When we refuse to forgive someone, it is as though we have a cancer. Cancer-like, our anger can spread and take over our body and spirit. Cut it out. Don't let it remain to poison your soul.

Terry Anderson is a journalist who was held captive in

the Middle East for over seven years by terrorists. After his release he was asked "Do you have any bitterness towards the people who held you for so long?"

His answer was a lesson in forgiveness. "I don't have any time for it. I don't have any need for it. It is required of me as a Christian to put that aside, to forgive them. I pray for them. I wish them no ill in their lives. My life is very, very busy—it is full of joy. The world is fresh and bright and beautiful."

Do you know someone you need to forgive? How about adding that F to your eternal report card?

F Equals Following Father in Heaven, Jesus Christ, and the Prophet

"Can we follow Jesus save we shall be willing to keep the commandments of the Father?" (2 Nephi 31:10).

My dear young friends, there is only *one* pathway to the celestial kingdom. It takes *Faith* to find it; it takes *Fellowshipping* to help others find it too. It takes *Feasting on the Word* to remain on the pathway and *Fasting* and *Fervent Prayer* and *Forgiving*. At the end of that pathway you'll find a *Forever Family*—just for you. *Following* the pathway outlined by Father in Heaven and Jesus Christ and our living prophet means living the commandments daily. It means being baptized, receiving the Holy Ghost, going on a mission, and repenting of your sins. It means preparing for eternal marriage in the temple and attending church and seminary and fulfilling your callings to the best of your ability. Following that path and achieving that reward requires obedience on your part, but that obedience brings so much freedom!

Father in Heaven loves you so very much. I hope that you have a testimony of that truth. Jesus Christ loves you more than you can ever imagine—just look at what he did for you in the Garden of Gethsemane. President Benson loves you with all his being—he truly loves each and every one of us.

I also love the youth of the Church and want you all to know that by including these F's in your life, you will find joy, peace, and fulfillment beyond your wildest imagination. Just choose one that you have a hard time with. Try and live it the best you can, asking Heavenly Father's help. Practice it daily for three weeks and then it will become a habit.

Remember, these F's will help lead you to the celestial kingdom. Cultivate them in your life. Always remember that this is the only true Church on the earth today. I know it and you can know it too.

Suzanne Ballard teaches early-morning seminary in Vancouver, Washington, where she lives with her husband, Russell. They are the parents of four children. A certified childbirth educator, Sister Ballard was named National Young Mother of the Year in 1985. She has served in leadership positions in Young Women and Relief Society and enjoys traveling, being with her family, public speaking, and "anything to do with the youth!"

3

AVOIDING THE APPLE SYNDROME

ART E. BERG

The *apple syndrome* is a phenomenon which has existed since the beginning of time. However, it seems that today more than ever, it has been responsible for the destruction of self-confidence, character, and eternal relationships.

In order to understand the *apple syndrome*, you have to go back thousands of years with me, to a beautiful garden in a place called Eden. Adam and Eve had been strictly forbidden to partake of the fruit of the Tree of Knowledge of Good and Evil. For whatever reason, a time came when both the man and the woman partook, and they began almost immediately to experience the consequences. God came down to the man, Adam, and in essence asked, "Why Adam? Why did you eat of the fruit of the tree?" And *what* did Adam say? "The woman! [We're going to take a little poetic license here.] The woman did cause me to eat." God turned to Eve and asked, "Why Eve, . . . why did you eat of the fruit of the tree?" Eve's response? "The serpent beguiled me."

You see, it is human nature to account for behavior by blaming other people, circumstances, or our environment, especially when our behavior is unbecoming. The ancient Israelites even had a tradition of selecting a goat, aptly termed a *scapegoat*, on which they symbolically loaded the sins and burdens of the people. Though we no longer use a literal *scapegoat*, many people in the modern world look to excuse their behavior by blaming it on someone or something other than themselves. Failure to accept personal responsibility for what we do results in spiritual retardation. M. Scott Peck has written: "Life is difficult. This is a great truth, one of the greatest truths. It is a great truth because once we truly see this truth, we transcend it. Once we truly know that life is difficult—once we truly understand it and accept it—then life is no longer difficult. Because once it is accepted, the fact that life is difficult no longer matters.

"Most do not fully see this truth that life is difficult. Instead they moan more or less incessantly, noisily or subtly, about the enormity of their problems, their burdens, and their difficulties as if life were generally easy, as if life *should* be easy" (*The Road Less Traveled* [New York: Simon & Schuster, 1978], p. 15).

As Dr. Peck further relates, it is when we seek to avoid our problems and difficult circumstances that we inherently begin to point fingers of blame. By so doing, we ignore the remedies and solutions to our struggles and begin to lay a foundation for imbalance in our personal, mental, and spiritual lives. Struggle, difficult circumstances, and pain are all essential to growth in this life. When we fall victim to the *apple syndrome,* by attempting to shift responsibility for our lives to conditions, circumstances, and behavior outside of ourselves, we deny ourselves opportunities to learn, grow, and become.

As a young man, I was out driving my father's car with some friends of mine. I was driving a little too fast and the roads were still wet from an earlier rain. As I took a sharp corner, the car slid out of control and into the side of a curb. The impact bent both wheels on one side of the car quite severely. As I drove the limping car home, I had just enough time to come up with a really good story for my dad.

I raced inside the house shouting, "Dad, Dad, you're not going to believe what just happened." (That was more prophetic than I imagined at the time.) I continued, "As I was driving home from school *by myself, observing the laws of the road*, I *gently* went around a corner, when a small child darted out in the road between two vehicles! Because of the skills which you have taught me and the genetics of my body, I was able to avoid hitting the child, but I struck the curb, and damaged your car. Aren't you proud of me?"

I got the same response you might be having now. My father just grinned and said, "Son, when you are ready to tell me the truth, why don't you come back?"

I stormed off to my room thinking, "I can't believe that my own father doesn't believe his son!" And then I thought of a new story! Reapproaching my father, I admitted, "You're right, Dad, I wasn't being completely honest before. There was no small child in the road, . . . it was a little dog! But aren't they important too?" Well, he didn't buy that story either. He finally dragged the truth from me, and then he made me pay for the damage.

Now, it is important that you understand this experience, because it was a few weeks after that event that as I was driving my father's other, *undamaged* car home from work, and had stopped at a traffic signal, someone rear-ended me. This was a truly exciting experience! You see, in all my limited driving experience, for the first time, . . . it really wasn't my fault! And I had the evidence to prove it!

I raced home. Perhaps too gleeful in my approach, I boldly declared to my father the circumstances surrounding his newly damaged car. My father, not changing his expression simply stated, "Son, it's your fault."

I couldn't believe what I was hearing! I said, "You must not have understood what I was saying. We're not communicating. I was an innocent victim of circumstance. There was nothing I could do—no place I could go. What do you expect from me?"

Calmly, my father responded, "Son, let me ask you a few questions. Did you decide to get up this morning?"

"Yes Sir, I did."

"Did you get yourself dressed, or did your mother have to do it again?" (Sarcasm intended.)

"Well, I got myself dressed, Dad."

"That's obvious. Did you drive yourself to work, Son?"

"You know I did. You know it's too far to walk." (That's about the time you get the story about how he walked ten miles to school in the snow, uphill both ways!)

"And Son, did you decide to stop at that light?"

"Yes Sir, I did."

My father then concluded, "Son, you need to take more responsibility for your life."

I didn't understand what he was trying to say. And quite frankly, I was just a little upset. However, it was ten years ago that I think I finally understood what my father really *meant* to say. It was ten years ago, while driving from California to Utah to get married, the driver of my car fell asleep at the wheel and our car hit a cement embankment. Ejected immediately from the rolling mass of twisted metal and broken glass, I broke my neck on a desert floor and was left a quadriplegic, paralyzed from the chest down. While lying in that hospital bed, what my father had said made so much more sense. What my father really meant to say was this: "Son, when you are ready and willing to take one hundred percent responsibility for your life; for the conditions, circumstances, and behavior of your life, it is then, and only then, that you truly have the *power to change your future.*" And that one simple truth saved this young man's life forever.

I suppose that it would have been easy those ten years ago to have blamed my condition and pain on circumstances and people outside of myself. I suppose I could have been angry at God. But, He didn't fall asleep at the wheel, did He? And besides, He has been the giver of every good thing in my life, before and since. I guess it would have been human nature to have been bitter towards my friend who fell asleep. But, it was just an accident, that's all. I imagine I could have blamed my pain on life. However, I have found that despite the circumstances of my life, life is sweet and good. And besides, I have gotten into the habit of breathing and I kinda' like it!

The saving truth I learned, was that by pointing fingers of blame for my condition at any person, thing, or environment outside myself, removed the power I had within me to learn from my experience, to make changes in my behavior, and to ultimately grow. I believe that when we are in a constant state of learning, growing, and changing, we are happy.

As I travel the world, about 150,000 miles each year, speaking to young and old alike, my greatest concern is the lack of self-confidence people are experiencing. This lack of self-confidence translates itself into their occupations, personal relationships, and spiritual growth. People who lack self-confidence often experience an overwhelming sense of hopelessness and a feeling of uncertainty about their future. I believe this has become an alarming problem and is another manifestation of the *apple syndrome.*

Psychologists have discovered that self-confidence stems from *perceived control.* When we perceive that we control our destiny, happiness, and spiritual future, we tend to have a greater sense of confidence in ourselves and our world. The greatest damage inflicted by the *apple syndrome* is the surrendering of our perceived control.

By taking 100 percent responsibility for the conditions, circumstances, and behavior of our lives, we put ourselves back into the driver's seat. When we have a habit of pointing fingers of blame, what we are really saying is that we have little or no control over our destiny. We are driven by the winds of fate. Without taking 100 percent responsibility, it is impossible to look for solutions, resolve conflicts, or grow spiritually. Instead we focus on the behavior of others, insisting that "when they change, . . . then I'll change."

This attitude is more pervasive than you may think. How often have you said or heard others say: "The *devil* made me do it," or "*You* make me so mad," or "If only *she* would be more supportive," or "I'll never get ahead as long as *he's* around," or "I *couldn't* help myself," or "If *they* just hadn't kept pushing me"? Such statements put us in a mental condition of surrendering to circumstance and resigning ourselves to *fate*. I believe that we have more control than that.

I do not mean to insinuate here that outside circumstances or other people do not play a role in our lives, and that some responsibility should not be laid at their feet. The Lord has declared that the sins of the children would be upon the heads of their parents if they, the parents, did not repent. Certainly, there are many factors that contribute to the conditions we are now experiencing. However, if we make these factors into excuses, we forfeit the growth we can experience by taking responsibility and learning from our mistakes.

The Apostle Paul stated that "God hath not given us the spirit of fear; but of power, and of love, and of a sound mind" (2 Timothy 1:7). Fortunately, we live in a physical and spiritual world that is governed by law; a world where "God is not mocked: for whatsoever a man soweth, that shall he also reap" (Galatians 6:7). A world where we are given power to "Act [and not] be acted upon" (2 Nephi 2:13). Because of these laws, we can, as Paul declared, come "boldly unto the throne of grace" (Hebrews 4:16). That is true, eternal, self-confidence.

Jacob and Joseph, brothers of Nephi, took 100 percent responsibility in their lives when they committed, "and we did magnify our office unto the Lord, taking upon us the *responsibility*, answering the sins of the people upon our own heads if we did not teach them the word of God with all diligence." By taking this stance, they found strength to do the work required: "Wherefore, by *laboring with our might* their blood might not come upon our garments" (Jacob 1:19; emphasis added).

When we are fully willing to take 100 percent responsibility for every aspect of our lives, we become capable of asking more empowering questions. Those who are caught in the *apple syndrome* find themselves asking "why" all the time. "*Why* can't I ever get ahead?" "*Why* did this have to happen to me?" "*Why* doesn't God love me?" Or, "*Why* doesn't anybody like me?" The problem with asking "why?" all of the time, is that it almost always focuses on outside influences or conditions, it seldom results in solutions, and the answers our minds give in response are generally negative and disempowering.

The person who has decided to take control of his destiny and life by assuming 100 percent responsibility, generally asks questions beginning with the words, "What" or "How." "*What* can I do to improve my station in life?" "*How* can I influence other people to like me more?" "*What* do I need to do to inherit God's power in my life?" These kinds of questions lead to positive solutions and realistic self-assessment. As we answer such questions and apply what we learn, we can take action and experience maximum growth. People who continually blame others never benefit from the hard experiences that come into each of our lives.

William Ernest Henley, while in the prime of his life, was struck down with a crippling disease. Left in a hospital where it was presumed he would die, he penned these immortal words entitled "Invictus."

Out of the night that covers me,
Black as the Pit from pole to pole,
I thank whatever gods may be
For my unconquerable soul.

In the fell clutch of circumstance,
I have not winced nor cried aloud;
Under the bludgeonings of chance
My head is bloody, but unbowed.

Beyond this place of wrath and tears
Looms but the horror of the shade.
And yet the menace of the years
Finds and shall find me unafraid.

It matters not how strait the gate
Nor how charged with punishment the scroll.
I am the master of my fate;
I am the captain of my soul.

After eighteen long months, William Henley walked out of that hospital.

I believe the Lord desires for each of his children to become masters of their fate and captains of their souls. By avoiding the *apple syndrome* of laying blame at the feet of the world, and by accepting 100 percent responsibility for our lives, we can obtain the strength that comes through overcoming adversity. Then, with the help of the Savior, we will possess the power to walk boldly before the throne of God.

Art Berg is a businessman and president of Invictus Communications, Inc. A professional motivational speaker to business, church, and youth groups, he is the author of a book entitled Some Miracles Take Time. *He enjoys wheelchair racing, parasailing, boating, and traveling. Art loves working with youth and has served as a Sunday School teacher, Aaronic Priesthood adviser, and a seminary instructor. He is married to Dallas Howard Berg, and they are the parents of one child.*

4

FEELING GREAT EVERY DAY

DIANE BILLS

Have you ever said to yourself, "I would feel so good about myself if . . . "? If I could just make the varsity football team. If I could win a student-body office. If I could be a cheerleader. If I could make the basketball team, volleyball team, or any team. If I could just get straight A's or make the honor roll or get a good scholarship. I'd feel so great, if I had more friends, or if I could just run around with "that group." Life would be great if I were sixteen and could date, or (for those of you who are sixteen) if I could just get a date! I'd feel so great if I could be in the jazz band or orchestra, or dance club, drill team, a cappella choir, madrigals, or the school play. If only they'd chosen me to be in my Young Women class presidency or quorum presidency. If only I had been chosen for seminary council. If I just had my driver's license and a car to drive. "Mom, I know these jeans cost $80.00, but I'd feel so great if I had them." And on and on and on. I'd feel so great if only . . .

I had one of those "I'd feel so great ifs" when I was your age. I'm almost embarrassed to tell you what it was, and yet, because of this desire, I had an experience that changed my life.

When I was in high school, I wanted to become the

queen of something—anything! You're probably amused, but, seriously, I wanted so badly to become the queen of something. I grew up in a queen family. My cousins were queens of everything. One cousin even went on to compete in the Miss America Pageant.

One of my closest cousins was my age. When we became teenagers, it seemed as though she was elected the queen of just about everything. I graduated from high school, not being the queen of anything. I wasn't jealous of my cousin, just the opposite. I was excited every time she won. It was like having my sister win, and I'd say, "Yes!! Way to go!"

After graduation from high school, my cousin Cami and I became roommates at BYU. Our sophomore year, Cami made head cheerleader. That same year I made it into one of BYU's singing and dancing groups. We were loving life.

Toward the end of the school year, it was announced that BYU was going to conduct the biggest "queen contest" the school had ever had. This particular contest would be held in conjunction with the bicentennial celebration of our country's birth. The winner would be named the "Bicentennial Belle of the Y." She would not only be Homecoming Queen and Belle of the Y, but she would reign as BYU's queen for the entire year! She would get a full-ride scholarship *and* she would become the official school hostess, the escort for any dignitaries who visited BYU campus. She would also have four attendants. Sounds kind of exciting doesn't it?

Now guys, I know you can't relate to the queen thing, so imagine for just a moment that this was going to be a Bicentennial All-Star Basketball Team with one player chosen to be the BYU Athlete of the Year. He would receive a full-ride scholarship as well as be the official school athlete to welcome all the other teams or athletes who visited the campus. Does that sound exciting to you?

I couldn't believe such a neat opportunity was being offered. I definitely wanted to get involved. As I checked the requirements, I found out to my dismay, that the contest was going to last five weeks—five weeks!! My singing and dancing group had practiced all year long for our spring tour, which was scheduled to begin in just four weeks. I was disappointed that I wouldn't be able to try out.

My cousin came home from school one day, all bubbly and excited about something. She announced that she was going to try out for the Bicentennial Queen.

"You're so lucky," I said "I would love to do something like that."

"Why don't you try out with me?" she asked.

"I can't, the contest lasts five weeks and our singing group is going on tour in four weeks," I told her.

"Hey, don't worry about that," Cami said. "Come and get into the contest with me. We'll make lots of friends, and for fun just see how far we can go. We probably won't make it that far anyway."

"You know, she's right," I thought. "It would be fun, especially doing it together. Let me think about it," I said.

I decided to pray about it first, and depending on how I felt, I would follow those feelings. As I prayed, I felt a sweet peace inside. I could hardly wait to tell my cousin.

"Sign me up! I'm in." I blurted.

Cami was pleased with my decision.

To the best of my recollection, the contest began with around one hundred and thirty girls. Each week, there would be a competition, and then a cut would be made for five consecutive weeks. After each cut, the campus news-paper, *Daily Universe,* would print the names of the top three girls for that week's competition. The judges would also keep an overall running score of how well each girl had performed. This was the score that counted, because it determined who made it that week and who didn't. After the final cut, the five remaining girls would become the royalty, with the student body voting for the winner.

The first competition was to determine modeling, poise, and posture. As soon as it was over, I knew I hadn't made it. I didn't even want to go look at the board where the list was posted of who made the cut.

Cami hurried home from school to tell me we both had made it! I was shocked! I was so sure that I hadn't made it. Cami's name appeared in the newspaper as one of the top three for that competition.

The second competition was to bake a cake from scratch and also make an article of clothing or craft project of our choosing. Once again, I was sure I hadn't made it. I was nervous as I looked through the fifty posted names, and then I saw it! My name was there! I couldn't believe it. It was really there!

The third event was a speech competition. We each wrote and then delivered a ten-minute speech about BYU, and then gave an impromptu speech. As I recall, it took most of the day to do our speeches. Then came the next cut to twenty-five girls. The most surprising news came when my name appeared in the newspaper as one of the top three for that competition, and consequently, I made the third cut.

The fourth part of the contest was the part we all dreaded the most—the in-depth cultural interviews! These were "one-on-one" interviews on art, literature, music, philosophy, and religion.

That Saturday morning we were all uptight for the interviews. Just before they began, I asked myself why I was so nervous? After all, it was the end of the fourth week of competition, and my singing group was going on tour in two days—I knew I had to go on tour. The contest was basically over for me. I might as well go to the interviews and have fun. When we arrived, I remember cheering everyone else on to do well. As I interviewed, I felt totally relaxed. At this point it didn't matter how well I did.

As soon as the interviews were over, I went to the woman in charge of the contest and explained to her that I was going to have to drop out because of my singing tour. I also explained that I had never thought I would make it this far. She was surprised, and said "Let me just go and see how you did today."

Would you want to know how you did that day if it were you in the contest? Guys, if you were in basketball try-outs, would you want to know how you did? You bet you would!

So she left. She was gone for what seemed an eternity. I can still visualize in my mind the experience that followed. She came back through the door, looked at me, and said, "Don't go on tour."

"I have to," I said.

"Don't go on tour."

"But, I have to."

"Diane, please don't go on tour."

"You don't understand," I said, "I'm in a singing-dancing group with guys and girls as partners. We are paired for our performance."

"Diane, I shouldn't tell you this, but today, you got the top score on the interviews."

"I what?"

"You got the top score on interviews! Because of today's score you are now in first place in the overall running score of the contest. You've made it! Right now you're practically guaranteed to make it into the royalty. Just stay until Tuesday night to do your talent, then fly out, and meet your singing group on Wednesday."

I stood there in shock. "I can't believe this!" I said. "This is amazing!" On the outside I tried to act calm, but my insides were all churning.

"I'll be there Tuesday night," I said. "You can count on it! I'll do what ever it takes to be there."

I ran to my tour director's house about a mile off campus and explained to him my dilemma. He and I tried to figure out a way for me to stay until Tuesday night and then fly out to meet our group on Wednesday. As we looked at the tour itinerary, we could see that the schedule was too tight, with practically two performances a day. On Wednesday, the group would be nowhere near an airport.

"It won't work," he said. "There's no way we can come to get you at any of these airports. They are hours away."

Finally, he told me I could stay home from tour and finish the contest instead.

"Thank you, thank you, thank you," I said.

Obviously, he could sense what I wanted. As he walked me to the door, he said, "Wait a minute. There's something I hadn't even considered. What about your partner? If you stay, your partner and the couple opposite you on stage won't be able to perform on tour."

We both stopped. He was right. I knew he was right. Everything our group did was symmetrical. There was no backup to take my place.

"You can still stay to do your contest, Diane, but if you do, they won't be able to perform," he said. "I'll let you make the decision."

Now I ask you, my young friends, "What would you do?" Here you are, a girl who would have been thrilled to be in the royalty of even a stake dance, and now, a rare chance to be part of BYU's Bicentennial Royalty. If you stay, three people in your singing group won't be able to perform on tour. Girls, what would you have done if you were me? Guys, what would you do if you had a chance to be on the All-Star, BYU Bicentennial Team? What would you do?

Well, I did what every one of you would probably do . . .

I called my dad and mom and asked them what I should do!!

My parents were surprised and pleased that I had made it into the finals. My mom said, "Oh, my little Diane could be BYU's queen." My dad said, "The scholarship sure sounds good!" They told me to come home to Salt Lake City so we could talk. Dad and Mom were waiting with open arms when I arrived. We laughed, cried, and talked, desperately trying to figure out a way for me to finish the contest and still go on tour. The solutions weren't coming. We kept running into a dead end. Finally, Mom said, "Diane, it looks like you have a decision to make. We can't make this one for you. However, I would suggest you go in your bedroom and talk to the person who *can* give you the guidance you need."

Mom was right. I needed to talk with Heavenly Father. He would let me know what to do. Late that afternoon I went into my bedroom and got on my knees to pray. I truly wanted an answer and decided I would pray until I got one, but nothing happened. I prayed on for a while longer, and still nothing happened. So I continued to pray.

Have you ever wanted an answer so much, but nothing happens? That 's happened to me many times. It's not that Heavenly Father doesn't care—He does care, and very deeply. I've learned that in His wisdom, He knows the best way and the best time to give an answer to each of us. Perhaps we aren't asking for what is best for us at that moment in time, or maybe we just aren't listening well enough for the answer. It is also possible that we need to humble ourselves more. What ever the reason, He does hear and He does care.

With still no answer, I began to pray more intensely and with a more tender heart. I shared with Him all my feelings; how I had always wanted to be a queen, how so many of my cousins had been, how I would feel so good inside if only. . . . As I humbled myself, I wept and prayed on. I don't recall how long my prayer lasted. I do know I had never prayed with such intent and humility. The answer finally did come. It was clear, it was beautiful. I knew without question His will.

The following Monday morning, I was on a bus headed to California. Yes, I did drop out of the contest. And, yes, my cousin did make it into the royalty. I know some of you are going "Ohhhhhh." But wait, wait until you hear the answer to that prayer. The answer is the whole reason I am sharing this story with you. You see, the answer isn't just about me, it's also about *you*. For a brief moment, in a tender, spiritual way that Saturday evening, Heavenly Father let me know who I am—it is also who you are. He let me feel in my heart that I didn't need to be BYU's queen to feel good about Diane, for I was already a queen in His sight. And then He let me understand what He has in store for *each of us* if we live worthily.

Oh, my young friends, **DO YOU KNOW WHO YOU ARE?** Do you have any idea who you are? You are sons and daughters of a Heavenly King, heirs to all that He has. Someday to become Kings and Queens. Those few, brief moments of spiritual communication in a quiet bedroom, on a Saturday evening, changed my life. The feelings of self-worth that swelled up inside me have been indelibly imprinted on my heart. I found out that night that I could not have felt better about myself, even if I had been crowned queen of BYU or been made BYU's student body president. I learned that there is not an award, an honor, a presidency, or a queenship that man can bestow upon man, that even begins to compare to the stature we already enjoy in the sight of God.

I discovered that true self-esteem doesn't come from being popular out in the world, but that true self-esteem comes from God. It is not the *image* of the world that matters, but rather, as Alma asks, in speaking of the Savior, "Have ye received *his image* in your countenances?" (Alma 5:14).

Who are you? You of the chosen generation. You righteous sons and daughters of God. You are heirs of all He has.

A group of students was hurrying to seminary class one day. They went up the steps into the building, and found Brother Asay standing at the door to greet them as they came in. He was to address all the classes that day. The teenagers couldn't wait to hear him, for he was a spiritual giant in their eyes.

Brother Asay was a kind and gentle man. He was along in years and deeply spiritual. He had been a stake patriarch for many years.

As the students sat waiting for class to begin, Brother Asay walked in. He had tears in his eyes. He spoke softly. "Today, my young friends, I have had one of the most spiritual experiences of my life." The students listened with genuine interest. "As you came up the steps into the building, the Lord lifted the veil from my eyes and let me see who you are."

A hush came over the students as they felt a sweet Spirit in the room. Then came words that pierced their hearts. Brother Asay said, "I felt as though I wanted to bow down before you." Tears filled their eyes. This man, their leader, their friend, had been privileged to see their spirits; to experience from God the worth of these young people.

And so, I ask again, "Who are you? Do you know?"

There **IS** a way to feel great every day. That way is to draw close to the Father and His Son and to come to understand more fully who you are. You were chosen to come to the earth now, at this most difficult time. Your spirit must have been strong. You must have been mighty. You must have been righteous! As you come to understand more fully who you are, your feelings of worth will increase.

This way has been discovered by others who have gone before; people like Abraham, Moses, Nephi, Alma, and others. They had many trials, but they knew the source of their strength. It's easier to understand how a man like Joseph Smith could be persecuted and harassed so often and yet remain strong. He understood that true feelings of worth don't come from peers, but from God.

The Savior is the perfect example. In spite of persecution and ultimate betrayal by a friend, His eyes and heart were always turned heavenward. He also understood that true feelings of worth come from God.

It can be the same for you. When friends hurt you or betray you, when you don't make the team or win the school office or get the date, when others try to tempt you or harm you , or when life seems too difficult and the world seems cruel—turn to your true source of strength. Turn to the one who knows and loves your spirit. Turn, humbly, to your Heavenly Father in prayer.

Diane Bills describes herself as a "full-time homemaker," but she is also a professional motivational speaker who enjoys writing, crafts, and calligraphy. A returned missionary from the Belgium Brussels Mission, she has served as a leader and teacher in Primary, Young Women, and Relief Society. Diane graduated from the University of Utah and has performed nationally and internationally as a singer and dancer with various entertainment troupes. She is married to Christian V. Bills, and they have three children. Her essay is taken from the talk tape "The Secret to Loving Yourself," by Diane Bills, produced and published by Covenant Communications, Inc.

5

RECEIVING THE MIND AND WILL OF THE LORD

RANDALL C. BIRD

Several years ago in a seminary classroom, a student raised his hand and asked, "How can a person say he knows the church and gospel are true?" Several other students said they had the same question. Seeing that this was important to the students, we embarked on an experience that I will always remember. I had just finished two weeks of in-service training with the Church Educational System. During that training we had discussed some of the principles involved in receiving revelation. How grateful I was for that training. It helped me teach my students the principles governing revelation and testimony. I would like to share with you some of what happened in the classroom that day.

The President of the United States once asked the Prophet Joseph Smith how our religion differed from other religions of that day. Joseph explained that Mormons differed in the way they viewed the gift of the Holy Ghost (see *History of the Church*, 4:42). In other words, revelation by the power of the Holy Ghost is a prime characteristic of the true Church. I find it interesting that the Prophet Joseph answered in such a manner. Often, when a seminary teacher asks LDS students how the Church differs from other churches, students cite such things as: temple marriage, the Word of Wisdom, the concept of three degrees of glory, or some other point of doctrine unique to The Church of Jesus Christ of Latter-day Saints. Why, then, would the Prophet Joseph respond by mentioning the Holy Ghost?

To understand Joseph's answer, I think we must first define revelation. First, revelation is the means by which God communicates intelligence (light and truth) to man. The Lord has said, "The glory of God is intelligence, or, in other words, light and truth" (D&C 93:36). The scriptures also teach that "whatsoever they [the servants of the Lord] shall speak when moved upon by the Holy Ghost shall be scripture, shall be the will of the Lord, shall be the mind of the Lord, shall be the word of the Lord, shall be the voice of the Lord, and the power of God unto salvation" (D&C 68:4).

Next, revelation (light and truth) is communicated in an essentially spirit-to-spirit process, although some of our physical senses may be involved. The Prophet Joseph taught, "All things whatsoever God in his infinite wisdom has seen fit and proper to reveal to us, while we are dwelling in mortality . . . are revealed to us in the abstract, and independent of affinity of this mortal tabernacle, but are revealed to our spirits precisely as though we had no bodies at all; and those revelations which will save our spirits will save our bodies" (*Teachings of the Prophet Joseph Smith*, sel. Joseph Fielding Smith [Salt Lake City: Deseret Book Co., 1976], p. 355).

Third, revelation is one of the foundation stones the Church is built upon. Peter was once asked by the Savior, "Whom say ye that I am?" He responded by saying, "Thou are the Christ, the Son of the living God." Peter had received a personal revelation of this truth. Jesus then declared "Upon this rock I will build my church; and the gates of hell shall not prevail against it" (Matthew 16:15).

The Prophet Joseph taught that the "rock" is the rock of revelation (*Teachings*, p. 274).

Fourth, revelation is the only way for man to know God. Paul, in writing to the Corinthians, said, "For what man knoweth the things of a man, save the spirit of man which is in him? even so the things of God knoweth no man, but the Spirit of God" (1 Corinthians 2:11).

Finally, there are counterfeit revelations that can come from Satan or from our own emotions. I have heard youth and adults sometimes equate the spirituality of a meeting with the number of tears it caused; the more tears shed, the more spiritual the meeting. This concerns me. The fact that tears often accompany the workings of the spirit certainly doesn't mean that an experience which doesn't cause tears is not a spiritual experience. Elder Boyd K. Packer, an Apostle, said, "Be ever on guard lest you be deceived by inspiration from an unworthy source. You can be given false spiritual messages. There are counterfeit spirits just as there are counterfeit angels. . . . The spiritual part of us and the emotional part of us are so closely linked that it is possible to mistake an emotional impulse for something spiritual. We occasionally find people who receive what they assume to be spiritual promptings from God, when those promptings are either centered in the emotions or are from the adversary" ("The Candle of the Lord," *Ensign*, Jan. 1983, pp. 55–56).

Now that we have a little understanding of what revelation is, let's examine those principles that govern the giving and receiving of revelation. First: the Lord, not us, determines who receives revelation, when it is given, how it is given, and what is revealed. It's almost as though some people tell the Lord, "If this church is true, have my sister from California call me tonight." We cannot decide what answer we require or in what form it will come. The Savior gave us a great pattern when he said, "If it be possible, let this cup pass from me: nevertheless, not as I will, but as thou wilt" (Matthew 26:39).

Students often wonder why they do not see the Lord like Saul did, or why they are not visited by an angel, like Alma the Younger was, or even why they are not struck dumb like King Lamoni was. It's true that some people are converted in a remarkable manner, yet most testimonies aren't gained in such a way (see 3 Nephi 9:20). Most revelation comes through the quiet whisperings of the Spirit; the sensational and dramatic spiritual experiences are real, but they are the exception rather than the rule.

Speaking of the still small voice, Elder Boyd K. Packer said, "Occasionally it will press just firmly enough for us to pay heed. But most of the time, if we do not heed the gentle feeling, the Spirit will withdraw and wait until we come seeking and listening" ("The Candle of the Lord," p. 53). President Spencer W. Kimball said, "Even in our day, many people . . . expect if there be revelation it will come with an awe-inspiring, earth-shaking display . . . The burning bushes, the smoking mountains, the sheets [full of] of four-footed beasts, the Cumorahs, and the Kirtlands were realities; but they were the exceptions. The great volume of revelation came to Moses and to Joseph and comes to today's prophet in the less spectacular way—that of deep impressions, without spectacle or glamour or dramatic events. Always expecting the spectacular, many will miss entirely the constant flow of revealed communication" (in Munich Germany Area Conference, 1973, pp. 76–77).

And today, President Ezra Taft Benson has counseled that for every Lamoni, or Paul, "there are hundreds and thousands of people who find the process of repentance much more subtle, much more imperceptible. Day by day, they move closer to the Lord, little realizing they are building a godlike life" ("A Mighty Change of Heart," *Ensign*, Oct. 1989, p. 5).

Another factor that influences the reception of revelation is worthiness. Revelation is more readily given as we meet the personal conditions the Lord stipulates. We must submit our will to God, strive to be diligent, study the scriptures and the words of the modern prophets, and strive to be meek and lowly of heart. We need to learn from the experiences of Laman and Lemuel that due to wickedness, we can actually become "past feeling" and lose the capacity to hear the still, small voice prompting us (see 1 Nephi 17:45).

On one occasion, Oliver Cowdery desired to translate rather than act as scribe to the Prophet Joseph. He was not successful in his attempt, and was told by the Lord, "You took no thought save it was to ask me" (D&C 9:7). Not only do some "just ask," but they ask when the answers are already found in the scriptures and the words of the prophets. Elder Harold B. Lee, an Apostle, said, "It should not be necessary today for us to expect new written revelation on every point when we have these men [the Apostles and prophets] thus possessed of the same spirit of revelation. A brief review of the past instruction of our leaders should only serve to warn the disobedient and to encourage the obedient to continue faithful" (in Conference Report, Oct. 1941, p. 114).

Remember the Lord reveals His will to us in His own due time. We should not put time constraints or demands on the Lord. I feel it would be unwise to tell the Lord "I need an answer by Thursday or I will assume the answer is no." Elder Boyd K. Packer said, "It is not wise to wrestle with the revelations with such insistence as to demand immediate answers or blessings to your liking. You cannot force spiritual things. Such words as compel, coerce, constrain, pressure, demand, do not describe our privileges with the Spirit. You can no more force the Spirit to respond than you can force a bean to sprout, or an egg to hatch before its time. You can create a climate to foster growth, nourish, and protect; but you cannot force or compel: you must await the growth. Do not be impatient to gain great spiritual knowledge. Let it grow, help it grow, but do not force it or you will open the way to be misled" ("The Candle of the Lord," p. 53).

The Lord has blessed each of us with many talents and expects us to use those talents to do many things of our own free will (D&C 58:26–29). Elder Dallin H. Oaks, an Apostle, said, "The Spirit of the Lord is not likely to give us revelations on matters that are trivial. I once heard a young woman in a testimony meeting praise the spirituality of her husband, indicating that he submitted every question to the Lord. She told how he accompanied her shopping and would not even choose between different brands of canned vegetables without making his selection a matter of prayer. That strikes me as improper. I believe the Lord expects us to use our intelligence and experience he has given us to make these kinds of choices" (*Speeches of the Year!* [Provo: Brigham Young University Press, 1982], p. 26). Even the Lord has said on occasion that it "mattereth not" to Him on some items people are concerned with (D&C 60:5).

A frequently asked question is, "How can I discern between true revelation and its counterfeits?" In today's world there are many people claiming to be speaking for God. There are a few principles that need to be understood if we are to avoid deception.

First, the Spirit does not cause us to act in ways that are bizarre or out of harmony with the sacred nature of God. The scriptures teach "He that preacheth and he that receiveth, understand one another, and both are edified and rejoice together. And that which doth not edify is not of God, and is darkness" (D&C 50:22–23). The Prophet Joseph taught that false spirits are found in The Church of Jesus

Christ of Latter-day Saints. He mentioned on one occasion that:

> Soon after the Gospel was established in Kirtland, and during the absence of the authorities of the Church, many false spirits were introduced, many strange visions were seen, and wild, enthusiastic notions were entertained; men ran out of doors under the influence of this spirit, and some of them got upon the stumps of trees and shouted, and all kinds of extravagances were entered into by them; one man pursued a ball that he said he saw flying in the air, until he came to a precipice, when he jumped into the top of a tree, which saved his life; and many ridiculous things were entered into, calculated to bring disgrace upon the Church of God, to cause the Spirit of God to be withdrawn, and to uproot and destroy those glorious principles which had been developed for the salvation of the human family (*Discourses of the Prophet Joseph Smith,* comp. Alma P. Burton [Salt Lake City: Deseret Book Co., 1965], p. 92).

The Prophet Joseph further taught that what we sometimes assume are ministering angels in the Church are in reality Satan and those cast out with him, who can appear as angels of light. He told the story of a sister in New York who had a vision and was told that if she would walk to a certain place in the woods an angel would appear to her. The Prophet continued:

> She went at the appointed time, and saw a glorious personage descending, arrayed in white, with sandy colored hair; he commenced and told her to fear God, and said that her husband was called to do great things, but that he must not go more than one hundred miles from home, or he would not return; whereas God had called him to go to the ends of the earth, and he has since been more than one thousand miles from home, and is yet alive. Many true things were spoken by this personage, and many things that were false. How, it may be asked,

was this known to be a bad angel? By the color of his hair; that is one of the signs that he can be known by, and by his contradicting a former revelation (*Discourses,* p. 93).

We need to understand then that a true messenger from our Father in Heaven would not contradict truths already revealed.

Next, we need to understand that revelation comes through certain channels. Our Heavenly Father's house is a house of order. Elder Dallin H. Oaks, said, "Only the president of the Church receives revelation to guide the entire Church. Only the stake president receives revelation for the special guidance of the stake. The person who receives revelation for the ward is the bishop. For a family, it is the priesthood leadership of the family. Individuals can receive revelation to guide their own lives. But when one person purports to receive revelation for another person outside his or her own stewardship—such as a Church member who claims to have revelation to guide the entire Church or a person who claims to have revelation to guide another person over whom he or she has no presiding authority according to the order of the Church—you can be sure that such revelations are not from the Lord" ("Revelation," 1982, p. 25). When we follow our priesthood leaders, they will help us recognize revelation from our Father in Heaven.

Elder Bruce R. McConkie, said, "Would you like a formula to tell you how to get personal revelation? It might be written in many ways. My formula is simply this: 1. Search the scriptures 2. Keep the commandments 3. Ask in faith.

"Any person who will do this will get his heart so in tune with the Infinite that there will come into his being, from the 'still small voice' the eternal realities of religion. And as he progresses and advances and comes nearer to God, there will be a day when he will entertain angels, when he will see visions, and the final end is to view the face of God" (Bruce R. McConkie, *How to Get Personal Revelation*, Brigham Young University Speeches of the Year [Provo, 11 Oct. 1966], p. 6).

I believe the following poem by Edwin Markham best summarizes the step by step, line by line process of receiving revelation. The poem reads:

> *The builder who first bridged Niagara's gorge*
> *Before he swung his cable shore to shore*
> *Sent out across the gulf his venturing kite*
> *Bearing a slender cord from unseen hands*
> *To grasp upon the further cliff and draw*
> *A greater cord, and then a greater yet,*
> *Till at last across the chasm swung*
> *The cable—then mighty bridge in air.*
>
> *So we may send our little timid thoughts*
> *Across the void, out to God's reaching hands—*
> *Send out our love and faith to thread the deep—*
> *Thought after thought until the little cord*
> *Has greatened to a chain no chance can break.*
> *And we are anchored to the infinite.*

We need to next address how we should treat those special, spiritual experiences we have in our lives. The scriptures give us great counsel when they say "Remember that that which cometh from above is sacred, and must be spoken with care, and by constraint of the Spirit; and in this there is no condemnation, and ye receive the Spirit through prayer; wherefore, without this there remaineth condemnation" (D&C 63:64). Elder Boyd K. Packer said, "I have come to believe also that it is not wise to continually talk of unusual spiritual experiences. They are to be guarded with care and shared only when the Spirit itself prompts you to use them to the blessing of others" ("The Candle of the Lord," p. 53).

Lastly, now that we understand some of the principles upon which the receipt of revelation is based, what is our responsibility upon receiving promptings from the Spirit? Alma teaches us that if we don't accept God's word when it is given, we may lose what we have (see Alma 12:9–12). Brigham Young stated, "When a revelation is given to any people, they must walk according to it, or suffer the penalty which is the punishment of disobedience" (*Journal of Discourses*, 12:127). Elder Boyd K. Packer told a personal experience wherein he suffered the consequences of not following the promptings of the Spirit. He said:

> I had been prompted several times, for the good of the work, to release one of my counselors. Besides praying about it, I had reasoned that it was the right thing to do. But I did not do it. I feared that it would injure a man who had given long service to the Church.
>
> The Spirit withdrew from me. I could get no promptings on who should be called as a counselor should I release him. It lasted for several weeks. My prayers seemed to be contained within the room where I offered them. I tried a number of alternate ways to arrange the work, but to no avail. Finally, I did as I was bidden to do by the Spirit. Immediately, the gift returned! Oh, the exquisite sweetness to have the gift again. You know it, for you have it, the gift of the Holy Ghost. And the brother was not injured, indeed he was greatly blessed and immediately thereafter the work prospered ("The Candle of the Lord," p. 55).

I hope that as each of us strives to gain a stronger testimony of Jesus Christ and his gospel, we will reflect upon these principles. The only way a person can know that the gospel of Jesus Christ and this Church are true is by personal revelation. I pray that we will ponder the scriptures and the words of the prophets and Apostles. Then, as we are privileged to receive the promptings of that "still, small voice"—the Holy Ghost, we will follow them.

Randall Bird has taught seminary for more than twenty years and is now manager of seminary curriculum in the Church Educational System. Brother Bird maintains a life-long interest in athletics—during his high school years, he was named to the Idaho all-state teams in football and track. He has been a high school coach in both sports and also enjoys fishing, collecting sports memorabilia, reading, and being with his family. He and his wife, Carla Aikele, have six children.

6

MANY ARE CALLED, BUT WHO IS CHOSEN?

DAVID L. BUCKNER

It was a cold December morning, and the skies were blue and clear. The two feet of new powdery snow that had fallen throughout the night muffled the sounds of the city in the distance. A day like this is what ski dreams are made of—one of those rare times when all the elements come together perfectly. I took a deep breath and smiled with anticipation. "Okay, class, this is it. Remember to make your 'pizza pies' around the turn and your 'french fries' across the hill," I barked out to my ski class.

I had learned as a young ski instructor, that kids always relate well to food. So in order to get them to ski properly, I would have them chant, "Pizza pies around the turn, french fries across the hill, pizza pies around the turn, french fries across the hill." To anyone observing us, this "Fast Food Midget Brigade" would have looked and sounded really strange.

As we turned the corner in true "pizza pie" fashion, I heard a faint, female voice crying out for help. "Please, anyone, help me!" The cry came once again. "Can anyone hear me? Please, please help me!" I counted my students, seven, eight, nine. They were all there. "Help me, please, is anyone there?" The frantic cries were now mere whimpers and the voice was fading. It was coming from a cluster of trees a short distance away. Surely, something must be wrong, I thought. If she were all right, she would have come back to the trail and waited for help there. She must be hurt. I instructed my students to ski down to the next tree in the middle of the ski run and wait. "Don't go beyond the tree," I repeated. "Stay right there, and I'll be right back," I told them with even greater emphasis.

I began to work my way through the deep, untracked powdery snow that had fallen the night before. The trees were thick, but the voice was constant. "Help, please help," came the muffled cries. Finally, I saw a red jacket and followed the ski tracks to the base of two very large pine trees. A woman sat, curled up in a ball, surrounded by various pieces of discarded ski gear. As I broke through the last vestige of thick brush she turned her eyes toward me. She began to cry when she saw me coming toward her, wearing my jolly-green-giant ski instructor's suit. "Are you all right?" I asked. I was anxious to find out if she had run into the tree she was sitting by. My years of experience as a skier had taught me that human flesh and hard wood generate pain when they collide. Especially when one of them is traveling at a high rate of speed.

Her response was puzzling. "I'm all right. But how did you ever find me so far out here?" It didn't make sense to me. We were only one hundred feet from the trail. As I removed my skis and began to help her collect her belongings, I asked her why she hadn't just carried her skis and poles back to the trail and started down again? The tears were now flowing more freely. "What trail?" she asked. "The trail must be miles away. I left it long ago and wondered if anyone would ever find me way out here."

Helping her to her feet, I turned her toward the open ski hill. The silence of the morning was broken by my students' laughing and taunting each other. "Those voices, they are so close. They must be lost, too," she said. I pointed in the direction of the voices and immediately she caught a glimpse of my students waiting on the trail by the tree. Tears welled up again in her eyes as she realized how very close she had been to the pathway. She was not miles away from civilization, just moments. Yet she had wandered from the safety of the open trail, had become frightened, given up hope, thrown off her skis and poles, and quit. She began to mutter to herself, "I was so close, so very close, and I really thought I was going to die."

Feelings of hopelessness and despair are some of Satan's greatest tools. More than anything in the world, he wants us to quit, give up, abandon our faith, throw away the helps the Lord has given us to get home, and declare ourselves lost. The adversary would have us believe that if we make mistakes, we cannot return to the path of righteousness. He would have us believe that the gospel of Jesus Christ is a country club for Saints, not a hospital for sinners. He must take pleasure in watching us quit, abandon our missions in life, and declare ourselves lost when we are standing only a few feet from the pathway of righteousness.

But why? Why does the adversary work so hard on the youth of today? Why does he obscure the pathway of righteousness with trees of hopelessness and despair? Why does he strive to make us feel we have strayed far from the pathway, when in reality, we are very near?

Answers to such questions become clear as we begin to understand where we are in the great plan of our Father in Heaven. With each passing day, we see more and more of the signs of the times described by our elder brother Jesus Christ while he was on the earth. Events which will usher in the Second Coming are reported every day on our television news broadcasts. "And they shall hear of wars, and rumors of wars. Behold I speak for mine elect's sake; for nation shall rise against nation, and kingdom against kingdom; there shall be famines, and pestilences, and earth-quakes, in divers places. And again, because iniquity shall abound, the love of men shall wax cold" (Joseph Smith–Matthew 1:28–30).

Reports on the wars that have plagued Yugoslavia, Somalia, Haiti, and even our own inner cities, are now daily fare on our news broadcasts. The floods in the Midwest, the devastating fires and earthquakes in California, and the horrible violence that is terrorizing neighborhoods every-where, are no small reminders that the Lord saw our time and knew what we were going to experience. He issued this warning: "Verily, I say unto you, *this generation,* in which *these* things shall be shown forth, shall not pass away until all I have told you shall be fulfilled . . . So likewise, mine elect, when they shall see all these things, they shall know that he is near, even at the doors" (Joseph Smith–Matthew 1:34–39; emphasis added).

"Even at the doors."

"Even at the doors."

"Even at the doors."

The thought ran around and around in my head. Could these really be the last days? And if they are, am I doing all I am supposed to as a spirit saved for this time, chosen to come down and make final preparations for the Second Coming? Am I helping people get back on the right path?

My thoughts were interrupted by the crash of the emer-gency room door flying open. It was another day at the ski resort, but the day was somehow different. I was sitting beside the bed of a young girl I had brought into the ski patrol infirmary, as another unlucky victim was brought in on a stretcher, after an unfortunate encounter with a tree on the bunny slope. "The tree jumped right in front of me, I promise," exclaimed the new arrival. My student, a ten-year-old girl named Elizabeth, lay next to me, complaining about her aching leg. She really wasn't hurt, but today had been designated as her "bad ski day." She was tired and had had enough of skiing for the day. So after a harmless fall, we made our way to the ski patrol emergency center to find her a bed and to let her rest for a while.

Once again the door in the corner of the room crashed open, and in walked a tall man with dark, curly hair. I immediately recognized him. I had seen him in many movies and knew that he skied frequently at the resort. As he walked toward me, I stood to introduce myself. My palms were sweaty and my pulse raced. I had to keep cool. After all, I was the ski instructor—calm, cool, and in control. I extended my hand and stammered, "I'm David Buckner, and this is . . . " I was just about to introduce Elizabeth, but it wasn't necessary. A smile lit up her face. Tears started down her cheeks, and she stretched out her arms for a hug. "Daddy, oh Daddy, I'm so glad you're here," she said, meeting him with the kind of hug only a ten-year-old girl can give to her dad.

After comforting his daughter, he turned to me and said something I will never forget. "You are so lucky!" Taken back for a moment, and looking around to see if he was really speaking to me, I couldn't believe it. "Me lucky?" How could he possibly think so?

He walked to the window and looked out at the pristine mountains covered with a new blanket of snow, and repeated his comment. "You are so lucky!" By this time, I realized he was really talking to me. I almost blurted out, "Would you like to trade 'luck' for a week? I'll go live in your Beverly Hills mansion or even your Malibu beach house for a week. I'll star in the movies and be rich, and you can live in my one-bedroom, basement apartment in Provo, Utah and teach school for me. Wanna trade, wanna trade, wanna trade?"

But just before my mouth got ahead of my thinking, he turned to me and said, "I have to plan months in advance

to spend just one week with my family in this beautiful setting. And you are here every day. You are so lucky." Wow, I
had never really seen myself as particularly lucky.

As I drove home that night from the ski resort, I thought
a lot about the events of that day. "Lucky. Am I really
lucky?" I thought. Could it be that I really had something
in my life that would make a Hollywood moviestar envious
of me? The more I thought about it, the more I reflected on
the Savior's words.

"Even at the doors."

"Even at the doors."

"Even at the doors."

I began to ponder, what are the chances of my being
here today, in this dispensation, at a time when so many of
the signs of the Second Coming are being fulfilled? As I
thought about all the people on the face of the earth today
who do not have the gospel in their lives, who don't even
know who will be coming through those doors when He
comes, I began to realize how lucky I really am—how lucky
we all are.

Consider this:

• You have *1 chance in 17* of being born in the United
States of America (6 percent of the world's population).

• You have *1 chance in 34* of being born the gender you
are, in the United States of America.

• You have *1 chance in 34,000* to be a member of The
Church of Jesus Christ of Latter-day Saints, born in the
United States of America, the gender that you are.

• You have *1 chance in 60* to have been born in this century (assuming 6000 years since the days of Adam).

• You have *1 chance in 2,040,000* to have been born in
this century, in the United States of America, the gender
you are, and to be a member of The Church of Jesus Christ
of Latter-day Saints.

• If you're happy to have been born in the decade in

which you were, the chances of you being here are even
more remote. Combine all the factors together, including
being born in your decade, you have *1 chance in 20,400,000*
of being where you are today.

Are you here by chance? Would you like to go back and
start all over again facing such monumental odds? As I
pondered these questions, I began to realize what had been
said to me that day was really true. I *am* so very lucky. I'm
not here by chance. I have been chosen to come down at
this time to prepare for the Second Coming of my brother
Jesus Christ. I can even imagine the faces of those 20,400,000
people who I represent at this time in history, many of
whom are looking to me to help prepare for the return of
the Savior.

Every day, we come face to face with some of those
20,400,000 we represent. Yet, I will never forget the day I
met one of them—a young lady sitting on the steps of a
museum in Prague, Czechoslovakia, who taught me in just
a few words how lucky I am.

My wife and I had arrived early that morning by train
to see that beautiful European city and learn of its people. I
had never been there before, and I couldn't even spell the
name of the country with any degree of confidence. As we
walked around the old city on a cold November day, the
mist from the river filled the small, narrow streets in which
the townspeople were hustling to work and to market. We
made our way to the steps of the National Museum where a
small demonstration was taking place. At first, only a few
people gathered around the statue in the square. Then,
more and more began to arrive. Hundreds and then thousands filled the square as we watched. As the crowd grew, I
asked several people around me what was going on. No
one could speak English, except for the young girl who was
sitting on the steps, watching the chaos. I asked her, "What
is happening?" Her response was simple. "This is our, how

do you say it . . . our '1776.' This is our two-year celebration of freedom." She paused, then continued in a powerful and most heartfelt tone, "We have had TWO years of freedom. You have had TWO HUNDRED!"

Face to face, I met my sister—one of those 20,400,000 I represent. All my life I have enjoyed the freedom to make choices, and I have had the gospel of Jesus Christ in my life. She had enjoyed the freedom to choose for only two short years, and she is still awaiting the gospel of Jesus Christ.

My dear young brothers and sisters, many of our eternal family members have strayed off the pathway leading to eternal life. Some of you have likewise found yourselves off the path, lost in heavily wooded areas of deception and despair. Many have discarded the guidance equipment the Lord has provided to help us remain on the path—aids such as prayer, the scriptures, and repentance. Some have given up all hope of ever returning, feeling they are too far off the track to find their way back. This is not the case.

Our Father in Heaven wants us home with him. He sent our elder brother Jesus Christ to provide a way for us to get home again. He has held back for these final days, the noblest and most valiant spirits. The youth of today are those spirits. You are not here by chance or by mistake. You were chosen to come at this time, to represent those 20,400,000, during a critical time in the history of the world. That calling is enormous! The weight on your shoulders is great! You must remember the Lord's challenge to you: "So likewise, mine elect, when they shall see these things, they shall know that he is near, even at the doors; . . . Therefore be ye also ready, for in such an hour as ye think not, the Son of Man cometh" (Joseph Smith–Matthew 1:39, 48).

My prayer is that you will stay close to the pathway of righteousness. *Learn of your calling, feel the urgency* of that enormous responsibility, and decide now to *make a difference* as a chosen spirit in this, the last dispensation of time.

David Buckner was a professional ski instructor for six years at Deer Valley Ski Resort and is a part-time faculty member at Brigham Young University. A certified emergency medical technician (EMT), David enjoys scuba diving and mountain biking as well as traveling and attending Broadway theater productions. He is working on his master's degree in international relations and law at BYU. Brother Buckner is a counselor in a bishopric and particularly enjoys working with and speaking to the youth. He is married to Jennifer Jackson.

7

THIRTY DAYS, THAT'S ALL WE ASK

JOHN BYTHEWAY

What are you doing? Reading a book? How boring! Aren't you supposed to be hanging out at the mall, or something? Isn't there a television set or a Nintendo game nearby? Isn't that what an average teenager would be doing right now? Well, maybe an average teenager, but you, my friend, are *not* an average teenager. You are every bit as wonderful as you've been told you are. So, congratulations for going against the grain and reading a book, but I have to warn you about something: this is a chapter with a challenge; and you are such a remarkable teenager that you will probably accept the challenge and finish it to the end. I gave this challenge once to a gathering of LDS youth at a stake meeting in Alberta, Canada and was overwhelmed to see about six hundred teenagers rise to their feet, signaling their willingness to accept. I still haven't finished reading their letters. I've given this challenge many times in the form of a talk, but never in a book. I don't know if it will work in a book. I guess we'll find out.

What is the challenge you ask? Well, I'm getting to that. You've heard the debates about television—you know, whether or not the violence and immorality we watch really affects us. Over the past few months, I've collected tons of newspaper and magazine articles, containing arguments on both sides of the debate. I have some really good ones. If I had enough space here, I could reprint all these articles and make a pretty convincing argument that much of television is hurting us. But I think I'm going to try a different approach.

When Moroni inscribed his last words on the gold plates he didn't provide a lot of proofs that we could look at to tell if the book was true. He didn't come up with a lot of facts or talk about the archaeological or anthropological evidences for the book. He just said, in effect, "Read it for yourself." Maybe that's the best approach to take with the TV issue. Ask yourself these questions: How does it affect me? Does it affect my spirit? Does watching it make it harder for me to live the gospel? Then you decide—not for everyone else—but for you.

Whenever television producers are accused of providing harmful programming, they always say, "Well, if you don't like it, just turn it off." Exactly. And that's what I'm suggesting you do. That's what I did. For a month. No TV, no movies, no videos. (Okay, I picked February, which is the shortest month, but it's still a month.) I thought I knew what it would be like, but I was wrong. It was quite an experience. The first few days were difficult. But little by little, I began to find alternative things to do with my time. Using my memory and some notes from my journal, I've put together a "play by play" account of what it was like to give up TV for a month.

Day Four

I began to notice how much more time I had! Every day when I would get home from school, I would think, "Hmm, what should I do now?" Before, I used to just plop down on the couch and "watch TV" for a few minutes. But a few minutes would often turn into an hour, or two, or three.

And then I'd scratch my head and wonder how I was going to get my homework done. Well, after four days without TV, I had made a list of all the things I was going to do during my "TV fast." I had books to read, places to go, projects to complete, and so forth.

Day Ten

On day ten, something hit me that I didn't expect. I suddenly noticed that I was having a much easier time controlling my thoughts! I realized that the main place where "the truth and values we embrace are mocked on every hand" is on television! I was no longer hearing off-color jokes on a daily basis. I was no longer being an eyewitness to illicit situations that made me feel like a Peeping Tom. And, of course, all this was having a positive effect on my thoughts! Satan is relentless. Most of the input from the world makes it hard to keep our thoughts on a higher plane. Is it important to control our thoughts? Are we accountable for our thoughts? Oh yes. "For our words will condemn us, yea, all our works will condemn us; we shall not be found spotless; and our thoughts will also condemn us; and in this awful state we shall not dare to look up to our God" (Alma 12:14).

Day Fourteen

Okay, here's the hard part. It was really hard not to judge the TV-watchers around me. I stopped watching TV for two weeks, and it seemed like that's all everyone else ever did! Sometimes I'd walk into my apartment where all my roommates were parked on the couch in front of the tube and think to myself, "Everyone seems so lazy all of a sudden—did I used to waste time like that?"

Day Sixteen

Have you ever been preparing to give a talk or attend church and felt like you needed to take a minute to clean out your brain? You know, a time-out to clear out all the stuff you've seen and heard in the last few days and move to higher ground? I think you know what I mean. Well, on day sixteen, I was preparing to give a fireside, and it seemed so much easier! I didn't have to clear out my brain, because it was already clear. I didn't have to work around all the clutter from the media, because it wasn't in there! Bad stuff gets in the way of good stuff. Listen to Elder H. Burke Peterson: "When we see or hear anything filthy or vulgar, whatever the source, our mind records it, and as it makes the filthy record, beauty and clean thoughts are pushed into the background. Hope and faith in Christ begin to fade, and more and more, turmoil and discontent become our companions" ("Touch Not the Evil Gift, Nor the Unclean Thing," *Ensign*, Nov. 1993, p. 43).

Day Twenty

On day twenty I'm thinking, "I'm having fun. I've read several books, I've written tons of letters, my room is cleaner than it's ever been, I've been exercising more consistently, and I feel closer to the Lord. Why didn't I try this before?"

We are all so hyper about what we put into our bodies. We want to be drug-free, alcohol-free, and tobacco-free. If someone says "You are what you eat," we agree! We don't argue about it! But, what about our spirits? If we're so concerned about what we put into our bodies, why aren't we equally concerned about what we put into our minds? "For as [a man] thinketh in his heart, so is he" (Proverbs 23:7).

Day Twenty-Eight

"Well, tomorrow I'm done with the TV Termination Test. That went by fast. Do I really want to watch again? I don't know. I know I'll be more selective that's for sure."

It's interesting the number of ways we protect ourselves

from things. We put dead-bolt locks on the doors, motion-sensor lights in the yard, and buy a burglar alarm. To keep things warm inside, we install double-paned glass, insulation, and weather stripping. Then we kneel down as a family and ask the Lord to "protect us from harm or accident." But Satan is clever. He can find a way into your house. He can come right through the antenna (or the cable). Or, we can actually pay money to "rent" his influence from the video store. Listen again to Elder H. Burke Peterson:

> Brethren, I plead with you to leave it alone. Stay away from any movie, video, publication, or music—*regardless of its rating*—where illicit behavior and expressions are a part of the action. Have the courage to turn it off in your living room. Throw the tapes and the publications in the garbage can, for that is where we keep garbage. . . . Again I say, leave it alone. Turn it off, walk away from it, burn it, erase it, destroy it. I know it is hard counsel we give when we say movies that are R-rated, and many with PG-13 ratings, are produced by satanic influences. Our standards should not be dictated by the rating system ("Touch Not the Evil Gift, Nor the Unclean Thing" p. 43).

My experiment was over on February 28, and I started watching TV again in March. It was interesting. Things bothered me more than they did before. My vacation from TV increased my sensitivity to certain things.

Over the years I guess I had gotten used to hearing the language of television. Now, with the TV on again, I was hearing the Lord's name in vain and other crude language and innuendo, and it bugged me more than before. My spirit was saying, "Yuck, this is sick." Listen to Elder Boyd K. Packer: "Profanity is more than just untidy language, for when we profane we relate to low and vulgar words, the most sacred of all names. I wince when I hear the name of the Lord so used, called upon in anger, in frustration, in hatred" (Boyd K. Packer, in Conference Report, Oct. 1967, p. 128).

To put it in a nutshell, my experiment worked. I didn't need to clip out any more articles. I had proved it to myself. The TV did have an effect on my spirit, and I knew it. All the printed research in the world wasn't as powerful a persuader as my personal experiment. Someone once said, "A friend is someone who makes it easier to live the gospel of Jesus Christ." As a result of my experiment, I know that if someone were to ask me, "Is the television your friend?" I would have to say "No—its more like an enemy." There's no way I could honestly say that watching television has made it *easier* for me to live the gospel.

Well, I'm sure you know what's coming next. You're right—the challenge. Some of you will accept this challenge. I hope all of you will. Here goes (imagine this next sentence coming from a deep voice with an echo). I challenge you to give up TV, movies, and videos for a month! (Imagine a clap of thunder and the ground shaking). I know you can do it, because I did it. Try it! Prove it to yourself. Keep a journal and take note of how you feel and of what happens to your spirit. It could change your life. Every youth who has accepted this challenge and written to me about their experience has had great things to say. If you need some further persuasion, listen to Lindsay from Clayton, California:

> I liked what you had to say about TV, and I decided to take the challenge not to watch TV for one whole month . . . and, well, to make a short story shorter, my whole family decided to go without TV. I think it was the hardest on my mother because she doesn't have a job and is home all the time, but she took up canning. So now we have every kind of jam and jelly you can think of. Name it, and we've got it in our freezer. My dad has suddenly found time to figure out our new computer system, and

all of us have been able to work on and develop our own talents. It's incredible to think back and realize how much we had been letting television monopolize our lives. Our home is much quieter and peaceful now. . . . But I think the neatest thing is, that the Spirit can be in our home all the time. . . . I'd like to thank you for giving us that challenge. My family and I have really benefited from it, and we've liked it so much that we're going to try to go for a whole year.

Here's another—listen to Laura from Delta, Utah:

> I don't know how I can thank you for this wonderful experience of the "TV Blackout." It has changed my life greatly for the better. I have gained a stronger testimony by using time to read the scriptures. . . . I found that I had uplifting thoughts, and it was easy for me because the garbage that is on TV didn't come into my mind. I earned a 3.994 in school this term because I found I had more time in the evening to study instead of watching TV. I have also lost fifteen pounds because I have been going to the recreation center instead of watching TV. I have decided that I should only watch the three shows that I really like. TV can be such a time waster. Because I have seen how much I can accomplish, and what a great effect this has had on me, I simply refuse to sit in front of the TV and do nothing.

Now, I don't know if you'll lose fifteen pounds, but I think I *can* promise you four things: **First,** you'll have much more time. (They say the television is on an average of seven hours, four minutes per day!). **Second,** you'll have an easier time controlling your thoughts. (You know what they say in the computer programming business—"Garbage in, garbage out!") **Third,** your spiritual sensitivity will increase. As you "deny yourselves of all ungodliness," you'll feel closer to the Lord (see Moroni 10:32). **Fourth,** you'll be more selective in the future. You won't just sit down to "watch TV." You'll choose carefully what you watch instead of punching the remote from a slouched position for three hours. Like everything else, any powerful tool can be used as an awful weapon. Of course there are some excellent programs on TV, but Satan has found a way to use the media as a weapon as well. We are foolish if we just sit there and let him parade all his evils before us.

Well, this chapter is over. It went by fast, didn't it? And so will your thirty days. There are many great chapters ahead, so keep reading! Once again, congratulations for reading a book. I've read a million of those "chosen generation" quotes about you, and I believe every one of them. I know you're working hard to live up to your potential and that it is not always easy. I hope you will accept this challenge to cleanse your spirit, and at least for a month, be TV-free. You believe in the thirteenth article of faith, right? Well, don't let Hollywood make you a hypocrite! May the Lord bless you to truly seek after those things that are lovely, virtuous, of good report, and praiseworthy.

John Bytheway is a popular participant in EFY and other youth programs. A genuinely funny public speaker, he says it is peculiar to have a prepositional phrase for a last name, and he enlivens even his spiritual messages with a lot of humor. John holds a bachelor's degree in marketing and is doing graduate work in communications at Brigham Young University, where he is an administrator in Continuing Education. His other interests include running, reading, and playing the guitar.

8

HOW TO T.A.B.B.ULATE YOUR OWN SUCCESS (THINK, ACT, BELIEVE, AND BECOME)

VIVIAN CLINE

As I've traveled and met people, I've noticed that successful individuals all seem to have something in common. These people have a formula that helps them be successful. They all THINK successful thoughts, ACT as if they are successful, BELIEVE in themselves, and then they BECOME successful.

The scripture in Proverbs that tells us that as a man "thinketh in his heart, so is he," is really true. No one has ever accomplished anything without first "thinking" that he could do it. To succeed, you have to be totally positive.

I grew up in Atlanta, Georgia. Beautiful as it was, there were no mountains there tall enough for skiing. I saw snow-covered peaks for the first time when I came to school at Brigham Young University. I can remember being in awe of the majesty of the mountains and frightened by their height. Try as they might, my roommates could never quite convince me that the mountains were safe places to be. For me, skiing was totally out of the question.

When I met my husband, Doug, I found out that he was an avid skier. I decided that was okay. We were too poor then to afford to go skiing. Besides, he could always go with a friend, and I could just sit and sip cider at the lodge, right?

Wrong! Ten years and three sons later, my husband gave me an ultimatum. "I am a skier," he said. "I have three sons who are going to be skiers. I'm afraid if you don't learn to ski, you are going to be left 'Home Alone!!'"

Suddenly, I developed a desire to ski!

Off to the slopes we headed, outfitted with all the paraphernalia necessary to stay warm and comfortable. Doug, being the smart man that I married, enrolled me in a ski school so I could learn the basics. This consisted of a two-hour bout with about twelve other snow bunnies in which we learned two key things. First, always fall toward the mountain, not downhill. Second, put your feet into a pigeon-toed position called a "snow plow."

The next thing I knew, I was in a chairlift headed up to the top of the Himalayas (or so it seemed)! Total panic gripped me when I realized that the chairs coming down from the mountain were empty. There was only one way down—on skis.

This could not be happening. You see, I didn't know how to ski. My mother didn't ski. My father didn't ski. None of my friends or relatives skied. I simply could NOT ski either.

As we got closer to the top of the chairlift, I felt my joints stiffen. Sure enough, when the time came to get off, I found myself permanently frozen to the chair. Now they would *have* to let me ride back down. I couldn't move.

Wrong! I suffered the humiliation of my life when they stopped the lift so Doug and another guy could pry me off the chair. Now I was doomed for sure. I couldn't ski down. I didn't know HOW to ski.

There I stood at the top of the mountain. I finally decided that it was me against the mountain, and I was determined to win. My only goal was to get down in one piece. Since all I knew was the snow plow, I positioned my skis accordingly. I made one adjustment, however. Instead of facing downhill, I placed my left leg parallel to the mountain and my right leg on a diagonal. This allowed me to put all my weight on my left leg, and I used my right leg to push against the mountain as I slid sideways down.

My husband tried to help me by giving me encouragement and instruction, but it didn't help. You see, I didn't know HOW to ski. I had thoroughly convinced myself of that. Doug finally laughed, and said, "You know, you are going to kill your left leg."

I replied, "Maybe so, but at least I will make it to the bottom of the mountain in one piece."

Finally, after what seemed like at least three hours of hard work and while Doug made at least ten runs past me, I arrived at the bottom of the slope. I had won. I had showed the mountain who was boss. I had survived. Funny thing though, I actually enjoyed it!

I decided to do it again. This time I didn't go down on my left leg. I put my feet into the snow plow position and took a very tentative zigzag path down the hill. My third and last time down, I made my zigzags shorter. I wasn't really skiing, but I was getting down much faster than I had originally.

A month or so later, my husband and I took an airplane trip back east. As we were soaring about twenty-five thousand feet above the ground, I began to think about my skiing adventure. I imagined myself at the top of the mountain in full gear. I began to go down the slopes in my mind.

Suddenly, it dawned on me. If I were facing downhill and put my weight on the ball of my left foot and took the weight off my right leg, I would turn right. In my mind I executed the move. Then, if I did the opposite by putting my weight onto the ball of my right foot and lifting the left leg, I would turn left.

Quickly, I turned to Doug, told him what I had just imagined, and asked him if that was the right way to turn. He laughed, and said it was.

You see, I didn't learn to ski on the top of a mountain slope but on an airplane twenty-five thousand feet above the slope. It was there that I began to *think* I could ski. If you don't THINK you can, you can't.

The next step in being successful is to ACT successful. "Act" is part of the word "action." You can think all the positive thoughts you want, but if you want to succeed you must act or work toward your goal.

I once heard a story about a young man who knew how to apply action to his positive thinking. This young man's family was poor, and he lived in a very humble home. He didn't do very well in school, and so he decided that he would drop out of school and find a job to help supplement the family income.

He found a job selling candy and newspapers on a train that ran from one town to the next. The only problem was that the train only made one run per day. It traveled from one town to the other in the morning and returned in the evening. That left him with the entire day to do nothing.

Although this young man could have hung out and pitched pennies with his friends, he choose to do something else. He found the only library in the town—it was only one room—and proceeded to read every book in it. Books on science and chemistry particularly interested him, and he began to do experiments.

Once, several years later, he performed one experiment ten thousand times. A friend finally said to him, "Why don't you just quit? You have failed ten thousand times."

"I haven't failed," he retorted. "I have only found ten thousand ways that it won't work."

Thank goodness for that man, who not only "thought" that his experiment would work, but who applied laborious "action" toward it. That young man's name was Thomas Edison, and he invented the electric light bulb that we enjoy so today.

After we "think" we can and apply "action" toward it, we must do the hardest thing of all. We must BELIEVE in ourselves, even if no one else does.

I know a story about a young man who believed in himself. His nickname was Sparky. He was named after a comic-strip horse by the name of Spark Plug when he was a boy, and the name stuck throughout his life.

Sparky was a loser and everybody knew it. He held the school record for being the worst student in the 8th grade. He flunked every subject that year. Straight F's.

No one was ever really mean to Sparky. No one cared enough to show him that much attention. He never dated in high school. He was so shy that he never asked a girl out. He was too afraid of being turned down.

Sports were not his strength either. Though he did manage to make the school golf team, he lost his only important match of the year.

Sparky was a loser. Everyone said so. After he had been called that long enough, he decided that it was just his fate in life to be mediocre. So he learned to live with it.

There was one thing, however, that was important to Sparky—his drawings. He loved art and was very proud of his art work. Naturally, no one else felt that way. He submitted some of his art work to the school yearbook, only to have it promptly turned down. Even though this was a great disappointment to Sparky, he still believed that his work was good and decided to become a professional artist.

After he graduated from high school, he applied to work for Walt Disney Studios. He sent some samples of his art work in for a proposed cartoon. When the reply came back from Disney Studios, it was "Thanks, but no thanks." Again, he had been rejected.

At last Sparky decided to write his autobiography in cartoons. He drew pictures and wrote about his childhood, about being the little boy who was an underachiever, about always being a loser. Soon his work became famous all over the world. You see, the little boy who failed every subject in the 8th grade and who was always known as the "loser," was none other than Charles Monroe Schultz. He created the comic strip "Peanuts" and the little boy whose kite would never fly—Charlie Brown.

At the height of Mr. Schultz's career, he was making thirty million dollars a year. A loser? I don't think so! I think he found that one of the secrets of being successful is to BELIEVE in yourself, even if no one else does.

I know another story that ends a little differently.

Bill was a young man from a large family who grew up on a farm in very humble circumstances. It was customary at that time to take the young men out of school and put them out in the fields to work as soon as they were big and strong enough to do so. For that reason, Bill was taken out of school in the 7th grade, at the age of twelve.

When he turned nineteen, he decided to leave the farm and go into the armed services. There was a war going on, and he wanted to do his patriotic duty.

While in the service, he found out that he could earn a general education diploma, which could be substituted for a high school diploma. He knew this would be a wonderful opportunity for him, so he took advantage of the program and made super grades.

After leaving the armed forces, Bill found that he was now eligible for a veteran's benefit that would help pay for a college education. He knew that a good education was important and decided to apply to a college. Oddly enough, he decided to apply to one of the most prestigious institutes of technology in the United States.

Amazingly, he was accepted! Here was a poor boy who

only finished the seventh grade, who never went to high school, and who only received a G.E.D. in the military. He passed the entrance exams to a very selective university. Miracle of miracles? No. Bill was just plain smart!

Before Bill could enter the university, however, he had to meet with a counselor who would help him plan his curriculum. After meeting with Bill and finding out about his background, the counselor proceeded to tell Bill how hard it was going to be for him. Because of his weak background in math, he would have to take remedial classes in order to prepare him for the more advanced classes.

By this time, Bill was married and had a child. He would have to work to support his family while going to school. He was also active in his church where he held leadership positions that took part of his time as well. With all of these considerations, the counselor told Bill that it would be all but impossible for him to make it through college.

Bill thought it over carefully and decided that the counselor was probably right. It really would be too difficult to accomplish such a task. Though he was a hard worker, Bill's lack of education limited the type of jobs he could get. He made an adequate income to support his family, but never the income he might have made had he obtained a college degree.

What was the difference between Sparky and Bill? Sparky believed in himself, and Bill didn't.

Winston Churchill, who was the prime minister of England during World War II, led his nation to victory. He once rallied his countrymen in a speech where he declared, "Never give up. Never give up. Never, never give up!" The person who *won't* be beaten, *can't* be beaten.

The last factor in our formula for success is to not only BECOME successful, but to BECOME the BEST.

We live in a world today in which mediocrity is the norm. Many of us not only fail to truly excel in school or at work, but we often just "get by" with the lowest possible grade or a minimal job performance. Once the United States produced the best goods in the world. Its workers made the best cars, manufactured the best steel, and created the best clothing. Now, not only is the U.S. not number one in the world, but it is way down the line, passed up by many countries who make superior products.

My husband and I had the opportunity to attend a Salt Lake City Chamber of Commerce meeting a couple of years ago. Charles Osgood, the famous news commentator, was the guest speaker. In the course of his speech, he shared with us a poem that he had written on mediocrity. Not only did he receive a standing ovation, but when the meeting was opened for questioning, the first question asked was, "Mr. Osgood, would you please share that poem with us one more time?"

The poem is entitled, "Pretty Good."

There once was a pretty good student,
Who sat in a pretty good class
And was taught by a pretty good teacher,
Who always let pretty good pass.
He wasn't terrific at reading;
He wasn't a whiz bang at math;
But for him education was leading
Straight down a pretty good path.
He didn't find school too exciting,
But he wanted to do pretty well
And he did have some trouble with writing,
And nobody had taught him to spell.
When doing arithmetic problems,
Pretty good was regarded as fine;
Five and five needn't always add up to be ten,
A pretty good answer was nine.
The pretty good student was happy
With the standards that were in effect,
And nobody thought it was sappy
If his answers were not quite correct.

The pretty good class that he sat in
Was part of a pretty good school,
And the student was not an exception;
On the contrary, he was the rule.
The pretty good school that he went to
Was right there in a pretty good town
And nobody there ever noticed
He could not tell a verb from a noun.
The pretty good student, in fact, was
A part of a pretty good mob,
And the first time he knew what he lacked was
When he looked for a pretty good job.
It was then, when he sought a position,
He discovered that life can be tough,
And he soon had a sneaking suspicion
Pretty good might not be good enough.
The pretty good town in our story
Was part of a pretty good state,
Which had pretty good aspirations
And prayed for a pretty good fate.
There once was a pretty good nation,
Pretty proud of the greatness it had,
But which learned much too late,
If you want to be great,
Pretty good is, in fact, pretty bad.
(THE OSGOOD FILE, CBS Radio Network,
     Copyrighted by CBS, Inc., all rights reserved.)

My young brothers and sisters, you were not sent here
to be mediocre. You were sent here to excel. You were sent
here to be the best.

Bishop H. Burke Peterson once said of you: "My dear
friends, you are a royal generation. You were preserved to
come to the earth in this time for a special purpose. Not just
a few of you, but all of you. There are things for each of you
to do that no one else can do as well as you. . . . If you will
let Him, I testify that our Father in Heaven will walk with
you through the journey of life and inspire you to know

your special purpose here" ("Your Life Has a Purpose," *The New Era,* May 1979, p. 5). Our dear prophet, President Ezra Taft Benson, has said, "You are to be the royal army of the Lord in the last days. You are 'youth of the noble birthright'" ("To the 'Youth of the Noble Birthright,'" *Ensign,* May 1986, p. 43).

It is my prayer that you will T.A.B.B.ulate your own success throughout your life. I hope that you will THINK successful thoughts and always be positive. I hope that you will establish honorable goals and ACT and work toward them. May you BELIEVE in yourself even if no one else does. And may you BECOME the successful generation that will indeed become the "royal army of the Lord in the last days."

Vivian Cline was a professional model for fifteen years and is now an image and business consultant. She is an accomplished public speaker who often addresses business conventions and especially enjoys her involvement in EFY and other youth activities. Vivian is the author of Dating, Dining, Dancing, and Other Teen Dilemmas *and serves as a Gospel Doctrine teacher. She likes to travel, read the scriptures, and watch her five children play sports. Married to S. Douglas Cline, she was named Mrs. Utah America in 1980.*

9

"THEY" CAN REALLY BE MEAN.
ARE YOU "THEY?"

TROY DUNN

THEY called me Chubby.
THEY called me Troy "Dumb."
And *THEY* even said I ran like a girl!

You know who *THEY* are. *THEY* are always someone who is faster, better looking, skinnier, older, and, by self-proclamation, cooler than *THEY* think you are.

Sure, I'll admit it. I *was* a little chubby. I was born chubby. My Huggies didn't hug. In fact, they didn't even shake hands! I seemed to be a little attached (pardon the pun) to my baby fat . . . and to peanut butter and marshmallow creme sandwiches. But, SO WHAT?

Troy "Dumb"? Now, attacking my physique is one thing, but attacking my family surname is quite another. I used to tell them, "It isn't over 'til it's over . . . and when it is, you will be finished, and I will be DUNN!" *THEY* were too dumb to get it! But, SO WHAT?

As for saying I ran like a girl . . . that really hurt . . . because even the girls were insulted! I remember that experience as one of my all-time lows. However, I have to mention that *THEY* seemed to have forgotten all their teasing and put-downs when, a few years later, I was the starting running back on our 4A State Championship football team and was being widely recruited by some of the best universities in the country. . . . But, SO WHAT?

The really upsetting thing to me was that even when my family moved to a different state, and I began going to a new school, . . . THEY were there too! Different faces, but it was definitely THEM!

I eventually realized that I was not their only victim. THEY thoroughly enjoyed humiliating anyone THEY could label in some way: "Zit Heads." "Dumb Jocks." As well as the "Geeks" in band and debate. THEY would roll their eyes and laugh derisively at anyone whose clothes, hairstyle, or car was considered by them as "not" rather than "hot."

Membership in their exclusive club required beauty, bronze, and/or money! THEY were the royalty above us commoners.

Fortunately, I didn't always buy into their mentality. But, unfortunately, some kids did. And what is even more unfortunate, THEY are still around. In fact, THEY have spawned a whole new generation of self-proclaimed critics with inflated superiority complexes.

Do you know who THEY are?

More importantly, is it possible THEY could be you?

Now, before you too quickly and self-righteously take yourself out of the running because you are quite sure that you would never label anyone and you are certain that you would never treat anyone as inferior to yourself, . . . realize that you just did exactly that! Yes, I just helped you see yourself as different from and better than THEY are. Oops!

You must understand, an attitude of superiority is a very insidious kind of cancer. Little noticed at first, it can quietly grow into an ugly, self-perpetuating, full-blown social tumor. It can begin with one little insensitive, unkind remark or a disdainful glance. Then, once started, the habit of passing judgment and ridiculing others can escalate.

When it gains any kind of momentum, it is hard to stop it or even slow it down.

Let's define insidious. Something is insidious if it has a gradual and cumulative effect. Here is an example. Did you know that you could accumulate over ten million dollars in just thirty-one days, by saving one penny today and doubling it tomorrow and then continuing to double the amount every day for thirty-one days? Ten million, seven hundred and thirty-seven thousand, four hundred and eighteen dollars, and twenty-four cents!

That's how insidious works!

Well, the good news is that if a negative attitude of superiority can grow insidiously and multiply, so can a humble, Christlike attitude.

There really aren't any secrets or tricks to bringing about such a "mighty change." It may not be easy, but the process is simple. If we hope to change our deeds, we must first change our hearts.

As I have been involved in speaking to youth around the country for the last several years, I have heard some very sad stories from youth who have suffered because they have been put down by others. These young people have been humiliated, demoralized, and demeaned by other young people who have felt superior for one reason or another. Too often this pain has been inflicted not by the unkind people of the cold, heartless world, but by other LDS youth!

Think of it. Our own brothers and sisters tearing down one another; deliberately trying to elevate themselves at the expense of someone else. How can members of the Church, who regularly partake of the sacrament and commit themselves to always remember the Savior and keep his commandments, go around ridiculing or belittling other people? It's not right. If Heavenly Father, the greatest of all, is no respecter of persons, how can we possibly justify feeling superior to *anyone?* Obviously, we can't.

The rich are not superior to the poor.
The strong are not superior to the weak.
Homeowners are not superior to the homeless.
The fit are not superior to the fat,
Nor the tall to the short.
The healthy are not superior to the handicapped.
The white are not superior to the black,
Nor are the young superior to the old.
Seniors are not superior to sophomores,
And LDS are not superior to nonmembers.

Excuse me a moment while I take a well-known scripture out of its context: The Lord did not command us to *divide* and *diminish* the earth. Rather, he commanded that we *multiply* and *replenish* it! The Lord teaches us principles that magnify, multiply, and add to our worth. It is Satan, the father of lies, who diminishes and divides—persuading us that people we meet who are different from us are somehow inferior to us.

Consider the example of the Savior. Though he could walk on water, turn a stone into bread, heal the sick, and even raise the dead, he did not put people down. Instead, he lifted them, reinforced their self-worth, and confirmed their self-esteem. He communicated by everything he said and did that every individual is unique and valuable in God's eyes. Indeed, it is his work and his glory to bring to pass the immortality and eternal life of man; and Jesus laid down his precious life for us—that we might be one day resurrected and redeemed from the effects of our sins.

He demonstrated his love, concern, and humility by kneeling before his disciples and ministering to them by washing their feet (see John 13:4–17). You might like to think for a moment about living conditions at the time this impressive event took place. Given the climate of the Middle East, the dusty roads, and the kind of footwear these men likely wore, to wash another's feet was a significant act of service as well as a demonstration of humility.

Read that scripture, young people. It is so powerful. "For I have given you an example, that ye should do as I have done to you. Verily, verily, I say unto you, The servant is not greater than his lord; neither he that is sent greater than he that sent him. If ye know these things, happy are ye if ye do them" (verses 15–17).

LDS youth, you know these things. Please do them. If a fleeting moment of self-importance tempts you to belittle someone else, humble your heart. Consider the stars in the heavens, the mountains and the seas, a butterfly, a rainbow, a newborn baby, and, yes, even chubby me. All of these things are the products of God's creative genius, just as each of us is. He is the master designer, and we all wear the ultimate designer label—Child of God.

I recently attended my high school reunion. I was impressed that no one seemed to be checking out what anyone else was wearing or driving. Instead, all of us were admiring each other's family pictures. I'm pleased to say that no one called me "Chubby" or "Troy Dumb" or accused me of running like a girl. We seemed to have grown up and out of the need to ridicule each other. Most of us had learned to say what I had been saying all along . . . SO WHAT?

It's nice to be important, but it is surely more important to be nice. It is my prayer for you, my young brothers and sisters, that by your words and actions, you will treat everyone you meet with the respect and kindness that grow out of knowing that every person is a child of God.

Troy Dunn remembers being picked on and ridiculed as a boy, a situation he remedied in part by taking up weight lifting. He attended Pitt State University and is the founder and president of his own company, International Locator, Inc. His hobbies include scuba diving and other sports. A popular youth speaker, Troy serves as a stake Young Men president. He is married to Jennifer Farrell, and they have three children.

10

BLESSED ARE THE PEACEMAKERS

SUE EGAN

Have you ever been guilty of passing along gossip about someone? Has anyone ever made you so mad that you vowed never to forgive them? Have you ever laughed to yourself when you saw the way someone was dressed? On the other hand, when was the last time you gave someone an honest compliment? Are you often the first to make up after a disagreement, even when it's not your fault? Within the past seven days, have you told someone in your family that you love them?

Nephi was given a vision of our day, and he tells us what he saw. He writes that, "[Satan] shall . . . *rage* in the hearts of the children of men, and stir them up to *anger* against that which is good" (2 Nephi 28:20; emphasis added). Yet, Nephi also saw a group of people, "who shall seek to bring forth my Zion at that day, for they shall have the gift and the power of the Holy Ghost; . . . [and] shall publish peace" (1 Nephi 13:37). Will you and I contribute to that rage and anger that is prophesied, or will we be among those who "publish peace?" Let's take a few moments and evaluate which side we will be on.

How do we publish peace? Justin is a good example. He is eleven years old. Weighing over nine pounds at birth, he's a born athlete. Justin can dunk a basketball, block a punt, or kick a soccer ball better than almost anyone else his age. Justin rarely loses where sports are concerned. A few months ago Justin had a chance to really show off his ability. He was playing basketball with his fifteen-year-old cousin, Nate. Nate is my son, and he was born with developmental disabilities and autistic tendencies. Nate is great at mowing lawns, and he is a superb worker, but he isn't good at sports. We have a basketball hoop in our garage and never once has Nathan thrown a ball through it for fun. He's simply not very good at it.

Nathan was spending the day at his cousin's house. Justin's mother, Heather, had taken time to remind each of her children what Nathan's strengths and weaknesses are so that he would have a good experience while visiting them. One at a time, the cousins were taking turns interacting with Nathan. Justin had been warned about how sensitive Nathan is when it comes to competitive sports, so when Justin came running up the stairs and announced to his mom that he had just finished playing a game of basketball with Nate, his mother was sickened.

"Justin, didn't I tell you that Nate can't play basketball?"

"But Mom, you've got to hear about my incredible game! I started dribbling the ball and I was all over the court."

"Justin, how could you take advantage of your cousin like that?"

"Mom, I was terrific. I was dribbling the ball under my leg and switching hands and driving down the court like you wouldn't believe!"

"Oh Justin . . . ," his mother winced.

"And then I got to the basket, and I was ready to do the world's most incredible slam dunk, and I hung there in the air just like Michael Jordan!"

"Justin, how could you . . . "

"Let me finish, Mom. I held the basketball above the rim until Nathan could bat it out of my hand and knock the ball through the hoop. And Mom, Nathan made a basket! Nate was cheering and jumping up and down, he was so excited! And do you know what I said to him then, Mom? I said, 'First basket wins!!!' Nathan won his first game of basketball, Mom! You should see how happy he is!"

"First basket wins . . . " Of course, if you have "ears to hear" (Matthew 13:43), you will know that I'm not just talking about a game of basketball. I'm referring to treating one another with tenderness and kindness and not taking unjust advantage of others because of our talents, strengths, or opportunities. King Benjamin explained it best when he said, "And you will not have a mind to injure one another, but to live peaceably" (Mosiah 4:13). Just as Justin did, we need to follow our Savior, "The Prince of Peace" (Isaiah 9:6), and not heed Satan, "the father of contention" (3 Nephi 11:29).

It's hard to show love and kindness toward someone when they have something that you wish you had. This is when Satan works overtime, tempting you to rage. But you don't have to listen to him. I remember Anne, my friend in high school. The dream of at least two hundred Highland High sophomore girls, including Anne and me, was to be a "Lassie" during our junior year. Lassies were members of the pep club. From our point of view, if you were a Lassie, you had it made. You were popular, you had seventy-nine instant friends, and your life couldn't be better. If you didn't make it, you might as well move to Siberia to hide your shame.

Needless to say, the day of the tryouts, all the "wannabe" Lassies were nervous. But everyone knew one thing for sure: Anne would make it. Anne would probably be our president. Anne did everything well. If we were just half as skilled as Anne, we wouldn't have to worry.

When the time arrived for the results to be posted in the gym, we all ran through the doorway searching for our name on the wall. My name was there! I didn't need a passport to Siberia! Yeah! There was a lot of screaming and hugging and tears of joy as each new Lassie celebrated her assurance of popularity. Then I saw Anne. She was crying. But they weren't joyful tears. I looked on the banner trying to find her name, but it wasn't there. She hadn't made it. That couldn't be possible. Anne was the best. I scanned the names again. Her name simply wasn't there. None of us could believe it.

That night I drifted in and out of sleep as I thought about my bittersweet victory. I wondered what kind of a night Anne was having. Within a few hours I knew. As I was leaving my house early the next morning, I saw something on my porch. It was a homemade treat with a note attached from Anne. It read:

> Next year, while you're marching on the football field, I'll be in the stands, cheering for you the loudest of all! Congratulations, Lassie!
>
> > Love,
> > Anne

Anne had every reason to be disappointed, to envy us, and to feel sorry for herself. But she rose above that. She was happy for *us*. She knew the meaning of the scripture, "Every man seeking the interest of his neighbor, and doing all things with an eye single to the glory of God" (D&C 82:19). At age sixteen, Anne had discovered the secret of peace. True peace doesn't come from having every wish fulfilled. Peace comes from keeping the commandments and doing as the Savior would do, "at all times and in all things, and in all places" (Mosiah 18:9). Just as Anne did, it is possible for you to learn to react peacefully in difficult situations.

Elder Marvin J. Ashton gave a talk in the April 1992 General Conference. It was entitled, "The Tongue Can Be a Sharp Sword." One sentence from that talk really had an impact on me. How would you fill in this blank? "The best and most clear indicator that we are progressing spiritually and coming unto Christ is _____" (*Ensign*, May 1992, p. 20). What do you think the answer is? This is what Elder Ashton said: "The best and most clear indicator that we are progressing spiritually and coming unto Christ is *the way we treat other people*" (emphasis added). Does that surprise you? How are you doing according to this measurement?

When we look at all the murders, gang violence, beatings, and other indisputable evils that go on in the world, the behavior problems the rest of us have may seem mild in comparison. But one of Satan's strategies is to encourage blatant evil so that other improper and sinful things don't seem so bad after all.

There are many subtle ways that we allow rage and anger in our lives, and perhaps we don't realize the seriousness of our behavior. Look at this list. Try to identify those things that you might be doing that Satan wants you to think are acceptable. Are you guilty of:

1. Making fun of other people?
2. Feeling secretly pleased when others fail?
3. Gossiping?
4. Holding a grudge?
5. Criticizing or judging?
6. Taking advantage of the weaknesses of others?
7. Losing your temper?
8. Trying to hurt someone's feelings?
9. Watching violent entertainment?
10. Yelling at other drivers?

Ouch! Did you recognize yourself somewhere on that

list? All those things are manifestations of rage or anger and they have no place in the life of a Latter-day Saint.

So, how do we go about "having [our] hearts knit together in unity and in love one towards another"? (Mosiah 18:21.) Let's look at another list that points us in the right direction:

1. Refusing to judge others
2. Defending someone who is being picked on
3. Finding joy in the success of others
4. Admitting mistakes and correcting them
5. Finding a positive alternative when disappointed
6. Controlling our temper
7. Showing kindness to *all* family members
8. Forgiving quickly
9. Looking at both sides of a disagreement
10. Paying a sincere compliment or writing a note of appreciation

As you strive to be a peacemaker, you must remember that you're not alone. Heavenly Father will help you succeed. Remember my son, Nathan, whom I introduced earlier? Because of Nathan's multiple disabilities, he often can't do that things that kids his own age are doing. Last summer, I received a call telling me that Nathan's application had been accepted for a series of courses at the Independent Living Center in downtown Salt Lake City. These courses are designed to give adolescents with disabilities instructions on how to become more independent from their families and more capable of functioning on their own. The first requirement of the course was for each student to master riding a bus to the center all by himself. This meant that Nathan had to transfer busses. I was concerned about having him ride a bus without supervision. The fact that he had to make a number of connections, coming and going, really had me worried. So this is what we did:

The first day we got in the car and drove to the bus stop.

I showed Nathan where he would be crossing the highway and exactly where to wait for the bus. Several busses stop at that bench, so I reminded him that the only bus he was to get on would have the number 8 on the front of it. We sat in our car at the bus stop, waiting until the number eight bus came.

"Tell me when you see the number eight bus, Nathan."

"There it is, Mom."

"That's the bus that you'll be riding next week."

Following the bus in my car, I began pointing out to Nathan familiar landmarks that the bus would be passing each day. As we neared the place for the transfer, I pointed out a fast food restaurant parking lot. When he was within sight of the parking lot, I told him that he was to pull the cord on the bus, and that the driver would stop and let him off. I then pointed out where he would cross the busy street and wait for the next bus. On the only bus he was to get on there was the number 32. I even had Nathan draw a 32 on a piece of paper so I was assured that he could recognize the numeral. We proceeded through the rest of the bus route this same way, following the correct busses and reviewing where to stand to catch each bus he was to get on. Then we drove the path again and rehearsed the same thing.

The following day, Nate and I rode the bus. As we walked from our house to the bus stop, we reviewed all the numbers and locations he would have to remember. The next day, we rode the bus together, again, except this time I didn't coach Nate. He showed me how to get to the bus stop, which buttons to push to cross the street, what bus number we were waiting for, and how to watch for familiar landmarks so we knew that we were on the right route.

After this, Nathan said, "Mom, I think I'm ready to ride the bus alone." I said, "Great, Nathan! Tomorrow, you ride the bus all by yourself and I'll follow you in the car to be sure you remember all the things you've learned."

The next morning I parked the car across the street from the bus stop and watched as Nathan waited for the first bus. I was feeling nervous. But I knew that I had taught him all that he needed to know, and that if he would just remember what he had learned, he would be successful. From the time I watched him wait on the bench alone, until he got off at his last stop and walked down Main Street toward the center, I offered a silent prayer. I prayed that all he had been taught would be brought to his remembrance. Finally, as he entered the Living Center, I breathed a sigh of relief that he had made it. Nathan had learned his lesson well and could now be given more freedom. The next day, he rode the bus alone, successfully!

Is our Heavenly Father as anxious for us to succeed as I was for Nathan to accomplish mastering the bus route? Of course He is! He has given us information, in the form of commandments, that we will need to know if we are to make a safe journey through this life and return to his presence. He has promised us that he won't leave us alone. As he promised the missionaries in 1832, he also promises us that as we strive to live righteously, "there I will be also, for I will go before your face. I will be on your right hand and on your left, and my Spirit shall be in your hearts, and mine angels round about you, to bear you up" (D&C 84:88). Remember that, the next time you have to face a difficult challenge!

As you strive to be a peacemaker, our Heavenly Father will strengthen you and give you the power to resist the rage and the anger that Satan desires you to partake of. Our Father is anxious for you to succeed. I humbly testify to you as Paul testified, "Be of one mind, live in peace; and the God of love and peace shall be with you" (2 Corinthians 13:11).

Sue Egan has attended both BYU and the University of Utah. She has been a professional vocalist and a teacher and is presently a homemaker. An avid student of the scriptures, Sue also loves watching "Dragnet" reruns on TV and "cruising" with her husband in his red sports car. Sister Egan is a popular presenter at EFY and serves in the Church as a stake Young Women president. She and her husband, Richard, have six children.

11

TO TEMPLE-BOUND TEENS: SURVIVE THE SEARCH FOR THAT SOMEONE

MARK ELLISON

I'm very romantic. In first grade, I used to ride my bike by Meredith Pinching's house and imagine that if it were on fire, I would rush in and rescue Meredith and her whole family. I would not only be on the six o'clock news, but I would also receive a warm handshake from Meredith's dad, who would ask how he could *EVER* repay me.

One day I got up all my nerve and asked Meredith, "Will you marry me?"

"Sure," she replied casually.

Our engagement was going along just fine until a few days later, when Katie Stymacher ran up to me on the school playground and squealed, "You're going to marry Meredith!" The whole first grade was watching. I panicked, quickly denying everything, insisting that I never wanted to marry Meredith, that in fact Meredith "stank" (this does not help a relationship, I might add), and the whole thing was off.

Then there was third grade, and a little angel named Tracy Martinez. One day Mrs. Fletcher taught our class a folk dance, and after we had all practiced it, she announced, "Tracy and Mark were the best couple!" Ah, I'll never forget the way Tracy smiled at me that day. It was a smile that said, "I vow to marry you."

She and I never did get around to tying the knot, and that was okay. But I never stopped wondering whom I would one day marry, being the romantic guy that I am. "I wonder if it's someone I already know," I would think when I was a teenager. "What if I end up marrying one of the *Mia Maids?* What if it's someone I haven't even met yet? What if she's living halfway across the world right now? What if Tracy Martinez joins the Church?" (Katie Stymacher did!)

I did at least have a goal to marry a faithful LDS young woman in the temple. In fact, I even wrote her a letter one day. I want to share some of it with you. I began: "To My Future Wife." Since I didn't know who or where my future wife was, I decided I would save the letter and give it to her on the day we got married. I wrote:

> I guess I should introduce myself, although I've probably already done this, if you're reading this as my wife, huh? Hi! My name's Mark. (Smile, shake hands.) Nice to meet you!

Then I got more serious:

> I don't know who you are yet, but I do know that when I enter the house of the Lord with you, it will mean some very profound things. I know that I'll love you more than anything in all the world. I know (because I've got confidence in my judgment and I'm not marrying no dud) that you're an absolutely terrific person and I just think the world of you. I'll always be loyal to you. You and I will be a team—you will bring out the good things in me, and I will bring out the good in you. We will lift each other. You will inspire me to be a better man, a better priesthood holder.

That was exactly what I wanted our relationship to be like.

I wrote my feelings about the Los Angeles Temple. I had been there and had felt the power of the Lord there. I knew that in the house of the Lord, the priesthood power could seal and bless the most sacred of family relationships, for this life and for the next.

> More than anything, I want to be with you forever. That's why I'm living the way I am now. I'm keeping my standards high and preparing for the day you'll read this.

Just thinking about my future wife made me want to live to be worthy of her, to be true to her always. It set the standard for what my dates should be like with other girls. I thought for a few moments about dates I had been on. Some had been great fun, others had been pretty disappointing:

> Have I ever told you about when Bridget O'Bryan asked me to the Junior Prom, and how I didn't plan ahead for the date and couldn't take Dad's Cougar XR-7, but at the last minute got stuck with the Lynx station wagon? But it didn't matter much. Bridget had only asked me out to make her ex-boyfriend jealous.

Finally, near the close of the letter, I wrote this:

> You know what I do sometimes? I pray for you. I figure, life must get challenging for you sometimes, just like it does with me. I just pray that you'll be comforted and given strength as you need it, and that Father will take care of you until I'm there to be with you.

I signed my name to the letter, put it in an envelope on which I wrote "To My Future Wife," and tucked it in my journal. I felt really good about the commitments I had made. Every so often, I would take the letter out of its envelope and reread it to remind myself of my goals.

Time went by. I served a mission, and though I didn't know it at the time, I was called to serve in the exact area where my future wife was living! Lauren and I never met while I was a missionary, but when we talked about it later, we realized that at one point—hold on to your hats—we had been in the same room! Well, it was a big room. Okay, it was an auditorium. She was a Laurel in the Oakland Temple Pageant, and my companion and I had brought some investigators to the pageant that year. So during the performance, my future wife and I were, technically speaking, in the same room (along with several thousand others). Someday, in the spirit world, Lauren and I will watch the video replay of our lives and see how close we came to bumping into each other among all the crowds of people there!

As it was, though, we didn't meet until two years after my mission. That summer at BYU, Lauren and her roommate, Julie, and I became good buddies. We played tennis together, went running together, rode bikes together, and went out for frozen yogurt together—always as a threesome. And strangely enough for a romantic guy like me, there was nothing really romantic going on. We were all just good friends.

One night, the three of us got together with a big group of friends and went out to a drive-in movie. We all pulled in and unloaded our cars of pillows, blankets, and lounge chairs, and watched the movies outside, under the stars. One guy even had a little hibachi barbecue. Donning an apron and chef's hat, he put some chicken on the flame and said, "Hey, who wants wings and who wants drumsticks?" We all sat around, chatting and eating and watching the movies. Sometime during the second show, Julie fell asleep.

"Julie!" we yelled, "You're missing the movie!" She mumbled incoherently and went back to sleep.

Now our threesome was down to just two: Lauren and me. We grew tired of the movie (it was a stupid film), so we got to talking. We had the *neatest* conversation, one that wound through various topics that now seem completely random: Our high school experiences, our favorite restaurants, what it would be like to lose one of our senses, things we would put in our dream houses, gospel principles, spiritual experiences, what we wanted to be when we grew up. . . . I remember looking at Lauren in the starlight and beginning to feel very romantic. She looked so beautiful. I was filled with wonder at what a fantastic person I was sharing this discussion with. I think that was when I first felt love for her, though I wouldn't know it for a while. All I thought was, "I've *gotta* ask this girl out on a date!"

The second movie ended, and we tried to wake up Julie. "Come on, Julie! Time to go home." This was bizarre—she was in such a deep sleep that we couldn't wake her up! Lauren and I had to practically *carry* Julie to my car and toss her in the back seat, where she sort of collapsed like a rag doll. As I drove the three of us back to Provo, it was like being alone with Lauren again. I asked her out right there.

"Okay!" she said in a happy, offhand way. Little did I know, Lauren was secretly crazy about me, and had been wishing for a long time that I would get interested in her. Inside, she was turning cartwheels, exclaiming "YES!" and generally rejoicing.

When we got to their house, we dragged Julie inside, and Lauren tucked her in bed. The next morning, Julie was happy for Lauren and me, but she couldn't remember a thing about the night before. We still tease her about that. I wonder if there weren't ministering angels who were trying to get Lauren and me together. "Let's get this Julie girl out of the way," they might have said. "THOU SHALT SLEEP!" ZAP—She was out.

The first date with Lauren led to another, and another. We loved being together, whether we were riding bikes, cooking stir-fry, or enjoying a stroll through the park. We grew in love. I realized that I didn't want to go through life without her. I wanted to be with her forever. "Could it be," I thought, "that it's actually that time in my life?" What a big step!

"What do you think about marriage?" I asked Lauren one night.

"I think it's great!" she replied, smiling.

I felt my heart pounding. "Do . . . do you mean, marriage in general, like, as a social institution, or like, marriage between y-y-you and m-m-me?"

"I think they're both great," she said, still smiling confidently.

I later went to the Lord in prayer, and felt assured that He had truly led me to this point.

Now for the actual proposal. I had always wanted to do this in a creative way. Late one night, I got a crazy idea. Lauren was taking a sign language class at BYU from a teacher named Jack Rose. At 11:30 P.M., Jack was awakened by an obnoxious phone call from me: "Hello, Jack? This is Mark! Say, I'd like to propose to Lauren tomorrow in your class. Is that cool with you?"

Jack groggily replied, "Mmrph?" I took that for a "Yes," and the next day, September 1, 1988, Jack (now fully conscious) announced, "Class, I've asked a fellow sign language teacher, Mark Ellison, to come in and demonstrate a translation of a song. I'm going to videotape this so I can show it to other students." There in the front row sat Lauren, right next to Julie (who was also fully conscious now). The camera started rolling. The music began to play the theme song from "Mr. Roger's Neighborhood"! The class thought, "How corny," and snickered as I attempted to sign poetically the idea that it was "a beautiful day in the neighborhood." Then came the last line of the song, which is usually "Won't you be my neighbor?" At that point, the music shut off, and kneeling in front of Lauren, I signed, "Won't you be my wife?" There were shrieks and applause. Lauren and Julie started hugging each other. I waited. Finally, Lauren looked at me and signed, "Yes!" Then she stood and hugged ME! Ah, yes. We've got it all on videotape. (That was Jack Rose's wedding present to us.)

On December 17, 1988, we were married in the Oakland Temple. I can hardly describe the beauty of the temple. It's a quiet, holy place, full of spiritual radiance, so unlike the gaudy glamour that the world thinks of as "beauty." Our parents, along with a few close relatives and friends, were with us there in the sealing room, all of us dressed in white clothing. Before Lauren and I knelt at the altar for the sealing ordinance, we heard some words of counsel from the temple sealer. Elder Boyd K. Packer has written some thoughts similar to those that were shared with us at that time:

> Today is your wedding day. . . . Temples were built as a sanctuary for such ordinances as this. . . . The things of the world do not apply here. . . . We have come out of the world into the temple of the Lord. This becomes the most important day of your lives. . . . You were born, . . . baptized, . . . ordained to the priesthood, [and given] your endowment. . . . But all of these things, in one sense, were preliminary and preparatory to your coming to the altar to be sealed as husband and wife for time and for all eternity. You now become a family, free to act in the creation of life, to have the opportunity through devotion and sacrifice to bring children into the world and to raise them and foster them safely through their mortal existence (*The Holy Temple* [Salt Lake City: Bookcraft, 1980], p. 69).

That evening, as Lauren (now "Sister Ellison!") and I drove out of the Bay Area towards Lake Tahoe, I reached over to the glove compartment and took out an old, slightly faded envelope whereon was written, "To My Future Wife." "Honey, this is for you," I said, handing it to her.

She smiled excitedly, opened the envelope, took out the old letter, and began to read it aloud. It was a moment I'll never forget. She laughed at the part about my junior prom. She cried when she got to the part that said:

> I pray for you. I figure, life must get challenging for you sometimes, just like it does with me. I just pray that you'll be comforted and given strength as you need it, and that Father will take care of you until I'm there to be with you.

And then she reached into her purse and took out another old, slightly faded envelope. On it was written, "To My Future Husband." Inside was a letter *she* had written to *me* when she was thirteen years old! Guess what she wrote to me about? Her testimony of temple marriage. Her desire to prepare for that sacred covenant. Her love for me. I can't tell you how much it means to me to know that the whole time I was growing up, struggling and learning, striving to live close to the Lord, and dreaming of wonderful things to come, she was doing the exact same thing.

It's a marvelous blessing for me to walk hand in hand with Lauren in this life, to learn and grow together. With her help and the Lord's, I might just make it "home" safely.

Young people, we are living in a society that for the most part is not only nonreligious, but *anti*religious. Nephi foresaw this: "At that day shall [the devil] rage in the hearts of the children of men, and stir them up to anger against that which is good" (2 Nephi 28:20). You can find many people among our national leaders, within the media, perhaps even among your educators who will tell you that the

traditional standards of morality no longer apply, that waiting for sex until after marriage is unnecessary, that loyalty
within marriage is optional. I believe that God will hold
such people responsible for leading His children astray (see
Matthew 18:6).

But there are many of God's children who valiantly
refuse to be deceived by the flattering lies that are currently
popular. I was thrilled to read that thousands of Christian
teenagers are following the lead of fifty students in
Nashville, Tennessee, who stood to publicly make this
pledge:

> Believing that true love waits, I make a commitment to
> God, myself, my family, those I date, my future mate and
> my future children to be sexually pure until the day I
> enter a covenant marriage relationship (*Time*, May 24,
> 1993, p. 60).

Make the pledge. Write it out, if it will help. Especially
make the pledge in your heart as you take the sacrament,
where you remember your baptismal covenant, and commit again to "keep His commandments which He has
given" (D&C 20:77).

I have a personal conviction of what the scriptures testify: Obedience to the Lord always brings happiness, and
sin always brings misery. When I have lived in harmony
with the will of God, I have felt lasting joy and peace. The
fondest hope of my heart is that I might endure in faith and
one day be worthy of the Lord's welcoming embrace as I
leave this life behind.

One of the Lord's purposes of marriage is to help us in
this very quest to endure in faith so that we might return
worthily to him. There is great strength that comes to a man
and to a woman who are trying to live righteously, who
walk with the Lord in a covenant relationship (see 1

Corinthians 11:11). I believe that is why the late Elder Bruce R. McConkie felt inspired to write:

> The most important things that any member of The Church of Jesus Christ of Latter-day Saints ever does in this world are: 1. To marry the right person, in the right place, by the right authority; and 2. To keep the covenant made in connection with this holy and perfect order of matrimony (*Mormon Doctrine*, 2d ed. [Salt Lake City: Bookcraft, 1966], p. 118).

May the Lord bless you as your prepare to make and keep the sacred covenant of marriage.

Mark Ellison teaches seminary in Springville, Utah. A former American Sign Language teacher at Brigham Young University and at the Missionary Training Center, Brother Ellison has served as a director of Especially for Deaf Youth. His hobbies include playing the guitar, the piano, and synthesizers, and he has worked as a guitarist in a dance band and even been a swimming pool digger. A triathlon racing enthusiast, Mark conditions himself in part by eating a dessert called "Death by Chocolate." Together, he and his wife, Lauren, enjoy teaching a class of Sunbeams in Primary.

12

FATHER'S EYES

KIM NOVAS GUNNELL

ey, Mom, I need some lunch money," I called. "My ride is here." Mom started digging through her purse while I grabbed my books. Just then my father came into the kitchen where we were standing.

"Hold on Kim," he said. "We haven't even had family prayer yet, and you're not going anywhere until you go back upstairs and change that dress."

"But Dad," I moaned, "this isn't short at all. It's just barely above my knee. You should see what all the other girls are wearing. I look like a pioneer compared to them."

Dad remained firm. "No daughter of mine is going to dress immodestly."

"But my ride is waiting," I said in exasperation.

"Then I'll take you." Dad opened the door and waved my friends on. I was upset. I didn't say another word. I just stomped upstairs to change.

Dad called after me. "Someday, you'll thank me for this."

I slammed my bedroom door. I felt quite sure that my father had just ruined my entire life.

Many years have passed since that incident, and my Dad was right—I have thanked him, often. At that time in my life, I was simply thinking about the moment at hand. Dad had a broader perspective. He saw things more clearly. He could see what was best for me in the long run even when I couldn't see it for myself. He saw with a father's eyes.

Ed Pinegar was one of my teachers when I attended Brigham Young University. He had a powerful and positive influence in my life. I'll never forget one day in class when he drew a diagram of a steep mountain on one side of the blackboard and a deep valley on the other. Then he pointed to the bottom of the valley and said, "You are here. You can only see what is immediately around you. It's not necessarily your fault. It is just where you are right now."

Then Brother Pinegar pointed halfway up the mountain and said, "Here are your parents and leaders. They have lived longer. They have a clearer view of things. They can see distant dangers and approaching problems that you may not be able to see from down in the valley."

Finally, Brother Pinegar pointed to the top of the mountain and said, "Here is our Heavenly Father. He has a perfect view of everything. He knows what is best for us now and in the future." Brother Pinegar didn't have to say anything more. His point was clear. Young people need to listen more carefully to the counsel and direction of parents, leaders, and Heavenly Father. They aren't trying to ruin our lives with their rules, commandments, and standards. They just see things a little clearer than we can with our limited view.

When my husband and I were living in Nashville, Tennessee, my husband started a tradition that he still carries on in our home. On certain Sundays throughout the year, he has a personal interview with each of our children. Our oldest son, Barrett, was about five years old at the time. My husband, Doug, invited him into the bedroom for his little interview and asked, "How are you getting along with your sister? Are you having fun with your neighborhood friends?" Barrett talked happily about his childhood world.

Then Doug asked Barrett what he wanted to be when he

grew up. Barrett's response was instantaneous. He said, "I want to be a pilot just like my Grandpas." Both of his grandfathers are pilots. One flew in the Air Force. The other is a stunt pilot and crop-duster. Barrett once had the opportunity of flying with his grandpa, the stunt pilot, and sitting right next to him in the cockpit of his plane. Barrett loved learning how the rudder works to keep the plane lined up on a particular heading and how the control wheel can bring the nose of the plane up or down. Barrett's grandpa even let him hold the wheel on the co-pilot's side of the plane and said to him, "Look, you're flying the plane."

Doug went on with the interview. "Barrett," he said, "I think it is wonderful that you want to be a pilot. You'll be a good one. But to reach that goal, you will have to work hard in school. You will need to know a lot about math and geography."

"But Dad," Barrett interrupted, "I already know how to fly. I flew grandpa's plane." In his eyes he was convinced that he already knew everything there was to know about flying airplanes. However, his father saw things a little clearer. If Barrett had been allowed to proceed toward his goal, trusting nothing but his own perceptions, it could be a dangerous and frightening situation. One day Barrett will be grateful that his father had a better view than he did.

I once spoke to a group of young women and told them to imagine themselves sitting on a grassy hill. I said, "Pretend it is a beautiful sunny day. You can see a river at the bottom of the hill. You can hear the water flowing swiftly in its course. There is a slight breeze and the sun is shining on your face." By now all the girls were very involved with this mental picture—especially because the actual weather outside was cold and rainy.

I continued, "Suddenly, you see a group of your friends coming down the river on a raft. They are laughing and having a great time. From your vantage point, high on the hill, you look down the river. The smile leaves your face.

You see clearly that your friends are heading directly into some rough water. You get up and walk along the hill in order to see even further down the river. There are terrible rapids ahead and a huge waterfall."

At this point I asked the young women what they would do. One girl said, "Depends on who is on the raft!" Everyone laughed. Then she said more seriously, "I guess I'd start yelling and waving my arms." Another girl said, "I'd try to warn my friends and tell them to get out of the river."

I continued the story. I said, "There you are on the hill. You know that you are the only hope of survival for your friends. Their fate is in your hands. Imagine that you start screaming, 'Hurry! Paddle your raft to shore. There's a waterfall ahead!' You are running toward them and yelling frantically." By now the young women were highly involved, even though it was just a story.

I continued, "Now imagine that one of your friends stands up on the raft and yells back at you, 'Bug off! You're always trying to ruin our fun. We can do whatever we want, so chill out.'" I asked the young women, "Would you forget it and say, 'Fine. Go ahead and drown. See if I care.'" They all agreed that they would try even harder to help their friends realize the seriousness of the situation. One girl said, "I would try to let them know that I could see further down the river than they could. They would just have to trust me even though they weren't able to see why, right then."

My lesson was over. These young women now understood a bit better the kinds of concern felt by their own leaders, teachers, and parents when they try to protect and warn them.

My brother-in-law, Brad Wilcox, once wrote, "The father who would go to any and all ends to save his drowning daughter at the local swimming pool wouldn't give a thought as to whether it was what his daughter might want. He wouldn't lose a single stroke while wondering if he were imposing on his daughter's free agency to drown. Is the same father going to sit helplessly by, sighing, 'It's her life. How do I know what's best for little Josephine?' when little Josephine begins dating too steadily, failing in school, attending R-rated films, and smoking? Too often we hear, 'Let him make up his own mind' or 'We shouldn't impose our will on him.' When it comes to lifesaving choices with eternal significance, aren't these rationalized excuses for weakness in our own conviction?" (*WATTS Under Your Bushel*? [Provo, Utah: Perry Enterprises, 1984], p.65).

Young people, please remember that when parents and leaders whip out the *For the Strength of Youth* pamphlet and start reviewing standards, it is not in an attempt to destroy freedom and ruin your life. Rather, it is an attempt to prepare, teach, and warn—to literally save your life.

When I was a teenager I sometimes saw my father's concern about the length of my dresses as being totally unreasonable. Now I understand that such involvement was an evidence of his love.

I often speak to groups about discovering hidden talents and challenging themselves to grow. I decided I needed to take my own advice. With the encouragement of some dear friends, I decided to enter the Mrs. Utah pageant. My husband agreed it would be a positive experience for me since the pageant was motivating me to improve myself. I was exercising, studying current events, and looking more deeply at different sides of political issues on which I would be asked to express an opinion.

As I prepared, I began shopping for the perfect gown to wear during the competition. It wasn't long before I realized that there were not many dresses available that were modest. When I found the right color, the dress had no back. When I found one with a back, the front was too revealing. Finally, a friend offered to loan me a dark royal blue evening gown that was modest. I have never felt that blue is my best color and because my friend is shorter than

I, the length of the dress wasn't quite right on me either. However, it was the only dress I had come across in weeks of searching that met my standards of modesty.

On the night of the pageant, I was asked the following question on stage before the entire audience: "If you could choose a role model, someone other than a family member, who would that role model be?"

I said the first thing that came into my mind and answered, "There is no better role model than Jesus Christ. Even though I have a long way to go, Jesus Christ is the person I most want to emulate."

The curtains closed. I'm sure that many in the audience may have felt my answer was inappropriate in that setting. I felt tears forming in my eyes—but these were not tears of embarrassment caused by what I had said. Rather, these were tears of sheer gratitude, shed because the gown I had chosen to wear did not contradict the first answer that had come into my mind.

I was not selected as the winner. But I felt very much at peace. The First Presidency has written, "You cannot do wrong and feel right. It is impossible" (*For the Strength of Youth* [Salt Lake City: The Church of Jesus Christ of Latter-day Saints, 1990], p.4). Brigham Young wrote, "The daughters of Israel should understand what fashions they should have, without borrowing from the impure and unrighteous. . . . We should lead in fashions and in everything that is right and proper; and not be led by the world" (*Journal of Discourses*, 12:220).

The following year, I decided to enter the Mrs. Utah pageant again. I felt more determined than ever to prove that no one needs to compromise the standards of the Church to reach a goal.

I began again to search for an appropriate and modest gown. My mother and I went into one store where the clerks commented that they had rented over one hundred gowns that week and they were low on merchandise. We scanned through the few dresses that were left on the racks. I spotted a white, chiffon-type, beaded gown that had obviously been overlooked next to the eye-popping gowns that had since left the store. Even though it looked a bit frumpy on the hanger, I decided to try it on.

I thought it was beautiful. I wanted to twirl around the room like a little girl. It was perfect. There was only one problem—it was cut a little low in both the front and the back. But it was nothing that couldn't be fixed with a little stitching.

Some people involved in the pageant thought I was making a mistake because the dress was not showy enough—in more ways than one. I remained unshaken in my determination to be modest. The simple elegance of this dress was what I was after.

"Would my father approve?" That is the question I often asked myself when I was younger. Now I asked a similar question: "Would my Heavenly Father approve?" I felt certain he would. I wore the dress. That night I was selected as the winner and that "frumpy" modest gown received the highest scores in the evening gown competition.

We cannot always see the end of every road as well as those who have a higher vantage point. The choices we make are important and have eternal significance. It is vital that we accept the counsel and advice of those who are higher up on the mountain—especially God who sees everything perfectly through a Father's eyes.

Holding a bachelor's degree in musical theater from Brigham Young University, Kim Gunnell is a professional singer and entertainer. She also teaches voice lessons and is a songwriter. Kim was the 1993 Mrs. Utah, U.S.A. Her interests include scuba diving with her family and home decorating. She has taught early-morning seminary, and she and her husband, Douglas B. Gunnell, currently work together in a stake calling as teachers of a missionary training course. They have three children.

13

SPIRITUAL HANDS

S T E P H E N   J A S O N   H A L L

Dear Father," I begged, "If I could only have my hands, I know I could make it. Please, Father, please. This is the time, here we go, my hands are going to move this time. It will be a miracle; I'll be in the *New Era* and everything."

I watched my hands, seeing them move in my mind, concentrating until it hurt, but, nothing, not a single movement. Again and again I would petition the Father on that dark, somber September night as I lay awake and alone, pleading within the confines of the University of Utah rehab unit #268, following a crippling Lake Powell diving accident. "Please Father, heal my hands, make them move, make them work." Each time, the same result, still nothing.

Oh, the intensity of my frustration, my anguish, my fear. It didn't seem too much to ask. Most kids at age fifteen worried about things like what they would wear the following day, but I was fighting death—uncertain whether I would even be alive the next day. Uncertain whether I would ever be able to move my limbs again. "I'm only a kid!" my soul would scream. "Keep my legs, Father; I just want my hands."

Such endless nights, spent alternately pleading with God and trying to move, were not rarities in the early stages of my paralysis. Even now I think often about those nights.

As I wheelchair through my life, I miss my legs, but I am constantly reminded of the absence of my hands. Each time I see someone helping another with groceries, planting a tree, shaking a hand, or teaching a child to play football, I long to be able to use my hands in service.

While at the University Hospital, I had resolved that in my daily therapy I would give everything I had. Hours upon hours I exercised, stretching and pulling, doing everything in my power to strengthen my remaining muscles. It was hard, but the time went quickly enough, and my daily progress made it all worth it—until Dan came.

Dan had been in an accident similar to mine in which his spine had been damaged and paralysis had ensued. But his case was different in that he had escaped with total use of his hands and partial use of his legs. He had access to a world that I could only dream of joining. Yet, he would sit there the entire therapy hour, whining and complaining that he was unable to totally use his legs.

"Today, let's concentrate on your upper body," the therapist would plead daily, only to hear Dan's all too familiar response: "I just wish I could move my legs. Maybe this is the day I'll be able to walk." There he would sit for the rest of the period, thinking about his legs, watching them for movement, rarely lifting an arm or pushing a weight.

This frustrated me to no end. My whole spirit would scream inside of me, "Don't you see what you have? Just look at all of the blessings and opportunities that are yours simply because you can move your hands. You have access to a freedom that I pray for, that I dream of, and you are too ungrateful to see it."

That same week I found myself in the room of my friend, Rich Hullinger, who was also a quadriplegic. I noticed that Rich wore leather braces on his wrists and hands. Near the beginning of my hospital stay, I had worn similar braces in order to stretch my tendons. But, as my wrists had gotten stronger, I was able to function without them. It seemed odd that Rich, who had been in the rehab unit longer than I had, would still be wearing them. Curious, I asked Rich about them. He explained to me that the break in his neck was one pinhead higher than mine, and that because of that, he was unable to move his wrist up and down, or even hold it against the power of gravity.

I returned to my room and prepared for bed. I didn't sleep much that night. Over and over, I thought of the lesson that Rich had taught me—of how blessed I was to make a simple movement. I found everything in myself that I hated in Dan. I had spent the bulk of my time concentrating on what I did not have, when I could have been focusing on what I did have. By centering my efforts on wishing for different circumstances, I had become totally oblivious of my life's many blessings. This oblivion caused my outlook on life to become tarnished. It had affected the way I was dealing with others, my zeal for life, and the way I felt about myself. However, with this new realization, I began to feel more blessed. As I felt more blessed, I became more thankful, and as I became more thankful, I developed a sense of worth, which brought with it increased ability to overcome.

All of this came from a man who, unknowingly, taught me that it does not matter what our physical situation is, but what does matter is the thankful spirit with which we receive the blessings the Lord affords us. The greater man is not the one with a hundred blessings that he takes for granted, but the man with one blessing who praises his God for his bounty.

Rich's spirit of gratitude taught me a lesson that all the object lessons of the seminary program had failed to. His lesson was quietly delivered, and it was only received when I chose to do so. It was powerful because he taught it with his spirit.

I have often reflected on this lesson and as I have, it has

forced me to reflect on others whose spirit has affected me for the better.

After spending time in numerous intensive care units and having my condition upgraded from critical to stable, I was still in traction and breathing with the help of a respirator through a tracheotomy. But, I was ready to move to rehabilitation. Upon entering this new room, I found that I was to share it with two other men, Zach and Troy. I wasn't too excited about the whole idea. Previously, in intensive care, the only roommate I had was the sound of my own respirator, and I kind of liked it that way. I became substantially more concerned when I learned that the two had sustained head injuries due to serious accidents.

I had heard of head traumas before, and what I knew frightened me. Zach had fallen off a mountainside, and Troy had been hit by a car while on his motorcycle. Together, we were quite a bunch. Zach, on the one side would yell, "C'mon, . . . c'mon" all night long until the nurses came in to see what was the matter, and then he would shout obscenities. This would continue until the nurse would finally leave, and he would begin the whole cycle over again.

On the other side, Troy believed that he was in Vietnam, and to make matters worse, there was an Oriental nurse on the floor. This made Troy extremely anxious. When he was not trying to kill the nurse, who he thought to be the Vietcong, he was headed for the helipad to go AWOL. Both Zach and Troy were strapped into bed, and they screamed all night long. When I was not lying awake scared to death of their next move, I was dying of laughter at their 3:00 A.M. battle with the nurse whose only wish was to give them their medicine and get home to bed.

I spent week after week with these two, and as I did, I watched their progress. I began to notice that their wailings and gnashings were manifestations of a still intelligent spirit, frustrated to the hilt by the damaged, fragile shell that it now resided in. The screaming and kicking were their inner selves pleading to be heard, and slowly, they were. Every time they lifted their spoon just that much closer to their mouth, their spirit would be heard. Every time they successfully slept through the night, their spirit would be heard. And every time that they spoke an intelligible sentence, it was their inner self, speaking loud and clear, showing that it was still alive. Each of these small victories was won after hours and hours of battle—battles in which their courage was severely tested.

I never saw either of them climb the highest mountain or swim the deepest sea; I barely saw them walk down the hall. I never had one meaningful conversation with either of them, and I am sure that neither of them would remember me at all. But, they taught me more about courage than any record-breaking athlete or adrenaline filled "hero" ever could. Just watching their daily struggle gave me the strength to fight to live another day. For their fight was not won by virtue of any physical prowess but by the determination of a dauntless spirit. My experience in the hospital taught me many things, but the lessons did not end with my discharge.

In my life, there are many people who lift me each day. Someone lifts me out of bed in the morning. People often lift me in and out of cars, up and down stairs, in and out of restaurants, and on and off platforms. Then at the end of my day, I have to be lifted into bed once again. And although I am most grateful to those who do this type of lifting for me, I have found that a much different kind of lifting is done every day by people who can barely move a muscle—people like Dawn.

Dawn is a student at BYU. I met Dawn during my freshman year, and since that time we have had only limited contact at best. The little conversation we have had has occurred while passing between classes, which, it turns out, is just enough time for Dawn to change a life.

Dawn is severely physically disabled, with a disability that has taken the majority of the motor control from her body. She works hard even to drive her motorized wheelchair. Studying for classes and taking exams takes days of extra effort, and she can only speak clearly as long as she concentrates and goes slowly. But, somehow, Dawn does it all. She is everywhere on campus, and she attends all of the events that she can. She is amazing.

While passing her one day, I noticed that Dawn was concentrating especially hard on something and seemed a bit preoccupied. Assuming that she was a little down and in need of some help, I thought that I would be the "big" one and brighten her day by saying hello. When I did, Dawn's whole countenance changed. She got so excited that her arms and legs went into a complete spasm, causing her to lose control. With legs and arms everywhere, she yelled out an excited, "Hi Jason!" Then, with the dignity of royalty, she regained her composure and was on her way.

I was in shock. In my attempt to lift Dawn, she had lifted me. My greeting consisted only of words, but hers involved her whole body and her spirit. I felt better that day than I had in a long while. I watch for Dawn on campus now, and when I find her, I race to say hello—even if it means that I have to go out of my way and be late for class. I have to. I need the lift that I feel when her spirit touches mine. In spite of her limitations, Dawn manages to lift others.

If I ever get discouraged because of my limitations, it is because of my inability to do "normal" things. I often think to myself, "I would really love to do that, if I were only physically able."

Feeling particularly limited one day, I went to speak to a Primary class on overcoming disabilities. The Primary leaders had invited four people with disabilities to teach the children about the various handicaps that different people face. Entering the cultural hall, I was still upset that it had taken me so long to get ready that morning, and that I had missed breakfast because no one had been around to cook it for me. I took my place in the front and began to sing the opening song that was already in progress.

Three of the invited guests that day were in wheel-chairs, and as I looked more closely I noticed that one of the men was a quadriplegic with an injury like mine. It seemed peculiar that two of us had been asked to come and bore the children by talking about the limitations that we shared. Confused, I continued to watch him, and as I did, I noticed that he moved his arms when he spoke. Looking closer, I was amazed at what I discovered. He was using sign lan-guage—the man was deaf! He had the same disability that I had, but he was also deaf. That meant he not only had to have someone help him get dressed, cook his food, and get into his van, but, on top of that, he had to do it while com-municating in sign language. As if that weren't enough, the sign language he used had to be a special one that involved only his arms, for his disability, like mine, had taken from him the ability to use his hands.

His spirit had refused to give up. He had more severe limitations than most people, but his spirit was constantly taking him outside his barriers. In my life since my accident, I have heard people say that it would be impossible to live with such an incredible physical disability and also be deaf. I am sure that there were slews of people who had told him the same thing—and maybe it was impossible—but his spirit yearned to live and to be functional, and so it was.

I will never forget that man. My life changed that day as his spirit inspired me to change. I left with a renewed belief in myself and in the things that I could do. He gave me the strength, so that when people said I could not, I just asked for the chance to try. He had an indomitable spirit, and when his spirit touched mine, I was inspired to be indomitable as well.

While each of these spirits affected me, their change was only part of a greater change that I experienced when my soul brushed with divinity.

My freshman year at Brigham Young University was lonely, very lonely. And as the time passed, it did not get any better. I remember one day looking at that majestic Y on the mountain and thinking, "That's a good question, WHY am I here and WHY aren't I at home?"

My roommate was very popular, especially with the girls, and that just made things worse. One night, I had had enough. I needed to find out. I needed to know if anyone cared. So I left and went to a place where I knew I could find out. I went to a little spot just above the Provo Temple. It was sunset and the lights on the temple and in the city below were just beginning to come up. I found myself deep in prayer. I fervently asked my Father in Heaven to let me know that he cared, that he loved me, and that I was his son. The answer I received is one that I will never forget. His spirit touched mine and let me know that he loved me. He encircled me about in the arms of his love (see 2 Nephi 1:15) and touched me with his spiritual hands.

It was with those hands that the Savior truly served. What mattered in his ministry was not that he walked with men or that he was a carpenter. What mattered was the service that he rendered with his spirit. When, like Rich, his spirit taught others to have a thankful heart as he praised the Father in all that he did. When, like Zach and Troy, his example lent courage to the hearts of men as he quietly let them drag him to a hill and nail him to a cross, while at his word awaited legions of angels ready to free their Lord. When, like Dawn, his spirit lifted the woman at the well by revealing to her the source of living bread and water. And when, like the man I met at the Primary activity, his spirit continues to inspire even the unbelievers who, regardless of their religious orientation, are inspired to live better lives by the way that Christ lived and loved. So it is with me.

Through the lessons taught me by Rich, Zach and Troy, Dawn, the man at the activity, and especially by the example of my Savior, I have realized that true service is never performed with our physical hands but with our spiritual hands. We extend those hands when we speak a kind word, proclaim a simple truth, or provide a good example. We extend our spiritual hands when we compliment someone on a job well done, or counsel with an ailing member, or love as Christ loved. This is the work in which we must anxiously be engaged. Robots, conveyor belts, and computers can bring in the groceries, plant a tree, and even teach football. But it is the spiritual service from the individual that can never be replaced. The work of such hands will change lives. Therefore, we must employ our spiritual hands in the service of our fellow man. And then, we will find ourselves in the service of our God.

I still pray for healing, and often watch for my hands to move. But regardless of how many of my faculties are restored, it is my prayer that at that last day, my spiritual hands will be those that tell the story of my life . . . by the calluses they wear.

Stephen Jason Hall graduated from Brigham Young University where he earned a bachelor's degree in English and where he served as an executive director in student government, as a member of the Honor Code Committee, and as student-body president. An Eagle Scout, Jason was junior class president and a member of his seminary council while in high school. He enjoys music, theater, public speaking, drama, basketball, and BYU football. A dynamic public speaker, Jason is a popular lecturer at EFY sessions. He is married to Kolette Coleman.

14

IF YOU BELIEVE YOU CAN, YOU CAN!

SUZANNE HANSEN

Two boys who had picked hundreds of hickory nuts in the woods stopped at a cemetery outside town to divide them. As one of the boys was counting, "one for you and one for me," two nuts rolled out underneath the fence. At the same time, a young man walking by heard the voices and raced back to town, terrified.

"What's the matter?" asked an older man he met in the street.

"The Lord and the devil are dividing up the souls in the cemetery!" the young fellow shouted breathlessly.

"I don't believe it," said the oldster.

"Come and listen."

Cautiously approaching the graveyard, the two heard a voice saying, "one for you and one for me."

"There," piped up the other voice. "Now, we're finished, except for those two nuts outside the fence. Let's divide those and we'll be even."

The older man *beat* the young one back to town.

As you can see from this fun story, the beliefs of the old man and young boy (although incorrect) were real for them, and those beliefs generated quite a lot of excitement—even fear.

What kind of beliefs do you have, especially about *yourself*? Are they correct or incorrect? Which of these statements sounds like you:

"Nobody really likes me. I have no real close friends!" or "I make friends easily. I enjoy being with people and they with me."

Is the way you feel about yourself dependent on your looks, body shape, money, clothing labels, or talents? Or, do you believe that you can accomplish anything you have a mind to because you know that your worth has nothing to do with superficial things and was established long before you were born? Do you see yourself as a royal child of God?

Well, whatever *YOU BELIEVE* about yourself *will be true for you*. Our beliefs are the sum of whatever *ideas and thoughts we accept as truth!* Always remember this important little rhyme:

> *If you continue to think like you have always thought,*
> *You'll continue to get what you've always got.*

When we were born on this earth, our minds (the place where we store our beliefs) were pure and unpolluted by the harsh world. We were innocent and untouched. The world is now full of loud, confusing voices that try to get us to question our beliefs, go against our consciences, and make the bad look good to us.

Vernon Howard wrote a story about a community of eagles that lived on a beautiful mountain range:

> The eagles were happy and found an abundance of food in the surrounding woods and streams. Their days were spent in lofty soaring in the beautiful blue sky, high above the world.
>
> But down on the dry prairie, there dwelt a band of devious crows. The crows had access to a low grade of

corn in glittering packages. They looked for unsuspecting travelers who they could get to eat the corn.

Now the eagles were smart enough, but careless at times. Though they were cautious at first, the corn looked pretty good. Besides, it saved the effort of hunting. So the eagles soared less and less and began dropping down to the crows' cornfield more and more. Of course, the less they flew, the less they felt like flying. Growing weak in their wings, they began to believe that they were meant to be down on the ground with the crows.

But there was one eagle who sensed something was not right. Besides, the corn didn't really taste as good as the crows said it would. When he tried to persuade his eagle friends to return to the mountains, the crows ridiculed him. Believing the crows, the eagles shunned their former friend.

Growing tired of it all, the lone eagle studied himself carefully. He tried his wings, and something deep inside told him he belonged in a higher place. So off he flew, back to the mountains. Then from dawn to dusk, he soared over his beautiful world, free to be what he was always meant to be—an eagle (*The Power of Your Supermind* [Englewood Cliffs: Prentice Hall, 1975], pp. 1–2).

The world is filled with blinding influences. If we are not careful, we can be deceived by the false beliefs and teachings being spread by millions of "devious crows." They are able to convince many to take the "easy street."

But we really are eagles. We are meant to soar. As children of God, our lives can shine forth and become a powerful influence and inspiration for good, despite the many "crows" around us. *If you believe you can, you can!*

The Influence of Belief

Bob Wieland has been an inspiration to the thousands of people whose lives he has touched.

Bob had both his legs amputated in Vietnam, but that

didn't stop him from *"walking"* across the country. It took him three-and-a-half years, taking 4,900,016 "steps" from Los Angeles to Washington, D.C. Bob used no crutches, or artificial legs—and of course, no wheelchair. He *"walked"* by supporting himself with his arms and hands—taking one "step" at a time and swinging his body along.

He proved the truthfulness of his favorite Bible verse, "For with God nothing shall be impossible" (Luke 1:37). He believed he could do it, and others believed in him and helped him along the way. He raised $305,000 on his trip to feed the hungry, and prayed personally with 1,488 individuals to strengthen their belief in Jesus Christ.

Bob never felt sorry for himself because he didn't have legs. But he believed he could do anything with God's help. *He turned his belief into action*—and never looked back (James Dobson, *Focus on the Family Magazine*, July 1986, p. 5).

How is your belief—in yourself? Perhaps you won't walk across the nation on your hands to raise money to feed the hungry, but do you believe you could organize a service project; or make the team; or be in the school play; or run for a school office; or get on the honor role?

Do you believe you could be kind to someone who has been mean to you, or resist talking negatively about someone who has offended you? Do you really believe Heavenly Father will help you master difficult tasks or overcome problems that seem insurmountable?

Belief—the Key to Accomplishment

Let's look at another true story. Bob Wieland lost both his legs. But Tony Melendez was born with *no arms*.

Tony's mother always believed, from the moment of his birth, that when *God created Tony he had something wonderful for him in mind*, and she never let Tony forget it.

Tony had a beautiful voice. When in his teens, he was able to sing in the church and school choirs. When Tony was fifteen, he decided to learn to play the guitar—with his feet! Dad's old Spanish guitar was a prized possession. For the next three years, Tony practiced four or five hours a day.

Tony would sit in a chair, with the guitar laid flat on the floor in front of him. Between the two larger toes on his right foot, he learned to hold the pick. He formed the chords by pressing the strings down with the toes of his left foot, while strumming with his right.

It wasn't easy to learn to play without the use of hands and fingers, but he played and replayed each chord (what must have seemed a million times) until the notes were clear and precise. After months and months of practice, he could finally accompany himself on the guitar as he sang *one* song.

But he continued to practice and practice, and perform on the street corners to earn extra money. He would sing songs of hope and love. He was invited to play and sing for the Pope, and he performed on national TV. Then he was asked to record a gospel album of his songs in English and Spanish. He has written a book and signed a contract for a television movie about his life. And he has now made concert appearances in Japan, Europe, Central and South America, and across the United States.

Tony wrote on the last page of his book, "I read a poster once that said, 'To BELIEVE in God is to know that the rules will be fair and that there will be many wonderful surprises'" (Tony Melendez with Mel White, *Gift of Hope* [New York: Harper & Row, 1979], pp. 3–5, 164–65).

Overcoming Fear with Belief

What kind of fears do you think Bob and Tony experienced to have their disabilities so visible to the general public? Bob was on the streets, and Tony sang before thousands. I'm sure they worried that there would be those who would ridicule or laugh at them. There are "crows" everywhere—

and "crows" don't like to see anyone do well or improve themselves—especially if they are doing better than the "crows."

But remember Bob's favorite scripture: "For with God, nothing shall be impossible" (Luke 1:37). When we truly believe that, and know deep in our soul that our Heavenly Father loves us and that Jesus Christ is interested in our success, fear will fly away from us.

Fear keeps us from receiving blessings the Lord is willing to grant us. Listen to what the scriptures say about that: "Ye endeavored to believe that ye should receive the blessing which was offered unto you; but behold, verily I say unto you there were fears in your hearts, and verily this is the reason that ye did not receive" (D&C 67:3).

Here are some more examples of people who overcame their fears by believing the Lord would help them no matter what. Their stories might even be referred to as "miracles."

> Ron Clark was a young Explorer Scout on a super activity. The truck he was riding in overturned on a mountain road, killing thirteen of the forty-five on board, and seriously injuring twenty more.
>
> Ron was among those injured. His left leg was crushed under the truck, and his jaw was severely knocked out of joint. The pain in his jaw was a lot worse than in his leg.
>
> Ron had a talent for singing, and his stake president, Ben E. Lewis, presented him with a request from the families of his slain friends. "Would you sing at the funeral service?"
>
> How could he do it? He couldn't even eat because of his badly swollen jaw, and the jaw was so rigid, he could barely speak through clenched teeth. Singing seemed out of the question.
>
> "You can do it," the stake president said, "if you will pray and if you really want to."
>
> He cast aside his fear and believed the Lord would bless him. His prayers continued right up to the time he was sitting in the funeral, still unable to move his jaw. Then suddenly, minutes before he was to sing, an over-

whelmingly peaceful feeling settled on him, and Ron
turned to his brother. "I can move my jaw!" he whispered. "It feels all right!"

His voice rose, beautiful and pure, as he began to sing.
The unwavering notes filled the Provo tabernacle and
soared to heaven on the summer breeze. As for the jaw—
immediately after the song, it locked back up, and weeks
passed before Ron could open it again. (Stan and Sharon
Miller, *Especially for Mormons*, 3 vols. [University Station:
Kelirae, 1976], p. 25).

A miracle? Some would say so. But the Lord blessed
Ron because his belief was stronger than his fear. His faith
overcame failure. Belief is what moves us forward while
fear holds us back.

Consider also the story of a Cheryl Prewitt, Miss America in 1980.

As a young teenager, Cheryl had been told that with
one leg two inches shorter than the other, there was nothing that could be done—that her left leg would never
grow. Somewhere in her heart she spoke to her soul,
"Well, God can make bone grow."

This simple belief worked in Cheryl over the months
as she sought a healing from God. Then one night, as she
was reading in John, she came to a verse that made her
heart do a little flip-flop. Jesus was speaking to his disciples, but he might as well have been addressing Cheryl.

"And now," Jesus said, "I have told you before it come
to pass, that, when it is come to pass, *ye might believe*."
(John 14:29; emphasis added).

"Amazing!" Cheryl thought. "Could this be what the
Lord wanted me to do with the healing I expected? Could
it be, he wanted me to somehow use it as a witness to his
reality in today's world?"

The next day Cheryl told her best friend, Dolly Cham-
bers, the story of the accident many years before that
caused her left leg to be two inches shorter than her right
leg. Then Cheryl said:

"My leg is going to be healed. I've been praying about it all summer, and I believe God can heal me. That's why I'm telling you this—so when it happens, you'll know *Who's* responsible."

Dolly grinned wryly. "I'll believe it when I see it."

"And you will," Cheryl said earnestly. "You really will!"

Cheryl had a similar conversation with about fifteen other kids by the end of the day. Cheryl gave herself no room for fear or doubt. She moved ahead with true belief burning in her heart.

Soon Cheryl was walking through the school halls without a limp, her pants hemmed perfectly even, because both of her legs were now the same length. Through the laying on of hands and the power, compassion, and love of God—and because of Cheryl's belief—a miracle had taken place. There had been no fear as Cheryl had notified her friends in advance of God's blessing—only belief.

Cheryl's friends' reactions were mixed. Some believed. Some didn't. The doctor didn't know what to think. But Cheryl's belief never wavered because of others' lack of belief. But Dolly whispered as she hugged Cheryl tightly, tears filling both their eyes, "I saw, and I believe."

This is the bigger meaning of the results of Cheryl's belief. There is a God—a living, powerful, personally involved God—who blesses the lives of those who believe in him without doubt or fear (Cheryl Prewitt, *Guide Post Magazine*, June 1980, pp. 2–6).

So how do you become more believing? How do you create in you the spirit that eliminates fear so God will bless you? Here is a four-step program that may help.

Step One—Be Like the Eagles—Elevate Your Thoughts

We come from God. Keep your eyes heavenward and your thoughts will follow. Remember, thoughts become reality. You can either think about the stars in the heavens or the mud on the ground. Remember, there are millions of "devious crows" who live in the mud, and they would have you there, too.

Listen to that still, small voice deep inside you that whispers you belong in a higher place. You are meant to soar above this world. So elevate your thoughts. *If you believe you can, you can!*

Step Two—Turn Your Belief into Action

Resist having a "pity party." That's where you feel sorry for yourself and wallow in it for days. Bob Wieland and Tony Melendez could have felt sorry for themselves because they didn't have legs or arms. They could have spent the rest of their lives lamenting all the things they couldn't do.

But they believed they could do *anything* with God's help. They believed that God created them *with something wonderful in mind*. They turned this belief into action—and never looked back.

You can do the same in your life. There is power in this moment, *right now*. It doesn't matter what happened in the past. The future will take care of itself if you begin, *right now*, to make your life better. *If you believe you can, you can!*

Step Three—Fear Keeps Us from Being Blessed—Belief Erases Fear

Write down on a piece of paper what you fear and why you think you have those fears. Be truthful with yourself. Then crumple up the piece of paper and throw it away. Put those fears out of your mind—they are gone. They no longer have power over you.

Are you afraid that the Lord won't bless you because of past problems you've had? Then you are cheating yourself of blessings he is waiting to bestow on you, right now! Belief is what moves us forward while fear is what holds us back.

So repent! Get your problems behind you. God is willing to forgive you. You need to forgive yourself and move ahead. Heavenly Father will not withhold blessings from you—even miracles! You can experience something as inspiring in your life as did Ron Clark and Cheryl Prewitt. *If you believe you can, you can!*

Step Four—You Can't Fail—You Will Succeed If You Believe You Can

The truth is, you can't fail in this life if you believe strongly enough that you will succeed. That's not to say that you won't make mistakes and experience setbacks. Mistakes are part of the growth process. Look at your mistakes as teachers and benefit by the experience they provide.

As long as you are striving to keep the commandments of God, your mistakes can serve as stepping stones, not stumbling blocks. You will succeed. *If you believe you can, you can!*

Finally, if God is for you, who can be against you? Someone has said: "I believe that the Savior loves you so much, that even if you were the only person alive in the world, he would have died on the cross *just for you!*"

Do you believe that you are that special to the Lord? I know you are. And to have this beautiful thought burning in your heart each and every day can be your greatest strength. All of Heaven believes in you. Now take flight—you were meant to soar. *If you believe you can, you can!*

Suzanne Hansen is a lecturer and a businesswoman. She has worked as a newspaper columnist, appeared on many TV talk shows, and written five books. Suzanne has several times been named one of the Outstanding Young Women in America. A former homecoming queen at Ricks College, she enjoys arts and crafts, flower arrangement, classical and new age music, and the study of quantum physics. She is married to Michael Hansen, and they have three children.

15

IT'S PROM NIGHT! WHAT'S MORE IMPORTANT—
THE DANCE OR SPIRITUAL TIME?

MITCHELL B. HUHEM

Because I was Senior Class President of my high school, my Senior Prom was a special event for me. It was also a time when I had to stand up for all I knew was right.

I'm Mitch Huhem. I was born in Brooklyn, New York, and raised in San Diego, California. I am a Jewish convert to The Church of Jesus Christ of Latter-day Saints. There were very few members of the Church at my high school—actually only two—my brother and me.

Anyway, I was telling you about my Senior Prom. As senior class president, I had been responsible for all the planning. Well, I love life, and I love people, and I really wanted to make this dance fun and something to remember. We had arranged to hold it on the top floor of an elegant hotel in the city. During that day, I had received tons of calls about the dance. "Where is it?" "How do I get there?" And so on. Everyone was anxious for the dance.

A large group of my friends, including one of my best friends, had rented a large motor home to drive to the hotel. The father of one of our friends had agreed to be our chauffeur. Although my friend Eric was not a member of the Church, he knew about my family's tradition of "Spiritual

Time." He knew that I could not leave the house until we had had "Spiritual Time." Since he knew this, he had decided to pick up everyone else, including my date, first, to ensure that I would be finished with "Spiritual Time."

Let me briefly tell you what "Spiritual Time" is and how it came about. During the first general conference held after my dad joined the Church, he was inspired by something President Spencer W. Kimball said about family life. Dad decided our family would do three things every day: sing a hymn, read from the Book of Mormon, and have prayer together. This was a long-range commitment for my father. Most people would decide to do something like that and maybe succeed for a little while but then abandon the plan. Not my dad.

Well, I didn't even catch the promise at conference, but after we got home from the meeting, my dad called us all in the living room. He pulled out this big cardboard box with "Spiritual Time" written on it. In the box there were a whole bunch of hymn books and copies of the Book of Mormon. Dad then introduced the process to us. We would first pick a hymn and sing it all together. Then, each of us would read a couple of verses in the Book of Mormon. In closing, everyone would kneel to pray, and then each of us would pray, from youngest to oldest.

I wasn't wild about the idea, but I thought that it would last a week at the most. A week went by and we still did it every day. I mean *every* day! The thing was, we couldn't have "Spiritual Time" until all the family was there, and similarly, you could not go to sleep or go out until we had had our "Spiritual Time." "Spiritual Time" went on for the next few weeks, then for the next few months, and for the next few years. Now it has been thirteen years, and every day my family still has "Spiritual Time." I have continued the tradition with my wife in our home.

I can remember coming home from church dances a

little late and going upstairs to my room. Just as I was finishing my prayers and getting ready to crawl into bed, the door would open and my dad would say in his raspy and firm voice, "We didn't have 'Spiritual Time' yet!" This meant he would wake everyone up at midnight, and we would have "Spiritual Time."

Now that I have told you what "Spiritual Time" is, I will return to my story. My friend Eric had picked up everyone, including my date, in the rented motor home. I was upstairs on the phone, still answering questions about the prom when I saw the big motor home drive up in front of my house. Eric darted out and ran toward the house in his tuxedo. I quickly hung up the phone and started to put on my bow tie. I heard the patter of his feet as he ran through the kitchen and up the stairs to my room. We were both *so* excited. We ran down the stairs, made a sharp right at the kitchen, and started down the long stretch of hall to the front door. About halfway down the hall, I heard a firm and raspy voice calling me.

I froze in my tracks as I heard these words: "Mitch, we haven't had 'Spiritual Time' yet."

My friend looked at me, stunned, and yelled, "You didn't have 'Spiritual Time' yet?" My close friends knew about "Spiritual Time" because many times they had been caught in "Spiritual Time" and they knew that I couldn't go anywhere until it was finished.

I turned white and said, "Dad, everyone is waiting. We are late. I have to go!"

My dad just looked at me and calmly asked, "What's more important—the dance or 'Spiritual Time?'"

I quickly snapped, "Dad, I know 'Spiritual Time' is, but everyone is waiting."

My dad just looked up and asked again, "What's more important?"

Imagine what I was feeling. The Spirit was saying,

"Come on, Mitch. You know 'Spiritual Time' is important."
But we were in a hurry. And I was afraid of being embarrassed.

I finally said, "Eric, just give me ten minutes. Tell everyone I will be right there."

I darted to the living room, got out the "Spiritual Time"
box, and started yelling to everyone: "Serena, Nicole,
Brigham, Victor, Mom, Dad; quick, 'Spiritual Time.' Come
fast!"

Everyone came in quickly, and I started throwing the
books at them. I mean everyone but my dad. Have you ever
seen the parent "slow walk?" "Dad, quick!" and he moves
even slower. "Come on, Dad, fast!" He then goes to his
"Super Slow Walk," like he is on the moon.

Finally, he gets there, and I hand him a hymn book. I
said, "What song? Come on."

My dad then looked at me and innocently asked, "And
your friends?"

I about had a heart attack. I could not believe it. I said,
"My friends?"

He said, "Yes, your friends. Why don't you invite them
in?"

I said, "Dad, you don't understand. They are not members of the Church. There are people out there who lie,
cheat, do drugs, and steal. You don't want them in our
house, do you?"

My dad just said, "And your friends."

I turned and faced the front door. It seemed like it took
an eternity just to get to the door. Looking out, I could see
the motor home through the screen door.

Romans, chapter 1, verse 16, "For I am not ashamed of
the gospel of Christ: for it is the power of God unto salvation," kept repeating in my mind. I almost chickened out
when I remembered another scripture in Ephesians, chapter 6, verses 10–14: "Finally, my brethren, be strong in the

Lord, and in the power of his might. . . . Stand therefore, having your loins girt about with truth, and having on the breastplate of righteousness." I looked again at the motor home. With all the courage I could muster, I went out to invite the whole group to come in for "Spiritual Time."

When I knocked on the little aluminum door, they opened it and said, "Great, Mitch! Let's go!"

I looked at them and said, "I need you to come in the house, quick!"

They looked at me as if I was totally crazy and said, "What for?"

I said, "We have to sing a song."

"A what?" they said.

I said, "A song."

All of them, the entire group of about fifty kids, came through the hall to our living room where my dad had hymn books for everyone. My friends looked at me like *"What* is going on here?" I tried not to look at them as I went to the piano where I would play the hymn, "Rejoice, the Lord is King!"

During the first verse, all I could hear was my family. The next verse, there were a few other voices. My heart filled with prayer and I plead to my Father in Heaven to touch their hearts. The third verse was fantastic! There was rapping and singing. It was booming and the Spirit filled the room.

After the song, they were all saying, "That wasn't too bad. It's over. Let's go."

But then, my dad began handing out copies of the Book of Mormon to everyone. My dad buys those blue, paper-back copies of the Book of Mormon like everyone else buys pens. We have them everywhere. Most of these kids had never even sung a hymn, let alone read from the Book of Mormon. But when my family had finished reading their verses, it was time for my friends to each read a verse. It is amazing to listen to people read scriptures who have never read them before. It was fun to hear them read about "Neh-fee" (Nephi) and how "It came to pass." The Spirit got stronger as each of them read their verse. I could almost see angels doing high-fives all around us, and I was feeling much better.

After reading—you guessed it—it was prayer time! In our house, that means *everyone* gets on their knees and prepares to pray. And *everyone* takes a turn. It doesn't matter if you are Jewish, a Buddhist, or what your religious preference is. If you are in our home during "Spiritual Time," you take a turn to pray.

Now, my friends were totally unaware of what was about to occur, so they just knelt with the rest of us. After my family members had each prayed, my dad looked up and said, "And your friends?" I had heard that one before. As I turned to look at my friends, each of them had a look of total terror and absolute shock on their face. It was like they were saying, "Mitch, no! No! No! Not me. Please, not this!" I knew most of them had never prayed before and so I stood up and taught them how to pray.

I said, "Prayer is like a sandwich! You have a top piece of bread and a bottom piece of bread. The top piece of bread is 'Dear Heavenly Father.' The bottom piece is, 'In the name of Jesus Christ, Amen.' In between, you can put whatever you want. You can ask for help and you can give thanks for things you have or have experienced. You can make a big sandwich or a small sandwich."

They looked at me, still in shock, so I had Eric start, because he had already experienced a couple of "Spiritual Time" treatments. He finished. Then the others followed. After a couple of the prayers, I wanted to see how they were doing, so I barely opened my eyes. No one was acting weird. Some were holding hands, and all of them were participating reverently. It was incredible to listen to them pray.

I knew many of them had never prayed before, so I mean *incredible!* When they were finished praying, I noticed that we had been in my home for more than two and a half hours. We floated down the hall to the front door. The Holy Ghost was present, and I felt absolutely happy and very confident.

Two big football players and I were the first to approach the door of the motor home. As we did, the door swung open and our chauffeur started to cuss us out.

"Where in the blankity, blank, blank, have you been? I have been waiting for you here blankity, blank." The football player to my right reached out and grabbed him by the shirt with a tight fist. The chauffeur looked shocked as the football player said, "Hey, you don't say those kind of words. We just got done reading the Blue Bible." As you can imagine, the Spirit was very strong!

The chauffeur quickly started the motor home and then drove us to the elegant hotel where the Prom was going on. The Spirit we had all felt at my house carried over, and many of the kids talked about wanting to live better lives— to do things that are right.

That's what the Spirit does. When we feel it, we are prompted to do what is right. It creates a desire which no one needs to force upon us. This is why having the Spirit when we share the light with others is so important. We can feel the Spirit by reading the Book of Mormon daily, praying continually, and living the commandments.

All fifty of us went into the Prom at the same time. There was only about half an hour left to dance. I had been dancing no more than five minutes, when someone came up to me and asked, "Is it true that Julie said a prayer in your house tonight?"

I told her, "Yes," and she said, "Julie? Are you sure?" and the girl walked away in awe.

Then a couple of minutes later, someone said, "Hey

Mitch, I need to ask you a question. Did John really read a Blue Bible in your house?" I said, "Yes," and again he walked away in awe. This went on for the rest of the night.

It has now been over six years since that night and I suspect NONE of my friends has forgotten the experience of "Spiritual Time" and the Spirit they felt. I love going back to San Diego, and when people see me they always say, "Remember when so and so sang, prayed, or read in your home?" What my dad made us do that night left a lasting impression on each of our lives. If I had been really brave, I would have had the chauffeur drop us off at the stake center for a pre-prom baptismal service.

I believe in you and your potential. You are fantastic! Although I may not know you personally, I know you are my brother or sister, and the fact that you are reading this chapter means you are a fellow disciple of Christ. "For I am not ashamed of the Gospel of Christ. . . ." Stand up for what you know is right and be firm in the faith. Isn't it good to feel the Spirit and have that overwhelming desire to just be good? To be a true disciple of Christ at all times, under all circumstances, wherever you may be? God loves you, and I am rooting for your success. *You can do it!*

Mitchell Huhem is a Jewish convert to the Church who was one of the youngest Eagle Scouts in America. He enjoyed wrestling in high school and has served a mission in Chile. A powerful public speaker, Mitchell has taught large weekly fireside discussions at the Missionary Training Center. He is the president of a company that promotes personal organization and time management for students through the use of daily planners. He also teaches self-improvement seminars and workshops at BYU. Mitchell is married to Patricia Villarroel.

16

THE GREAT GAME PLAN OF GOD

C U R T I S   L .   J A C O B S

Several years ago a pair of missionaries was about to give a first discussion to a family whose father was the leader of several congregations of another church. (Doesn't *that* sound like a fun evening?) The missionaries knew they'd be confronted with some hard questions. So, armed with all the scriptures they could find to "back up" their position, they took a deep breath and knocked on the door.

As the missionaries had predicted, the discussion soon evolved into a debate of doctrines. The minister finally said, "This is getting us nowhere. Do you have anything you want to tell us?"

The missionaries felt impressed to teach the "plan of salvation" discussion, a lesson usually kept until later.

As these young elders were teaching the plan to this minister and his family, something wonderful happened. The father's face came alive with interest. He even began to show his family other scriptures not used by the missionaries to show the truth of what was being taught. When the doctrine of baptism for the dead was brought up, the father literally jumped to his feet, and with tears in his eyes quoted 1 Corinthians 15:29 (which, as all you marvelous seminary students know, talks about baptism for the dead).

He then said, in so many words, "I have studied for years to discover what that scripture means. You two young men have made it perfectly clear. You have brought us the truth!" (Richard Cracroft, *Teaching the Gospel*, Brigham Young University Speeches of the Year [Provo, 29 June 1993], p. 41).

What is this "plan of salvation" that it has the power to take a difficult discussion and turn it into the conversion and baptism of an entire family? The scriptures have many names for this plan. It is known variously as "the plan of mercy" (Alma 42:15); "the eternal plan of redemption" (Alma 34:16); "the plan of our God" (2 Nephi 9:13); and "the plan of happiness" (Alma 42:16).

Most of you already know the basics of "the plan." Let me illustrate. If you're in a Sunday School or seminary class and the teacher goes up to the chalkboard and puts a nice-sized circle in the top left-hand corner of the board, what is that? Well, the premortal life, of course, right? What comes next? A little squiggly line (the veil). Next? Another circle (earth). Then a straight line (death). Another circle, one we always cut in half with a line (spirit world). Then a big "bar" (judgment). And, finally, three circles (the three degrees of glory).

To a nonmember, the three circles might look like a stoplight or a real "odd" snowman. Imagine what they might think if we told them this represented our "plan of salvation." To us, however, these are more than just circles and lines. What we are diagramming is God's plan for us, and to us there is no more significant message.

So, what do you remember about our premortal life? (Actually nothing. We "forgot," remember?) So, what have you been *taught* about our pre-earth life? You probably learned that we all lived with Heavenly Father as his spirit children. Do you realize how important it is to know that we are children of God?

When I was in college, I loved both gymnastics and girls, and so I became a cheerleader. Anyway, some of us had the opportunity to go to Santa Barbara, California, during the summer, to a "Cheer Camp." There we were, about forty guys and several hundred girls. (It was a very tough couple of days, but, hey, someone had to do it.)

One evening our coaches decided to have a "talent show." A "cheer camp talent show" usually consists of different cheerleader teams performing a cheer or a dance routine, to which the rest of the cheerleaders respond by screaming and yelling their approval.

Since all of us from Utah State University were LDS, we decided to join with the team of cheerleaders from BYU and perform together. But, did we just do a cheer? No, not us. We decided to "teach" a little principle to this rowdy, cheer-happy group.

We began by singing the first verse of "No Man Is an Island," to a guitar accompaniment. (I realize that's not one of your basic "top-40" hits.) Then we changed keys and began singing the first verse of a song you all know.

> I am a child of God,
> And he has sent me here,
> Has given me an earthly home
> With parents, kind and dear.
> Lead me, guide me, walk beside me,
> Help me find the way.
> Teach me all that I must do
> To live with him someday.
> (Hymns, 1985, no. 301.)

Then we sang the second verse of "No Man . . ." and then the final two verses of "I Am a Child of God." You know what happened? Instead of the normal yelling and screaming, these wild and crazy cheerleaders looked as if they had realized something about who they really are for the first time in their lives! They were "children of God!" After we finished, there was a moment of silence. Then, one began to clap, then another, and then another—until they were all applauding. Their response was incredible. It was as though they were saying thank you!

So what's the big deal in knowing that we are children of God? Let me ask you a couple of questions. What does a little kitten become? (A cat, in case you didn't know.) What does a calf become? (A cow.) How about a fawn? (A deer.) Now, wouldn't you really question my intelligence if I said a kitten becomes a dog, or a fawn becomes an elephant? Do you see? In every instance we know about, the offspring has the potential only to become like its parent. To say otherwise goes against everything we know and see around us.

So, if we are the "offspring of God" (Acts 17:28–29; D&C 76:24), then we have the divine potential to become like our Heavenly Father! Can you think of anything more awesome?

Meanwhile, back at the ranch (I mean in the premortal existence), we grew and learned until finally Heavenly Father called us all together in that great "Family Home Evening" in the sky. Our Father told us we were ready to move on to the next step in our eternal progression, earth life.

He told us about his plan. What did the "plan" include? Among other things, that we would obtain a physical body (some of you may think others got a better deal than you did, but just wait until the resurrection). He told us that, with the use of agency, we would be tested to see if we would keep his commandments while out of his presence. He knew that we would make mistakes, but that one would be chosen to be the Savior for the rest of us.

"Whom shall I send?" the Father asked. Our Savior, Jesus Christ, spoke. Elder Neal A. Maxwell has said of this event, "Never has anyone offered so much to so many in so few words as when Jesus said, 'Here am I, send me' ("'Jesus

of Nazareth, Savior and King,'" *Ensign,* May 1976, p. 26).
Lucifer tried to get his own plan accepted. He and those
who followed him rebelled, and there was "war in heaven."
You should know which side you were on. Don't forget that
before you were ever born into mortality, you fought for the
plan of our Heavenly Father.

So, we've come to earth without remembering that
wonderful place, but deep inside our spiritual self knows
our potential. Now we are here on earth to be tested. And
what is the nature of this test? President Spencer W. Kimball has said, "We knew before we were born that we were
coming to earth for bodies and experience and that we
would have joys and sorrows, ease and pain, comforts and
hardships, health and sickness, successes and disappoint-
ments, and we knew also that after a period of life we
would die. We accepted *all* these eventualities with a glad
heart, *eager to accept both the favorable and unfavorable*" (*Faith
Precedes the Miracle* [Salt Lake City: Deseret Book, 1976], p.
106; emphasis added).

We must have "opposition in all things" in order to
grow here on earth. Do you understand why? What if we
had come to earth with our agency, but were only given
good choices? How could we prove we'd do the right thing
if we weren't given the option of choosing the wrong thing?

Unfortunately, on earth we will each do some pretty
dumb things. The problem is, some of us don't know how
dumb those things are, and that's *really* dumb! Some poor
choices aren't that big a hindrance to our progression, while
others can really hurt us. Each of us will be tried, but there
are many forms of trials. Some trials we bring upon ourselves. One guy learned this principle the hard way when
he jumped from 190 feet up, with a 260–foot bungee cord.
OUCH! We must remember that each choice we make has
consequences. Whether those consequences are immediate
or come some time later, we must never think we can do

wrong and not suffer a negative consequence. Remember, it's a lie of Lucifer that we can "Eat, drink, and be merry; . . . and at last we shall be saved in the kingdom of God" (2 Nephi 28:8).

Other trials come from living in this telestial world. There are going to be broken bones, hurt feelings, people who can slam dunk and people who can't. (Trust me, at 5'7" tall, I know this from personal experience.)

It's not the nature of the trial, but how we handle the trial that matters. A young lady who is deaf, whom I've had as a student, once bore her testimony. She can speak, but very deliberately. "I don't fear being deaf," she said, "it has taught me so much about life." She went on to say, "One of my favorite songs is 'Because I Have Been Given Much, I Too Must Give.' I've been given so much from my Heavenly Father."

Another young lady, one confined to a wheelchair, was asked if she could change anything, what would it be? Marriage and normal family life appeared to be passing her by. Yet she responded, "I would really like to be healed so I could live a normal life. However, if in order to be healed, I would have to give up all the things I have learned and experienced as a person with a handicap, I do not think I would ask to be healed" (A. LaVar Thornock, "Do the Wicked Prosper While the Righteous Suffer?" *Ensign*, Oct. 1990, p. 15). The list could go on and on. Each of us must face trials, hard ones, but if we endure them well, we will become more like our Heavenly Father and his Son.

Then at some point here on earth, we will die. (It's hard to get out of this life alive.) One of the most difficult times in my life came years ago when my parents were killed in a car accident. But with my understanding that it was all a part of "the plan," I was greatly comforted. My parents had simply gone on to the next step in their progression. When our youngest son's school had a "Grandparents' Day," a day when grandparents are invited to come to school with their grandchildren, he explained to his friend that Grandpa and Grandma Jacobs lived in Italy and couldn't come. My wife said, "Jonathan," they're not in Italy, they're in heaven." "Oh yeah," Jonathan replied, "I knew they were someplace neat."

After death the spirits of the righteous are taken to a place "of happiness, which is called paradise, a state of rest, a state of peace, where they shall rest from all their troubles and from all care, and sorrow" (Alma 40:12). Granted, the wicked don't receive quite as nice a place, a place described as "a state of awful, fearful looking for the fiery indignation of the wrath of God" (Alma 40:14). Which place we end up in depends on the choices we make here on earth.

Then there is "Judgment Day." Those two words create all sorts of "visions" in my mind. You know the kind I mean. There you are, with your parents and grandparents. They're all eating popcorn because it's "family night at the movies," and **YOUR** movie is showing! Everything you've ever said or thought is right there in front for all to see. Are we having fun yet?

Hold it! Remember? Before we ever came to earth, Heavenly Father knew we would make mistakes. That's why we had to have a Savior. Because of the Atonement, we can get rid of our sins and their effects through repentance. Through that process, parts of our movie can be edited out, completely. (Thank goodness, right?)

It's not easy to repent, but it is possible to "change our movie" if we undergo a sincere "change of heart." As a bishop, I have witnessed this change. Some have had to change not only their hearts but also their friends or the places they usually go to have fun. It takes effort, sincere prayer, and a determination to sin no more. Yet, when they have done so, that marvelous miracle of forgiveness is finally given.

Do you understand what really happens on Judgment Day? We are simply rewarded, based on what we did on earth. Isn't that fair? Wouldn't it be unfair for those who haven't kept the commandments, who haven't repented, to receive the same blessings as those who have tried their hardest and repented? On Judgment Day, we, like Nephi, will know that "[God's] ways are just" (2 Nephi 26:7).

Those who have done their best, and who, when they have fallen short, have repented, can return and live with Heavenly Father forever. They have chosen to become more like him and, therefore, will feel at home in his presence.

Do you understand why Heavenly Father has given us commandments? Because, to become like him, we must not only know what is right, we must choose what is right. The commandments are given to show us what we must do in order to become like our Heavenly Father. Whether it is the law of chastity, the Word of Wisdom, or serving others, when obeyed, each act of obedience helps us reach our potential.

Will you please remember this great game plan of God? You are here to prove that what you really want is to become like him. Your destiny isn't a matter of chance but a matter of choice. Please choose wisely. You have the divine potential to do so. And by the grace of Jesus Christ and with his help, we can return to our heavenly home, to live there forever and enjoy the blessings of eternal life. That has been our Heavenly Father's plan all along.

Curtis Jacobs teaches at the institute of religion at Utah State University. Holding a master's degree in counseling and guidance, he has taught both seminary and institute in Arizona. Curtis enjoys playing racquetball, and he held a championship in the sport while residing in Prescott, Arizona. His other interests include basketball, piano, old movies and Les Miserables. *The bishop of a student ward, he is married to Jolene Keeler, and they have four children.*

17

GETTING ALONG WITH YOUR FOREVER FAMILY

STEVE JAMES

As the oldest of four children, I had a lot of responsibilities while growing up. I would baby-sit for my parents, do work around the house and the yard, protect my two younger sisters and my younger brother, and be a good example. Granted, I had my privileges, but at times, life became a struggle to survive, much like a wildlife documentary seen on the Discovery Channel. Sometimes, getting along with my siblings required real effort.

When I was eight years old, we were living in Salt Lake City, Utah. I was a subservient child, emanating a choirboy demeanor but with a mischievous twist. I was obedient though, and I respected my parents. My father was the teachers quorum advisor in our ward and made his living managing an Italian delicatessen. My mom was a homemaker extraordinaire who reminded me of a twentieth century Snow White. My two sisters were little angels (when in the presence of my parents), and my brother was still waiting to be born. I was the oldest child and felt the constant need to please and impress my parents and other grownups.

One day, I walked out the door to find that two members of my dad's teachers quorum were preparing to plant grass in our front yard. I walked across the freshly raked soil to the two young men, who, being teenagers, were my heroes.

"Excuse me," I said. "I just wanted you to know that although I am only eight years old, most people think I'm ten." I tried to act mature.

They laughed. "Oh really?"

"Yes," I returned. "And I came out here to tell you that if you need any help with planting my yard, I am more than willing to assist."

"Thanks," they smiled.

"Oh, by the way," I continued, "I also want you to know that I have never cried in my life!"

"No," they teased. "Not even when you were born?"

"No, never in my life . . ." I answered.

"That's a lie!" exclaimed a voice behind me. I turned to face my six-year-old sister, Tammy.

"I've never seen her before in my life," I insisted.

Tammy, my assertive six-year-old sister, who just weeks before had saved me from the neighborhood bully by chasing him off with a stick, was on the rampage. Hearing my tall story, she was indignant.

"He always cries, whenever he gets in trouble and . . ."

"Tammy, get out of here." I commanded.

As she stalked away, I continued my sophisticated conversation with my teenage friends. Again, I offered my services and began sharing stories of my incredible strength.

Suddenly, I felt the most incredible pain! I screamed in agony! Tammy had lugged a boulder so big she could hardly carry it and unceremoniously dropped in on my foot, breaking my big toe.

It hurt so bad, I began to cry.

"See," Tammy announced. "I told you he cries!"

Years have gone by, and Tammy and I have grown to be close friends. She does have a strong will. But I think that is

what eventually helped her to be an outstanding missionary. Her personality enabled her to teach in areas where
missionaries had previously never been accepted. I look
back and laugh at the way we acted as little kids and how
our relationships have transformed over the years. I have
seen a lot of change. Not that we didn't get along in our
early years, we were just kids being kids.

I remember when Mom brought newborn Wendy home
from the hospital. I was four and Tammy was two. Mom
came in the front door and immediately went over to
Tammy, kneeling down in front of her with the small
bundle in her arms. Tammy, no longer the youngest child,
watched as Mom lifted the blanket. Mom spoke lovingly.
"Look what I brought home to you—a new baby sister."
Tammy replied, "Okay, now I've seen her. Take her back."

Not long ago, our family gathered for a musical night at
the home of our grandmother. I will never forget the look
on Tammy's face as she listened to Wendy sing. It was a
look of admiration, respect, and love. They now are best
friends and share a bond that is rare in this world where
even brothers and sisters struggle to be friends and to love
each other.

As a child, Wendy was as uncontrollable as a whirlwind. I remember the day she ran outside in the snow to
play, without her shoes on. She knew that if she were
caught she would be in trouble, but she wanted to have it
her way. When my dad noticed her absence, he searched
throughout the house. Not finding her, he opened the front
door to see that she was riding her tricycle with bare feet.
He picked up a pair of her shoes and proceeded to scold
her. She turned around, looked surprised, and yelled out,
"Oh, Daddy, you found my shoes!" My dad was speechless.
As usual, she could talk her way out of anything.

Years later, while studying for a beauty pageant interview, Wendy asked if I would help her. I read her questions

that the judges might ask, and she practiced giving intelligent replies.

I asked her the first question. "Wendy, who was the person who sewed the stars and the stripes on the flag?"

She confidently answered, "Margaret Thatcher."

"No, Wendy, she's the prime minister of England," I said.

Laughingly, she attempted to excuse herself. "I know it wasn't Margaret Thatcher who sewed the stars and stripes on the flag!" She paused. "It was Betty Crocker!"

Although she was nervous, she did well in her interview, with the exception of "missing" one question. It related to a controversial moral issue. Wendy could have expressed a popular viewpoint, knowing it would impress the judge. But she refused to compromise her values. She confidently told the judge how she really felt, suspecting that he held a different opinion. She didn't win the pageant, but she did stand up for what she believed in.

Like all kids growing up in families, my sisters and I did not always get along perfectly. They had idiosyncrasies that used to bug me, and I had to learn to be tolerant—to accept the fact that it was okay to be different. One of the greatest lessons I had to learn was the need to work on my own weaknesses rather than focus on theirs. But as the years went by and we each grew older, I learned to accept my family members for who they were. I'm glad I felt close to my brother and sisters growing up. We were not only members of the same family—we were friends. And, as the oldest, I felt the responsibility to protect and watch over them.

I remember when Johnny came to our family. I was ten. Mom brought him home from the hospital and we all flocked around to see our family's new addition. I remember looking into his small, monkeylike face and almost wanting to cry because I was so happy to finally have a little brother, but I held back the tears.

Having a new baby in the family was a big responsibility for all of us. I sometimes think that Johnny grew up with five parents instead of two parents and three siblings. As Mom's right-hand man, I even occasionally changed his diapers, (wearing my swimming nose plugs, of course). I also tended him when my parents were gone.

One Christmas time, while I was baby-sitting, I asked two-year-old Johnny, "What do you want for Christmas?" He blubbered, "I wat my Mommy for Cwismas." As the baby of the family, he was dearly loved and occupied a privileged position.

Wendy liked to play "Superman" with Johnny. He would wear his Superman "Underoos" and a bath towel which was safety pinned around his neck for a cape. Lying on her back, she would hold his hands and push him up with her feet on his stomach, while shouting "Up, up and away!" Johnny would laugh and say, "Again, again."

One day, when they were playing "Superman," I heard, "Up, up and awaaaaa. . . . . . . ," then silence. I was concerned. I immediately ran into the room where they had been playing and found Wendy on her back, with her hands and feet in the air, lying on a bed next to an open window. Johnny was nowhere in the room. We were relieved to find him outside the window, giggling and unhurt saying, "Again, again."

I sometimes wonder how we survived our childhood, but we did. Now I look back and feel so grateful that we learned how to get along. There might be some of you who are thinking, "That's great, but I just can't get along with my family, my parents or brothers and sisters."

Building relationships takes a lot of effort and work. And good family relationships are worth working for. Now having "good" relationships doesn't necessarily mean having perfect ones. I realize that there are many dysfunctional families in the world and many children who are struggling. I understand. We all have our trials, including my family. But in order to have an eternal family someday, we must put forth as much effort as we can. Sometimes we have difficulties with certain members of our family. We seem to focus on each other's weaknesses, allowing them to get on our nerves. Occasionally we even judge others, concluding they don't measure up to our expectations of what we think they should be. We tend to forget that we are commanded to love unconditionally and to accept others for who they are and for the choices they make as free agents and as children of our Father in Heaven. "A new commandment I give unto you, That ye love one another" (John 13:34).

My grandmother always used to tell me not to judge other members of my family because I never knew what they might be going through. She taught me to love and respect them, even if they were making decisions and doing things that I didn't agree with. I didn't have to condone their actions, just leave judgment to God and make sure that I was living the gospel. She would say, "Stevie, the most important thing to me is that we all make it home to our Heavenly Father."

Last spring, I was speaking at a youth conference in Las Vegas. My Mom was traveling with me. Shortly before the conference began, she had a prompting to call my grandmother who was ill, suffering from cancer. When we called Grandmother's home, one of my aunts answered the phone and told us that an ambulance was just leaving, taking my grandmother to the hospital. She expressed an urgency for us to come home because she felt that Grandmother's time had come. We called the hospital and spoke to a nurse who confirmed my aunt's feelings, telling us that my grandmother only had moments left to live. While we were packing my car, Mom saw a blooming bush of gigantic roses. She said, "Oh Grandmother loves roses. I am going to take her some." I told her that they would never make it through the ride in the desert. But she insisted. She picked the roses, and we proceeded to travel to Salt Lake City.

On the way, we stopped in St. George, Utah, to pick up my grandmother's sister who couldn't make the drive by herself. I feel that the Lord allowed us to be nearby so we could bring her to see her dying sister. After seven hours of travel and making several stops to call the hospital to see if Grandmother was still holding on, we arrived and ran up to her room.

I'll never forget what I saw or how I felt. My entire family and all of my cousins on my dad's side were surrounding Grandmother's bed where she lay in a coma. My dad said, "She waited for you to come." Then Grandmother's sister went up to her. Grandmother responded by raising her eyebrows. I knew that she could hear us.

Her sister said, "Tell Mother and Daddy hello for me," and she kissed Grandmother and told her she loved her.

My mom followed and said goodbye, and then it was my turn. I walked over to the bed and looked down at her face. She had not only been a grandparent to me, but a dear friend. I knew that this couldn't be the end. I said, "It's okay, you can let go now. I love you, Grams."

Then my family asked me if I would sing to her. I sang some of her favorite hymns. First "How Great Thou Art," and then, "I Am a Child of God." During the second verse of the last song, everyone in the room joined with me singing, and we held hands. In the middle of the third verse, Grandmother's eyes opened widely and she looked toward the foot of her bed and upward. I would have given anything to see what she saw at that moment. Then she glanced over at us, looked up again, and, like a music box slowly unwinds, she gradually stopped breathing. Finally, the last breath left her mortal body. She was gone.

After a while, the nurses asked us to leave the room for

several minutes so they could prepare my grandmother. When we returned to the room, I noticed how peaceful she looked lying there, and to my surprise, in her hands were the roses that Mom had picked in Las Vegas. I had completely forgotten about them. The flowers hadn't died at all! They were in full bloom and unwilted. My mom turned to me, smiled lovingly, and said "Now she can see them."

It all seemed like a movie to me, some epic motion picture, and we were all characters. It was a happy ending. She didn't have to suffer any more. We all gathered around the bed where my grandmother lay and knelt down and had a family prayer. It was a serious moment, but I must admit, I peeked during the prayer. I couldn't help it. The feeling was so strong. I looked around the room at my grandmother's children and grandchildren, who were all present. There seemed to be an outpouring of love and hope in all of our hearts. I could feel it. I could see it in their faces. No one was worrying about getting along with each other or about who was living the more righteous life. We were together as a family on our knees, humbling ourselves before our Heavenly Father. All that seemed to matter was that we would someday make it "home" where we could be reunited with Grandmother again. "And because of meekness and lowliness of heart cometh the visitation of the Holy Ghost, which Comforter filleth with hope and perfect love, which love endureth by diligence unto prayer, until the end shall come, when all the saints shall dwell with God" (Moroni 8:26).

My life seemed to pass before me that day—all of my successes and all my mistakes, all of the happy times, the funny times, and the cherished memories of sad and trying experiences. I looked back on those years growing up with Mom, Dad, Tammy, Wendy, and Johnny, and I knew that there had to be a plan by which we could be together, forever. I knew that the gospel of Jesus Christ provided the fulness of that plan for our salvation. I knew that Grandmother was now waiting for me and all of us to come home, and that someday we would all join her. For the first time in my life, I wasn't afraid of death. I understood it more clearly; not with a perfect knowledge, but with a simple faith that we would be with her again. Seeing Grandmother die was one of the most beautiful experiences of my life.

My objective now is to return to my Heavenly Father's kingdom, bringing with me my wife and my children. I pray that we all will make it there. I love my family, in spite of their weaknesses and differences. I hope that they will overlook mine. I want to learn to love them unconditionally and to accept them for who they are and not judge them for not being who I want them to be. I want to build lasting relationships of trust with them as we learn to get along. I know that, eventually, my time will come and I will join with them and together we will progress into eternity. And that is a goal worth working for.

The end?

There is no end.

Steve James has been a professional entertainer since he was fourteen years old. He is a singer, composer, and producer who plays all keyboard instruments as well as the guitar. A dynamic youth speaker, Steve has performed for and addressed thousands of youth annually, challenging them through his presentation to make positive choices in their lives. He has also been a spokesman for Drug-Free Youth and numerous other youth foundations.

18

LISTENING TO THE STILL, SMALL VOICE

BARBARA BARRINGTON JONES

Sometimes I imagine that when we are tempted, it's like we have a little angel sitting on one shoulder, whispering in one ear, and we have a devil sitting on the other shoulder, yelling into that ear. While we are trying to decide what to do, the angel keeps saying, "Don't do it. Don't give in." But the devil is telling us lies. Here are three of the biggest lies he tells us.

"Once won't hurt."

"No one will know."

"Everybody's doing it."

I want to tell you the story of Susan, a friend of mine whom I met after she won a contest I held. She came to my house for a week of training I give to potential contestants for a pageant. She was a beautiful gymnast. She was popular and had a nonmember boyfriend whom she was crazy about. Things seemed to be going really well in her life. A few months later, she wrote me a long letter telling me what had happened since we had seen each other last. There had come a point where she had ignored the whisperings of the angel on her shoulder and had succumbed to the lies of the devil. Here is part of her letter:

On Friday night, some friends and I went out to the

desert and had a party. There was beer there, and I started drinking. We were all having a great time by this huge bonfire, talking and dancing.

A few of us decided to go back to this guy's house and get our cars. It was about 9:30, and I rode back with my boyfriend in my friend David's truck. I've known David since fourth grade and I had always trusted him, although I knew he had been drinking a little. There were four of us in the cab of the truck and three more in the back. We were driving way too fast and listening to really loud music. There was one hairpin turn that needed to be taken slowly. We were approaching that turn, and every-one in the truck started yelling at David to slow down. He didn't, and the truck rolled. I can still feel us sus-pended in the air, deadly silent. It seemed to take forever. Then the truck hit the ground on the driver's side. The sound of it hitting was deafening, and the truck rolled so fast, I could feel my head hitting the windshield although I didn't register any pain.

After the truck came to a stop, I looked at myself in the mirror. I was bloody over my entire face. I knew my teeth were messed up, and I kept saying that I couldn't see very well. An ambulance came, and I knew I was really hurt. I got sick and threw up over and over. I don't remember any of the ambulance ride.

My own doctor didn't even recognize me. My eyes were swollen shut. My jaw was hanging off to one side, and I couldn't close my mouth. My jaw was broken in three places and my skull in two. I had air in my brain, which is very dangerous, and they weren't sure I'd be able to see.

Susan spent weeks recuperating in the hospital and at home. Her jaw was wired shut. She had to have braces put on her teeth. Her memory and ability to concentrate were slow to return. She did regain her sight, but was left per-manently deaf in her right ear. She wrote to me that both she and her boyfriend knew ahead of time they shouldn't go to this party. The promptings of the Spirit were very strong. Both of their mothers didn't feel good about them going out that night and suggested that they stay home and watch a video instead.

As she was getting ready to go that evening, Susan's little sister begged her, "Please don't go out tonight. Please."

Susan asked her sister why. The little girl said, "I don't know, but please don't go."

After the accident happened, even though it was miles away from her home, Susan's little sister had come screaming into the living room. She was holding her ears saying, "Mommy, Mommy, I hear an ambulance."

Her mom said, "Honey, there's no ambulance."

"Yes, Mommy," she said, "I hear an ambulance. It's Susan."

Everyone involved seemed to have a premonition of trouble. In this case, the warning had been clear. But Susan didn't listen. She believed the lies, that just once wouldn't hurt, that no one would find out, and that everyone was doing it. Susan learned a harsh lesson, but she is grateful that she now understands the truth.

She wrote in her letter:

> At first this was very hard to accept. I didn't think it was fair. I asked, "Why me?" Lots of things are still hard, but I'm doing great. My balance has been affected, but I have confidence in the Lord. If gymnastics is in my plan, he will help me achieve it. This accident has helped me adjust my attitude about life and the obstacles we face. My family is very close, and my relationship with my Father in Heaven has grown immensely. If it took a tragic wreck to get me on track, then I guess I'm glad it happened.

We don't have to experience a terrible accident to stay on track. The promptings of the Spirit are so strong. Why can't we listen? Heavenly Father allows you to hear the still, small voice. It will always be there if you are trying to live like you should. At the time of your baptism you received the gift of the Holy Ghost, and part of the promise given you was that you would have the Comforter to be with you to help you overcome the temptations of your life.

Another young woman wrote a letter to me and enclosed several poems she had written about her experiences. I asked her for permission to print two.

The Devil's Game

It started out so innocent,
we all went for a ride.
But soon enough, I came to know,
the plan he'd kept inside.

Beginning with a playful game,
which I refused to play.
Forever putting off the hand,
that always seemed to stray.

We both became the players,
of a sport I'd never known.
I hadn't ever felt as scared,
or quite so all alone.

He turned into a stranger,
possessed by greed and lust.
I felt my hatred growing for
this boy I used to trust.

I fought him off as best I could,
he had more strength than I.
It didn't even faze him,
when I began to cry.

His mind was filled with darkness,
caused by mixing drugs and booze.
I wonder what he thought he'd gain,

from the virtue I would lose?

My pulse began to weaken,
my body numbed with fear.
I lost all hope, I needn't cry,
for no one seemed to hear.

Oh, selfish boy, you ruined my life.
I'll never speak your name.
I'll always hate the memory of
the Devil's evil game.

Never Stand Alone

So many times they'd warned her,
of a dark and sinful zone.
To keep it to a friendly date,
and know you're not alone.

She felt she needn't worry;
she had the truths they'd taught.
She'd never know the hole she'd dug,
the entrance Satan sought.

Her foolish pride did blind her,
to the warnings that they gave.
Her only hope, a heartfelt plea,
for the virtue she must save.

The self-control she valued,
soon left when face to face.
The apple of her father's eye,
now sat in cold disgrace.

She'd tried to do it all alone
despite pleadings from above,
But came to know she couldn't stand,
without the Lord's true love.

For this young girl, the devil's lies led to a horrible experience for her. She is struggling to once again become the girl she once was. Now, she anxiously listens for the promptings of the Spirit.

Here is one more example. A young man wrote this letter. Notice that he tells about the promptings of the Spirit and how he ignored them.

> I feel a need to presume upon your kindness and unload and ask advice. I messed up in a major way. I had never really seriously dated a nonmember until one girl came out to church, basically at my invitation. Unfortunately, we became involved. When the relationship started out, we kissed. And that was a major mistake. I never went any further until one night. I had walked over to her house with a friend. We sat around and talked until my friend had to leave. I felt very strongly that I should go with him, and he told me later he had felt he should stay. Both of us ignored what we felt. After a while he left.
>
> To make a long story short, you know what happened. Neither of us wanted to. We'd talked about waiting until marriage, but the kisses made that seem so far away. That and what followed were the worst experiences of my life. Luckily, nothing as far as pregnancy came of it, but there are worse types of hell.
>
> I went to my bishop. He is helping me work through my problem. He has made me feel like I can get over this, but it hasn't been easy. I was president of my quorum and had to be released. Do you know what it's like to be asked to say a prayer and have to refuse? To want to bear your testimony, but you can't? To love the sacrament, and you can't partake of it? To love the Savior and know you've caused a lot more pain to come upon him?
>
> Please use any of this to warn the youth you come in contact with. I don't want anybody to go through this.

This young man is in the process of repenting, but he wishes with all his heart that he had listened to what he knew was right. Once won't hurt, no one will know, and everybody's doing it are misleading and damaging lies that lead inevitably to pain, heartache, and sorrow.

There is another lie Satan frequently tells in his attempt to destroy us. He tells us that if we have made a mistake, there is no way we can be forgiven. He would like us to believe that things are hopeless and that there is no use trying any longer.

If we believe that lie, then we don't understand the atonement of Jesus Christ. The truth is, no matter what we have done, we can ultimately be forgiven. We will have to endure some pain and take some difficult steps, but it is possible to repent and put our lives back together.

If you are struggling with such a problem, go to your bishop and ask him for his help. He knows how repentance works and he can guide you through the things you will need to do to be forgiven. I know it is scary to think about making that phone call or to actually knock on the bishop's door. But I promise you that if you will trust the Lord and take that first step, there is a "miracle of forgiveness" waiting for you. Imagine getting rid of the fear, guilt, and sadness you may be feeling, and having that replaced by a sense of peace, confidence, and happiness.

Don't fool yourself by imagining that if you just wait long enough, or confide your problem to a close friend, or pray hard enough, you can make your pain go away. It doesn't work that way. But the Lord has an "agent" in the bishop. The bishop is the one authorized to guide us through the process of repentance. He will help you in a spirit of love and kindness. And he will welcome your call.

I promise you that you will not be left alone in your determination to live the commandments. You have been given a guide to help you tell right from wrong. Listen to those promptings. "For behold, again I say unto you that if ye will enter in by the way, and receive the Holy Ghost, it will show unto you all things what ye should do" (2 Nephi 32:5).

I love you all. I know that God lives, that Jesus is the Christ, and he leads this church. We are in the right place if we keep Him as our very best friend. Make him your partner. Live a righteous life, and you will have the still, small voice to guide you. Listen to it.

Barbara Barrington Jones is an international image consultant, author, lecturer, and fashion designer, as well as a former classical ballet dancer, actress, and professional model. A director of summer youth programs at BYU, Sister Jones grooms young women for competition in national and international beauty pageants. She enjoys walking, preparing and eating healthful foods, and working with the youth. Barbara and her husband, Hal, reside in Novato, California, and they are the parents of two children.

19

ARE WE NOT ALL BEGGARS?

GARY R. NELSON

After completing my mission, I worked part-time in my father's sporting goods store while attending Southern Utah University as a full-time student.

One Saturday morning, a middle-aged gentleman entered the store. He had in his hands and in his coat pockets, an assortment of permanent ink markers. He handed me a business card which stated, "I am mute. I am selling pens for a living. Please help by purchasing a pen for a dollar. Thank you."

I recognized his type, I thought. Stories about professional "street bums" who take advantage of kind-hearted people swirled through my head.

"I am not interested," I said, as I handed back his card and continued to restock the shelves with ammunition. As I turned around to retrieve more boxes of shotgun shells, he placed the card in front of me again. This time his countenance was more agitated. I knew my lack of interest was not making him happy.

My business courses at college had prepared me for predators like the one now facing me. The words "caveat emptor" or "buyer beware" flashed into my mind. This guy was out of his league. He had approached someone filled with the entrepreneurial spirit. I determined to work him down on the price. You know—the great American way— get the most value for the lowest possible price.

I thought that one dollar was too much to pay for one of those markers. I reached into my pocket and pulled out a buck and then held up three fingers, indicating the number of markers I wanted for my dollar.

He shook his head vigorously and held up just one finger. This guy was not going to budge. Emphatically thrusting my hand upward with my three fingers, I continued the bargaining process.

He grunted some incoherent sounds then angrily slammed three pens on the counter alongside my dollar bill and abruptly walked out the front door, without even picking up his money.

"Wow," I thought. "I wonder what his problem is? How rude. Oh, well, that's his fault for being so inconsiderate." I had three free pens! Shoving the new markers into my shirt pocket, I went about my merchandising. However, my conscience reminded me over and over during the day that I had offended one of God's children. Finally, I couldn't handle the guilt any longer. After work, I drove up and down the streets of St. George, Utah, in search of this person I had angered and whom I had also cheated. I could never locate him. The pens have long since been lost or discarded, but the memory of that experience has often reminded me of the responsibility I have to those in need.

Addressing the early Saints in the Book of Mormon, King Benjamin taught:

> Ye yourselves will succor those that stand in need of your succor; ye will administer of your substance unto him that standeth in need; and ye will not suffer that the beggar putteth up his petition to you in vain, and turn him out to perish.
>
> Perhaps thou shalt say: The man has brought upon

himself his misery; therefore I will stay my hand, and will not give unto him of my food, nor impart unto him of my substance that he may not suffer, for his punishments are just . . .

[But] behold, are we not all beggars? Do we not all depend upon the same Being, even God, for all the substance which we have, for both food and raiment, and for gold, and for silver, and for all the riches which we have of every kind? (Mosiah 4:16–17,19.)

As I continue to grow within myself, I have come to realize the profound truthfulness of King Benjamin's admonition—I am a beggar, too. No, I do not have to be homeless or penniless to be a beggar; nor do I have to wear tattered clothes and sport an unkempt beard to be a beggar; nor do I have to hold up a sign asking for money; nor eat out of soup kitchens, to be classified as a beggar.

No, outwardly I may not look the part of what society would label a "beggar," but what about inwardly? Remember, while man looks on the outward appearance, God looks on the heart (see 1 Samuel 16:7).

We depend upon God for everything—for the air we breathe, for everything we own, from the food we eat to the clothes we wear. We need to set aside our false pride and acknowledge that we rely upon our Heavenly Father for everything. Everything! Nothing really belongs to us. King Benjamin declared, "Your substance . . . doth not belong to you but to God, to whom also your life belongeth" (Mosiah 4:22).

We call upon the name of the Lord and beg for a remission of our sins. We do not beg in vain, for the Lord hears us and causes our hearts to be filled with joy (see Mosiah 4:21).

The Book of Mormon prophet Helaman shared additional insights into the insignificance of man when he said,

O how great is the nothingness of the children of men;

yea, even they are less than the dust of the earth. For
behold, the dust of the earth moveth hither and thither,
to the dividing asunder, at the command of our great and
everlasting God (Helaman 12:7–8).

Man, God's greatest creation, is lower than the dust of
the earth. Why? How could this be? The dust at least obeys
God's commands, but man will not.

While serving my mission in Brazil, I developed greater
feelings for the less fortunate. I saw much disease, sickness,
and poverty. People of all ages formed the ranks of God's
destitute, crying out for money and food. Some were content with the spiritual food the gospel offered, but most
cried out for physical help. Great spiritual discretion was
needed in the "giving process." One could not just simply
give money to the poor, as it would frequently not be used
for food. Instead, it would be used to buy liquor, cigarettes,
or drugs. As missionaries we would often invite these
struggling souls to a nearby hot dog stand, offering to buy
them food to appease their hunger pains. If they refused
our offer, we assumed they had other motives in asking us
for money.

Giving money to just anyone appearing needy on the
street should be discouraged. In a world full of deceit and
harm, caution should be used in even picking up hitchhik-
ers. The Spirit can assist us in assessing the needs of people.
In addition, the Church has provided "agent bishops" to
provide temporary help and assistance to members with
legitimate needs for food, clothing, and shelter. Our leaders
have counseled us to help the poor by making contributions
to the fast offering fund of the Church.

We simply do not have the money or services to help
everyone in need. When we don't help because we can't
help, our attitude ought to be, "I give not because I have
not, but if I had I would give" (Mosiah 4:24).

What we *can* give to those who are searching, are the spiritual riches that we possess. Such was the case with two missionaries laboring in Brazil over thirty years ago, in the city of Porto Alegre, in the state of Rio Grande do Sul. Finding a helpless old beggar in the gutter, they were prompted by the Spirit to take him home, clean him up, feed him, and teach him the gospel. Pedro Bortoloto joined the Church, overcame alcoholism, saved his marriage, and eventually started his own upholstery business. In February 1973, he was ordained a stake patriarch. An important key, once again, is following the Spirit. "And remember in all things the poor and needy, the sick and the afflicted, for he that doeth not these things, the same is not my disciple" (D&C 52:40).

In order to impress my seminary class about the importance of the beggar while we were studying the New Testament last year, I came dressed up as a "bum for a day." I sat in the doorway and asked for money by holding out a cup as my students passed by on their way to class. What an interesting experience! Staying in character all day was difficult, but by the close of the day, I had acquired almost $15 in bills and loose change. I was also given a guitar pick, a button, and an expired clothing discount coupon from my "charitable" seniors.

My good friend and colleague, Jeff Chapman, played the bum part the next day and collected nearly $10. We pooled all the monies and placed them in a manila envelope, sealed it, and began searching for a suitable person to give the money to. I felt prompted to find a local, disadvantaged person by the name of Evan. I had seen him around town, walking the streets for the past few years. After nearly a week of packing around the heavy bag of loose change and bills, without seeing him, I said a silent prayer. I prayed that I might be directed to find Evan or someone else the funds could benefit. Soon, I spotted Evan walking in front of a drugstore. My little truck screeched to a stop as I slammed on my brakes next to the weary walker. He was visibly touched by the generosity of the seminary students as I explained about the money in the bag. He told me the loose change would come in handy for buying hard candy and that the bills would help him with food. I wished him well and left him to wander off into the chilly night. As I began to drive off, a thought struck me, "What would Jesus do?" Rolling down the window I asked: "Evan, when was the last time that you had a good meal?"

"Well," he said, "it has been about three weeks." I also discovered that he had not taken a bath nor slept in a warm bed in six months. He could not even remember the last time his clothes were washed.

Following promptings within me, I invited him to my home for the evening to eat a nice home-cooked meal, have a shower, and get a comfortable night's sleep. I even offered to wash his soiled clothes. He accepted my invitation and climbed into the truck.

I enjoyed our conversation during the twenty-minute drive to my home. I learned that he had graduated from high school, attended college for awhile, and served in Vietnam. Upon our arrival at my home, I found a warm meal prepared by our ward Relief Society sisters awaiting us. My wife had gone for the week to assist a friend, and the wonderful sisters had blessed my family by bringing in several delicious meals. The children were still working on yesterday's casserole, so tonight's dish of spaghetti and bread sticks hadn't been touched.

After enjoying a nice hot shower with a new bar of soap and plenty of shampoo, Evan slipped into my pajamas and robe which hung loosely on his skinny body. His hair and beard were nicely groomed. He gobbled down the whole bowl of spaghetti in less time than it would have taken to boil the noodles. "This is perfect . . . just perfect," he declared. "Everything is just right. Thank you."

My warm king-sized bed and Merrill Jensen's music, "Beyond," had him snoring in minutes. Unlike Goldilocks, I knew who had been eating from my bowl and sleeping in my bed. As I thought about the comforts Evan was enjoying, I had a feeling like that portrayed in the Toyota "Oh, what a feeling!" commercials you see on TV. Grateful that I had extended myself in service, I had the feeling the Savior was also pleased.

It was difficult for me to drop Evan off on the highway the next morning. The weather conditions were rainy and overcast. Where would he find warmth and shelter? He said he would wander from awning to business overhang to stay dry. I gave him $2.50 for breakfast, a bag of my wife's chocolate chip cookies, and I expressed how much I loved him. He even accepted my offer to return to my house again.

Some concerned and generous Dixie High Seminary students made sure that he was taken care of for Christmas 1992. They raised $120 for him. In addition to donating some of their own clothes, they purchased $80 worth of apparel which included a new belt, two new pairs of pants, new briefs, thermals, and socks. They bought him a used radio/tape player and gave him several seminary tapes. Can you picture this guy swaying back and forth to the rhythm of "Free to Choose" while walking down the streets of St. George? Evan spent Christmas Eve and Christmas Day with my family. What a joy to hang out an extra stocking for him and to see him open his gifts with happiness and anticipation. He enjoyed the gifts and the extra $40 in cash.

Are we not all beggars? We beg for forgiveness for our sins. When we have wronged someone, we beg for mercy.

We plead for help from God when challenges come in our lives.

I have learned that this "attitude of gratitude" is vital to maintain a humble heart. We need to spend more time thanking the Lord for what we have and less time asking for things that we do not have. Just offering a thankful prayer especially helps—no asking, just thanking.

A good example of ingratitude may be found in the New Testament:

> [As Christ] entered into a certain village, there met him ten men that were lepers, which stood afar off: And they lifted up their voices, and said, Jesus, Master, have mercy on us. And when he saw them, he said unto them, Go shew yourselves unto the priests. And it came to pass, that as they went, they were cleansed (Luke 17:12–14).

After this monumental miracle, only one in ten cared enough to return and say thank you to the Man from Galilee who had healed their bodies and had given them hope for the future. "Such ingratitude is self-centered," said Elder James E. Faust. "It is a form of pride" ("Gratitude As a Saving Principle," *Ensign,* May 1990, p. 85).

I once had an experience where I was disappointed to observe a general lack of gratitude among a group of young people. Wanting to express my love to the students I had enjoyed in the five great ninth grade seminary classes I had been teaching, I decided to use my own resources to provide something of a picnic for the kids on the last day of school. Hungry students lined up for helpings of potato chips, cups of punch, and barbecued hamburgers topped with the best of condiments. As you might imagine, everyone seemed to enjoy the meal and many lined up for second helpings. But to my surprise, not even one student paused to say "thank you." That concerned me. The reason for the party was not to hear them thank me, but it occurred to me that if one hundred and fifty, fourteen- and fifteen-year-old youth are that careless about expressing gratitude for a hamburger, could it be possible they might also be careless about thanking Heavenly Father for the blessings he bestows upon them?

Elder W. Eugene Hansen has said, "The sin of ingratitude is more serious than the sin of revenge. With revenge, we return evil for evil, but with ingratitude, we return evil for good" ("Love," *Ensign*, Nov. 1989, p. 24).

"Selfishness and ingratitude are tools of destruction," commented Elder Robert L. Simpson. "The civilized world rocks and reels today because of selfish attitudes." I like the expression in an anonymous poem quoted by Elder Simpson:

> *Lord, help me to live from day to day*
> *In such a self-forgetful way*
> *That even when I kneel to pray*
> *My prayer shall be of others.*
> *Others, Lord, yes, others.*
> *Let this my motto be.*
> *Help me to live for others*
> *That I may live for thee*
> (*in* Conference Report, *Oct. 1962, p. 100*).

Yes, we are all beggars. Let's never forget to express the gracious, humble attitude that tells the Lord, and others, that we appreciate and are grateful for all of our blessings.

Gary Nelson is a seminary instructor in St. George, Utah, who has been a seminary principal, travel coordinator, insurance agent, roller rink manager, motorcycle and mountain bike salesman, and a taxi driver. A former collegiate football and tennis player, Gary was a sportswriter for the Daily Spectrum, *and he retains an interest in all sports. He enjoys writing, public speaking, singing, and going to BYU games. Brother Nelson and his wife, Christine, have seven children.*

20

YOU CAN'T REAP UNLESS YOU SOW: PREPARING NOW FOR THE HARVEST OF A MISSION

LISA HECKMANN OLSEN

By the age of eight, I knew I wanted to go on a mission. But I grew up in Provo, Utah, and as a result had very limited contact with members of other religions and little chance to perfect my missionary skills. My first significant missionary experience happened the summer after my first year of college. A friend's parents had invited our small group of friends to go on a business trip with them. We were leaving at 3:00 A.M. to start our long drive. I told my mom and dad not to worry about me in the morning—that I would of course get off fine. But when the horn honked, Mom followed me outside carrying a large box that she said was for our trip. She put the box in the back of the car and instructed us not to open it until we arrived in Cedar City. Long after we had passed through Cedar City, and just before we arrived at the vacation site, one of my friends suddenly yelled, "The box!" We had all completely forgotten about it. My friend anxiously pulled out the letter attached to the mysterious box, and he started reading. "Oh, my gosh. I can't believe it!" was all we could hear, over and over. After recovering from a dose of pure shock, my friend looked at me and said "I can't believe your mom!" He pulled a copy of the Book of Mormon out of the box and told us that my mom had packed ten copies and that she expected us to give away every copy while we were on our trip.

Several wonderful vacation days went by, but the thought of the books hung over our heads. I had never spoken to a stranger about the Church, and the whole idea scared me to death. I hoped one of the returned missionaries in the group would teach me the way to approach people. Once, while we were walking by the "all-you-can-eat-buffet," we saw a man with his wife. The gentleman was confined to a wheelchair. One of my returned-missionary friends walked right over to them and said, "I think that you'll like this book, " and then tossed it into the lap of the man and walked off. I knew there had to be a better way. Then a different returned missionary in the group approached a couple standing in front of a window display. Within a few minutes, they graciously accepted the book. That seemed more like what we were supposed to do. By the end of the week, I had not given away my copy. But I had made friends with the maid. Just before check-out, I wrote my testimony in the book and left it on the bed. I still lacked the courage to talk to her face to face.

After this experience, I learned that I needed to do a lot to prepare to be a missionary. During that summer I became very serious about this. Brother Todd Parker, my seminary teacher, was a pole vaulter. One day he brought his pole to our class. He pushed the end of the pole into a corner on the floor and pushed with all his might. The pole bent, but immediately snapped back, throwing Brother Parker across the room. "You get out of it what you put into it," he said as he started to bend the pole again. Then getting up a second time he repeated, "You get out of it what you put into it!" He then taught us the Law of the Harvest: "But this I say, He which soweth sparingly shall reap also sparingly;

and he which soweth bountifully shall reap also bounti-fully" (2 Corinthians 9:6). What an incredible lesson! I knew that if I was going to have a successful mission, I would need to prepare now (the sowing) for the reward later (the reaping). If I desired the reward to be bountiful, I would need to work even harder.

Prior to beginning his formal ministry, Jesus Christ spent his youth preparing. "And Jesus increased in wisdom and stature, and in favour with God and man" (Luke 2:52). In a talk he gave in general conference, Elder Robert L. Backman adapted that formula for growth to us, as he spoke of the need youth have to prepare themselves for missionary service in the following four ways: physically, socially, mentally, and spiritually.

Physical Preparation

"Who does your cooking, sewing, ironing? Who makes your bed? Who sweeps the floor; who does the dishes; who presses your pants, launders your shirts, shines your shoes? Who reminds you to get up or to go to bed? You would do well to become self-sufficient in these matters before you go on your mission. It is much easier to learn now . . . than to wait until you are forced to learn to survive" ("Called to Serve," *Ensign,* Nov., 1987, pp. 60–63). The Church Mission-ary Department has this to say about physical preparation: "The well-prepared missionary has good eating habits, is at the proper weight, exercises regularly, gets sufficient rest, and keeps himself, his clothes, and his surroundings clean and tidy. He has also had all medical problems cared for before reporting for missionary service."

Eating properly keeps missionaries well. It is important that they learn to cook before leaving so they don't have to live on macaroni and cheese for two years. I once received a telephone call from two desperate elders in my district.

"Sister Heckmann," they said, "We'll buy a roast, potatoes, carrots, and onions and pay you $25.00 if you'll cook a Sunday dinner for us!" I laughed, but I didn't cook them dinner. Other missionaries, like my younger brother who is now serving in the Arizona Tempe Mission, are better prepared. Adam was always curious about cooking. At a very young age he learned to bake snickerdoodles. He would bake a batch then hide them from his sisters. Little by little, he added new recipes to his repertoire. Now he cooks very well. He and his companions will not have to call on the sisters for a Sunday roast.

A mission also requires physical strength. Missionaries need to be well and fit. I served in the Switzerland Geneva Mission. All missionaries, including sisters (in dresses), rode bikes. Getting used to riding a bicycle every day is hard enough. I was glad I wasn't overweight.

Physical preparation also includes saving money. Switzerland and France were very expensive countries to live in. It cost about $600 a month just to make ends meet, and we lived a very humble life. With the new mission equalization plan, youth now know exactly how much their mission will cost regardless of where they are called. Many great blessings will come to youth who sacrifice NOW and start saving for their missions.

Social Preparation

This is the area where most teens are already very well prepared. But there are probably a few who were like me in high school—a little afraid and quite shy. It was hard for me to talk to strangers and to get to know people. I was a little like my good friend, John. We met in a young adult ward my first year of college. He had been a good, even a bold missionary in Italy. Returning home, his thoughts naturally turned to girls. He dated a lot and was quite popular in our ward. However, there was one girl in our ward, Beverly, who made him nervous. He often talked about her and wanted to get to know her but was afraid. Beverly was two years older than John, a professional nurse, very beautiful, smart, and strong in the Church. She had "everything going for her." Well, the story continues. John had promised to meet me and my friend, Ruth Ann, at a dance. But John stood us up, and I was mad. I told Ruth Ann that we had to get back at him somehow. So we drove to his house. He answered the door and we could tell he had forgotten about his promise. I smiled and asked, "John, do you trust me?"

"Sure," he answered.

I continued, "Do you trust me enough to let me take you someplace you've never been?"

"I guess so." (I think he thought we were going to take him to a surprise party). One final question, "John, do you trust me enough to let me tie you up?" Immediately after his "yes," Ruth Ann and I tied his hands behind his back, tied his knees together, and also blindfolded him.

We put him in the back of Ruth Ann's car and drove around until he was totally lost. Then we stopped at Beverly's apartment. We carried him to the front porch, laid him down, and put a blanket over his body. Then we attached a note that read, "For Beverly," rang the doorbell, and ran. I can only imagine what happened next because we were long gone. I can see Beverly opening the door and wondering, "What in the world is this?" And John thinking, "Okay, where's my surprise?" I wish I had been able to see his face when the blindfold came off. As it turned out, John was thoroughly stunned and had nothing to say to his secret flame.

I have felt that way before—being with someone and having nothing to say. It is crucial that potential missionaries learn how to be sociable, how to start a conversation with a complete stranger. The sooner the fear is overcome, the more effective the missionary will be. While I was in the

Missionary Training Center preparing to go to Switzerland, I heard a section in the Doctrine and Covenants quoted over and over. "Open your mouths and they shall be filled" (D&C 33:8). I knew I had to put this principle to the test to overcome *my* fears. I had studied and I felt I knew a lot about the gospel at the time. It was just the fear of talking to strangers that I had to overcome. I remember my last prayer before leaving the MTC. I asked the Lord to give me an opportunity to share the gospel with someone *before* I arrived at the mission home.

The missionaries in my group compared seating assignments after we arrived at the airport. All of us were seated in one big clump—except one—me. I was at the back of the plane for the flight from Salt Lake City to Denver. I sat by an English woman who I learned trained and showed horses for a living. I thought, "This is the opportunity I have prayed for." I jumped right in with, "I'm a missionary for . . ." and asked her if she wanted to know more. She said, "no," and fell asleep. I felt bad. She left the flight at Denver and no one was assigned to sit next to me for the flight to New York.

A few minutes after take-off, I was bored, so I went to talk to my companion. We were speaking in French when a little boy, about four years old, pulled on my jacket. "Lady, are you speaking French?" I told him yes and he said I needed to talk to his mom. He took my hand and led me to where she was seated, saying, "She speaks French." The woman was American, but fluent in French. She asked me why I was going to Europe. I told her about my mission and she was very interested. I asked about her life and learned that she owned a boutique in New York and made frequent business trips to France. I love tailoring clothes (and buying clothes) so we had a lot to talk about. Then she asked more about my mission. I asked if she wanted to know more about our church and she shocked me with a "Yes." For the rest of the flight, I taught her the first discussion. The other missionaries kept looking over their seats, envious that I had gotten the first chance to teach. I learned that she was Protestant and her husband was Jewish. They had decided to choose only one religion to teach their son. Neither wanted to convert to the other's faith, so they agreed to find a new religion and convert together. I was the first person she met after their decision.

I asked her at the end of the conversation if she would like to meet the missionaries in New York. She said she would. I was thrilled. The promise in D&C 33 worked! What surprised me most was how natural and normal the conversation felt. I know if we want missionary opportunities and pray for them, they will come. I ran to the pay phone during my layover and called the mission home in New York so she could see the missionaries as soon as possible.

Mental Preparation

I teach high school art classes and have noticed how heavily the media influences what my students choose to draw. Church leaders have often given us counsel about the media. "Whatever you read, listen to, or watch makes an impression on you. Public entertainment and the media can provide you with much positive experience. They can uplift and inspire you, teach you good and moral principles, and bring you closer to the beauty this world offers. But they can also make what is wrong and evil look normal, exciting, and acceptable. Don't attend or participate in any form of entertainment, including concerts, movies, and videocassettes, that is vulgar, immoral, inappropriate, suggestive, or pornographic in any way. Movie ratings do not always accurately reflect offensive content. Don't be afraid to walk out of a movie, turn off a television set, or change a radio station if what's being presented does not meet your Heavenly Father's standards. And do not

read books or magazines or look at pictures that are pornographic or that present immorality as acceptable" (*For the
Strength of Youth*, pp. 11–12).

The opposite is also true—whatever good you expose
yourself to will stay with you. Unfortunately, there is no
automatic transfer of gospel knowledge when you are set
apart as a missionary. The principle is simple—the missionaries who study more before their mission know more at
the MTC. The Lord has said, "Seek not to declare my word,
but first seek to obtain my word, and then shall your tongue
be loosed; then if you desire, you shall have my Spirit and
my word, yea, the power of God unto the convincing of
men" (D&C 11:21). The missionary department in Salt Lake
City has found that successful missionaries are those who
have had personal experiences with the scriptures and with
prayer. According to their studies, "successful" does not
necessarily mean lots of baptisms, but that the missionary
is happy with the work.

I was grateful that I spent time studying the scriptures
before my mission. While teaching the discussions, I often used
those seminary scripture chase scriptures. Or, if an investiga-
tor had a question, I would frequently remember something
from my personal scripture study that would help them.

This was the case with a man we taught in Dijon,
France. My companion and I had bundled up for a long day
of tracting. It was a very cold winter so we took the layered
look to new extremes: we wore sweats under our dresses, a
couple of slips, a skirt, a few blouses, a sweater, a coat, a few
scarves and then topped it off with a hat. We were working
in a government-subsidized apartment complex. The walls
were covered with graffiti and the elevator smelled like
urine. Most of the people were very poor and few took any
pride in their apartment building. All morning long we
were told, "Ca ne m'interresse pas!" (Not interested).

At some point, we met a young woman holding a baby.

We started our approach by saying, "Hi, we're in the area giving away copies of an important book . . ." She cut us off and said that she wasn't interested. We kept talking because we were anxious to teach her. She told us she was atheist and the only thing she cared about was her baby girl. After talking with her for about five minutes, we heard a man's voice yell, "Go away, leave!" After a few minutes he came stomping to the door, put one hand on his hip, and pointed a finger in my face. He said, "You are the most obnoxious woman I have ever met—listen to my sister and just go away!" I smiled and asked him if he would like to listen to our message. Alain laughed and said he was like his sister—also atheist—and that he believed in nothing. Then his sister chimed in, "Besides we are having a family reunion!"

Getting even more bold, I asked if we could teach the whole family. They laughed and to my surprise, agreed. We soon learned that we would be the entertainment for the evening. My companion and I sat in the center of the room with the family around us. We started the first discussion, talking about God and Jesus Christ. They laughed out loud. "You two left AMERICA to come to France to teach people about God while you are in the prime of your life?" They were baffled when we said that was our goal for eighteen months. We continued and tried to teach them the role of Joseph Smith. They laughed as if we had just told a fantastic joke in a comedy club. It was obvious they weren't going to take our conversation seriously, so we quietly decided it was time to leave. We bore our testimonies and left them a copy of the Book of Mormon with a challenge to find out for themselves. We thanked them for their time and told the family we would return in a week.

When we came back a week later, no one answered. We really weren't very surprised. A few weeks later we decided to work in a part of town we had rarely visited. After knocking on a few doors, we were shocked when Alain answered one of the doors.

"How did you find my door?" he asked.

We explained that we weren't looking for his door. Alain told us he had wanted to talk to us again but that he couldn't remember our names. Now here we were on his doorstep. He invited us in and walked us past his twin sisters who were sitting on the couch. They were smoking, but through the haze they saw us and hollered, "Joseph Smith!" and started laughing.

We followed Alain into the kitchen and sat at the table. He didn't have too much to say. At that point we knew he had felt something different that night at his family reunion or he wouldn't have invited us in. We asked him three questions: "Alain, do you ever wonder where you came from, why you are on earth, and where you will go after you die?" Pretty standard missionary questions, and he gave the usual response "yes." We talked briefly about the first two questions and asked, "Alain, have you ever had someone close to you die, and have you ever wondered where they are?" He had, and after a few more questions we discovered he was thinking about his mom. I asked if he could share his feelings about the experience. He said no and put his head down. The second time I asked, he was crying. He looked at us and said he felt strangely comfortable talking to us, and that he felt we might have some answers for him.

Alain shared the entire story. He and his mom had enjoyed a really good relationship. When he was sixteen years old, he and his mom were in a car accident. His mother had died and he had survived. "I held my mother in my arms as she took her last breath," he said while crying. Then he asked us a tough question, one we had heard often, "How can there be a God if a sixteen-year-old boy has to go through something like that?" We did the best we could to comfort him. Alain was ready for some gospel-centered answers.

We opened the Book of Mormon and read a few passages from the place where Alma discusses death and the resurrection: "Therefore, there is a time appointed unto men that they shall rise from the dead; and there is a space between the time of death and the resurrection. . . . Now, concerning the state of the soul between death and the resurrection—Behold . . . the spirits of all men, as soon as they are departed from this mortal body, yea, the spirits of all men, whether they be good or evil, are taken home to that God who gave them life. And then shall it come to pass, that the spirits of those who are righteous are received into a state of happiness, which is called paradise, a state of rest, a state of peace, where they shall rest from all their troubles and from all care, and sorrow" (Alma 40:9–12).

We both bore our testimonies that we knew his mom was still living in spirit and that some day he would see her again. For the first time in the conversation he looked at peace. "I *hope* you are right, I really hope that you are right."

I was grateful that I had studied the Book of Mormon before my mission and that I was familiar with the passages. I had no idea what type of questions Alain would ask, and in such a situation I think it would have been awkward and almost tacky to say, "Wait just a minute while I look through the Topical Guide to find that answer!" I believe that the more a missionary studies and knows, the more effective he will be.

What would happen if you were set apart as a missionary at this very moment? Can you picture yourself there? Are you prepared? Can you imagine yourself answering the types of questions Alain asked? It's best to study for those moments now.

Spiritual Preparation

President Spencer W. Kimball said "[But] we must prepare our [young] missionaries better, not only with language, but with scripture and above all with a testimony and a burning fire that puts power in their words" (Regional Representatives' seminar, Apr. 1976). The two greatest ways to gain spiritual power are through daily scripture study and personal prayer. While I was teaching at the MTC, Jay Jensen, an administrator, told me the Church did a survey a few years ago to identify the things which most help young people decide to go on missions. Personal experiences with prayer and scripture study were the most important factors.

Daily prayer and scripture study will best prepare a missionary to work with the Spirit and listen to its subtle promptings. At the end of my mission, I learned an important lesson about listening to the Spirit. Louis Lohassa was an older, paralyzed man we had been teaching for a few months. Though confined to a wheelchair, Louis was very stubborn and wanted to do everything on his own, including opening his own doors. However, he was afraid of committing to baptism and had cancelled all of his many baptism dates. My companion and I invited him to a baptism so he could see exactly what would happen.

Louis was sitting in a corner of the chapel close to the front. A beautiful young family the elders had taught was being baptized. The first speaker stopped in the middle of his talk and said something surprising.

"I think there is someone here who has just received an answer to his questions."

He then continued with his talk. Then he stopped a second time.

"I want you to know that you can be baptized today—no waiting."

The people in the audience were perplexed and started to whisper. Then the speaker asked, "Is there anyone here who would like to be baptized with this family?" Louis raised his hand, but he wasn't noticed. So he hollered out, "Yes, sir. I want to be baptized!" My companion and I were floored! He wheeled out to the foyer where the zone leaders quickly interviewed him. He was found worthy to be baptized.

He didn't want any help so it took Louis about half an hour to change into white clothes. Then I saw something—an image I'll never forget. Louis wheeled himself to the edge of the font, but at that point he had to be helped. Two elders gently lifted him from his chair and carried him into the water. One elder held him up as the other elder raised his arm to the square. Louis was baptized. After he was confirmed, I talked to Louis and asked him why he chose to be baptized after so many cancelled dates. He smiled, pointed his finger at me and said, "Sister Heckmann, when the Spirit tells you to do something, you just *do it*, and you don't ask questions!"

When Louis finally became familiar with the language of the Spirit, he wouldn't deny the prompting. I was reminded that the Lord's work is just that—his work, not mine. I am just an instrument. "Yea, I know that I am nothing; as to my strength I am weak; therefore I will not boast of myself, but I will boast of my God, for in his strength I can do all things" (Alma 26:12). The best time to prepare is now. A full-time mission will be one of the most profound experiences of your life if you choose to make it that way.

Lisa Olsen graduated from Brigham Young University with a bachelor's degree in art education and French. She teaches art at Timpview High School where she is also student government adviser. A returned missionary from Geneva, Switzerland, she has taught French at the Missionary Training Center. Lisa was a counselor for EFY before becoming an EFY speaker. She loves painting, drawing, and making stained glass, and she enjoys aerobic exercise, trips to Lake Powell, and house hunting. A newlywed, Lisa is married to Brent Olsen.

21

IS IT LOVE?
THE FEELING YOU FEEL, WHEN YOU FEEL YOU ARE
GOING TO FEEL A FEELING YOU NEVER FELT BEFORE

TODD B. PARKER

What is this thing called love? We've heard about it. People fall into it and out of it. It drives some people crazy, it inspires others. Some who are in it never want to get out of it, and some people who have been in and out of it never want to be in it again. It seems to be everywhere: in the movies, on TV, on the radio, on the magazine rack, and on the bookshelf. More time is spent on this word than almost any other. People like to write poems about it, sing songs about it, and just plain talk about it. Consider a few song titles: "I Will Always Love You," "I'd Do Anything for Love," "Love Will Keep Us Together," "Every Heartbeat," "I'll Never Get Over You Getting Over Me," "Everything I Do, I Do It for You," "How Do You Talk to an Angel?" and yes, even "Achy Breaky Heart" is about love! There are jokes about love. Someone said, "Life is just one dumb thing after another. Love is just two dumb things after each other." People write volumes about lost love, for example this little anonymous poem:

My love has flew
Her did me dirt
Me did not know
She were a flirt
To those in love
Let I forbid
Lest they be dood
Like I were did.

Many great names in literature have written about love. Shakespeare said, "This thou perceivest, which makes thy love more strong, to love that well which thou must leave ere long." Profound things are stated about love like, "Absence is to love as wind is to fire. It extinguishes the small. It enkindles the great." There must be something about this very thing called love which is transcendent, infinite, undeniably important, and nearly beyond our grasp. The scriptures are filled with references to love. They even say, "God is love" (1 John 4:8).

Since this topic of love is so immense, my purpose in this chapter is to focus on just one aspect of love. Since love is a feeling, I would like to teach something about it by telling a story about feeling. Some of you may identify with the feeling. Then, together, perhaps we can analyze this aspect of love.

As a youth growing up in Utah, I saw myself as a social derelict. I wanted to impress girls, but things never worked. My youthful countenance was the first stumbling block. In high school I looked like I was still in the third grade. My face also looked like the craters of the moon. A glance into the mirror each morning confirmed the feelings of the morning before, and the one before that. "Parker, you need help." Consequently, I didn't date at all. Oh, I liked girls, but when I tried to talk to them I not only put my foot in my mouth, I'd empty the entire shoe store. Things looked hopeless.

Then it happened. One day, during my junior year in

high school, a transfer student from Las Vegas walked into my American history class. As I cast my optics upon this girl, I felt as though I was at the feet of Aphrodite, goddess of love and beauty. My heart did a double back somersault, with a half twist. I was in love. I knew it. This was too good to be true. I had my friend, Doug, arrange a picnic so she and I would be together. It was heaven. I wasn't on cloud nine—I was above it. I was feeling a feeling I'd never felt before. I didn't want to leave her. I couldn't say goodbye. All I could do was think about her. After the picnic, I found myself missing her, longing to be with her, and wondering where she was, what she was doing, who she was with and most of all, was she thinking about me?

We dated for three months. I was crazy about her! She was my life. She was in my every thought, my every plan. Every moment we were apart was spent in anticipation of when we'd be together again. She was my walk and my talk. She was my inspiration. She created a zest for life in me that I'd never known before. But we never talked about love, and so I kept wondering if she was feeling what I was feeling.

One day I discovered, quite by accident, that she was not a member of the Church. I had assumed she was, because she lived with her aunt and uncle who were members of the Church. I knew her cousin well, and it never occurred to me to even ask—I mean we were in Utah—I didn't know any nonmembers. One night, after a walk beneath the orchard trees near my home, we began talking about life, death, and God. She said she didn't know much about the Church but would like to learn. I asked if she'd mind visiting with my seminary teacher. She said that would be fine with her. I arranged the meeting. By now I was sure I was in love—I mean, there was even a spiritual dimension to our relationship now. I still remember how openly she accepted the challenge to read the Book of Mormon and pray about it. I felt life couldn't be any better. Then my world caved in.

She called me and asked me to come over. I drove to her uncle's home thinking she'd decided we needed to talk about love and the future. I wasn't prepared for what I heard. She said, "My mother called last night. She wants me to come home—tomorrow." What? This couldn't be happening! Not to me. Not now. Everything was so good. It couldn't end like this. It just wasn't fair.

"Can we pray together?" she asked. "I've got a place picked out, sort of like where Joseph Smith went to pray." She directed me to drive to a little grove of trees. We walked hand in hand. "I'll pray," she said as we knelt beneath the trees. I felt a spirit I'd never felt before. After she closed her prayer, she turned and said, "I love you." I heard myself saying the same words to her, in a state of shock and disbelief. We were saying these words now, and she was leaving in the morning? I couldn't take this. My heart was going to break in two.

We drove to her uncle's house in silence. A lump in my throat made speaking impossible. The silence was awful. I turned on the radio. The song that was playing only added to my pain.

> *Perish is the word that more than applies*
> *Each time in my heart I realize*
> *That I am not going to be the one to share your*
>   *dreams*
> *That I am not going to be the one who shares your*
>   *schemes*
> *That I am not going to be the one to share what*
>   *seems*
> *To be the life that you could cherish as much as I do*
>   *yours . . .*

I fought back tears. The good-bye was short. I ran to my

car and drove into the darkness. I couldn't hold the tears any longer. They flowed down my cheeks, onto the steering wheel, all over my hands. Out of habit, my hand reached for the radio dial. Click. An unfamiliar tune—but the words—I'll never forget those words: "Cry softly, lovely one, it's over, it's dead, it's done." No! It can't be! I drove home. I poured out my heart to her in a twelve-page letter. This couldn't be the end! I wouldn't let it. She had everything. She was everything. She was beautiful. She was electrifying. She was tender. She was spiritual. And she *loved* me!

She left, and something died inside of me. Life held no meaning, except for the mail box. We'd write almost daily—long, long letters. We'd pray "together" every Sunday night at a set time. I was driving my friends crazy. They'd be at McDonalds ordering something at the counter, and I'd be sitting over in a booth. Doug would come over and I would say, "Oh, Doug. Nine weeks ago she touched this very table!" It would kill me to see other couples together, holding hands, arm in arm. I longed to be with her, just to touch her hands, her hair, and gaze into her eyes.

I never asked her if she dated other guys, but I needed to know. I had my sister write and ask questions about her social life. And then I'd read the letters she wrote my sister.

Time passed. We continued to write. She took the missionary lessons and was baptized. My senior year came and went. All my friends got their money together and paid to bring her from Las Vegas to Ogden for a surprise party for my birthday. For a weekend, I was in heaven. But when she left, my life felt so lonely. She eventually came to BYU to school. I was attending Weber State, eighty miles away. To make a long and painful story short, she started dating lots of guys. I acted the part of the lonely martyr.

I had to make a decision. Was this love? Had it been love and now it wasn't? Did I love her but did she not love me? Is there something that you think is love, but it really isn't? I felt feelings I'd never felt before, but I'd never been in love before, either. I'd heard once in seminary an odd word—"Infatuation." I was told it was a counterfeit of love. Was I only "infatuated?" What is infatuation and how does it compare to real love? Are all those songs on the radio about infatuation or about love?

Let's compare the two. In the case of mature love, physical attraction is only one component of the relationship. Infatuation, on the other hand, is based primarily on the physical aspect of the relationship. The dictionary describes an infatuated person as one "possessed with foolish passion." The following chart may be of some help.

INFATUATION	vs.	LOVE
1. Worry and suspicion		1. Trust
2. Rushed—someone else might steal them away		2. Calm—no hurry
3. Always want to be alone together		3. Able to enjoy group, family activities
4. The physical desire to be together is paramount		4. Friends first, sweethearts second

Let's consider each category separately.

1—Worry and Suspicion vs. Trust

Often a relationship based on infatuation is characterized by suspicion or jealousy. The boy or girl wonders where the other is, who they are with, and if they are being "true." The couple may be either consciously or unconsciously aware of some deficiency in the relationship. President Spencer W. Kimball taught:

> Every boy should have been saving money for his mission and be free from any and all entanglements so he

will be worthy. When he is returned from his mission at twenty-one, he should feel free to begin to get acquainted and to date. When he has found the right young woman, there should be a proper temple marriage. One can have all the blessings if he is in control and takes the experiences in proper turn: first some limited social get-acquainted contacts, then his mission, then his courting, then his temple marriage and his schooling and his family, then his life's work. In any other sequence he could run into difficulty ("The Marriage Decision," *Ensign,* Feb. 1975, p. 4).

I was too young. I hadn't been on a mission. I hadn't been to college. I wasn't really ready for everything that mature love brings with it. Often, young, infatuated couples, who know the gospel, feel uncomfortable because they know they are operating outside the "proper sequence" outlined by President Kimball. Worry also comes from the "unknowns" that are yet unexplored and still loom ahead. The very real questions regarding education, money, employment, housing, transportation, insurance, children, etc. seem overwhelming. They are set aside and replaced with emotional clichés such as "love will keep us together."

A more mature love has some broader experience at its foundation—experience in dating, experience with other relationships, and time spent with members of the opposite sex in platonic (nonphysical) relationships. Those months I spent writing my friend in Las Vegas were fraught with worry. Was she dating? Who was she with? Was she involved in any physical relationship? Much of the worry came from my wondering if she was involved with someone else the same way she had been involved with me—not in an immoral way but with lots of hand holding, hugging, and touching. Another part of my worry was that I knew our relationship was not in harmony with our leaders' teachings. President Kimball has said, "We recommend that people marry those who are of the same racial background generally, and of somewhat the same economic and social and educational background . . . and above all, the same religious background" (Spencer W. Kimball, "Marriage and Divorce," BYU Devotional, Sept. 7, 1976, p. 3). Our backgrounds differed greatly.

2—Rushed vs. Calm

Infatuation creates a sense of urgency. It is as though all of this is a dream—too good to be true—so one must capture it now or it will be lost for good. This feeling usually translates into a need to "go steady," to be "promised," to wear a ring, or to utilize some other method of announcing to others that this person is "taken." It's often based on jealousy and more often based on the physical aspect of the relationship. The announcement carries with it the message "I will now only hug, kiss, and embrace this one person." If the relationship is physical and is fueled by passion or lust, the scriptures teach "They shall not have the Spirit, but shall deny the faith and shall fear" (D&C 63:16). On the other hand, a virtuous relationship brings with it the Spirit as "a constant companion" and the couple's confidence will wax strong in the presence of God (see D&C 121:45–46). In infatuation, feelings are rushed. Mature love promotes peace and calm feelings.

3—Desire To Want To Be Alone Together

Often, an infatuated couple will claim they like to be alone a lot because of the deep discussions and feelings they enjoy when they are together. In reality, the deep discussions are often centered on questions and feelings related to physical desire. That kind of expression would be better avoided. If they were honest, many young men and women would have to admit that if the touching, kissing, and embracing were eliminated from the relationship, these "deep discussions" would lose their mystique. Erich Fromm has wisely observed:

> Because sexual desire is in the minds of most people coupled with the idea of love, they are easily misled to conclude that they love each other when they want each other physically. But if this desire is not stimulated by real love, it leaves strangers as far apart as they were before—sometimes it makes them ashamed of each other, or even makes them hate each other, because when the illusion has gone, they feel their estrangement even more markedly than before (*The Art of Loving* [New York: Harper & Row, 1956], pp. 54–55).

The acid test for couples who think they are in love, where a physical relationship is a primary factor, is to remove all physical contact for a substantial period (for example, six weeks) and see how the relationship fares. "Slipping" every once in a while will ruin the test. That would result in variable interval reinforcement (the same principle on which a slot machine operates) which will keep the relationship going—anticipation of additional "slipping." Removing physical contact from the relationship will permit a couple to explore other areas of common interest; the use of leisure time, working, studying, and doing routine chores. I've challenged many youth to try this. Without any physical contact to enhance their relationship, they often become bored with each other. In such cases the boy and the girl are "lovers" but maybe not even friends— which leads me to my last point.

4—Be Friends First and Sweethearts Second

Bruce Hafen offered this wise counsel to college-aged students:

Be friends first and sweethearts second. Relationships between young men and young women should be built like a pyramid. The base of the pyramid is friendship. And the ascending layers are built of things like time, understanding, respect, and restraint. Right at the top of the pyramid is a glittering little mystery called romance. And when weary travelers in the desert see this pyramid far off in the distance, maybe the first thing they see is that glittering jewel on the top; but when they get closer, they see all that must underlie the jewel of romance to hold it up so high. Now you don't have to be very smart to know that a pyramid won't stand up very long if you stand it on its point and expect the point to hold up everything else. In other words, be friends first and sweethearts later, not the other way around. Otherwise, people who think they are sweethearts may discover they can't be very good friends, and by then it may be too late ("The Gospel and Romantic Love," *Ensign,* October 1982, p. 67).

As I considered my relationship with this young lady, I realized we were sweethearts only, and not even friends. I'd never seen her at work, without make-up, in a bad mood, or in a boring situation. We would each spend hours getting ready to be together so that we would look our best. It was more fantasy than reality. When I was honest with myself, I realized that what really mattered to me was not very high on her priority list. I also realized that what really mattered to her didn't matter much to me.

In conclusion may I leave you the words of Elder Boyd K. Packer. Referring to eternal love he states:

A boy ought to love a girl. He ought to desire with all desire a life's companion. He ought to love fully and completely and righteously. He ought to be preoccupied with finding a sweetheart and, having found her, to love her—permanently. This power, this yearning to love and to be loved, is something so magnetic, so powerful, so compelling, and so important that it is not to be ignored.

Young people sometimes get the mistaken notion that the religious attitude and spirituality interfere with the experience of love. They assume that the requirements of the Church are interferences and aggravations which thwart the full expression of love. Oh, youth, if you could know, the requirements of the Church are the highway to love, with guardrails securely in place, with guide signs plainly marked, with help along the way. How foolish is the youth who feels that the Church is a fence around love to keep him out. How unfortunate to resent counsel and restraints. How fortunate is the young person who follows the standards of the Church, even if just from sheer obedience or habit, for he will find a rapture and a joy fulfilled ("Eternal Love," BYU Tri-Stake Devotional, Nov. 3, 1963, p. 9).

It is my desire that any young person who reads this chapter will be honest with himself. I hope you will consider the "proper sequence" outlined by President Kimball. I hope you will believe that the Church standards are the "highway to love." I pray that the experiences I have shared with you will help answer the question, "Is it love?"

Holding a bachelor's degree in English, an M.E.D. in counseling and guidance, and an Ed.D. in educational psychology, Todd Parker is an associate professor of ancient scripture at Brigham Young University. Dr. Parker was a seminary teacher for fourteen years, and he has also been an institute instructor. An athlete himself, he remains interested in distance running, pole vaulting, gymnastics, and in coaching track. He is married to Debra Harbertson, and they have eight children.

22

WHAT NOW?

KIM M. PETERSON

Life is filled with surprises. We can't guess the end of every story. Sometimes it seems as though we can't predict anything. Frequently we must ask, "What now?" After high school, graduates may ask, "What now?" At age nineteen or twenty-one, potential missionaries may ask "What now?" Young women and young men deciding to get married must ask, "What now?" When faced with serious temptation do we ask, "What now?" Fortunately, most of life's major decisions can be made ahead of time. Amid all other uncertainty, these two facts remain: sin causes misery and righteousness makes us happy.

What now? Let me take you on a trip. We'll go anywhere you would like. I'll be your traveling companion. I'll pay your expenses, including shopping, dining, and entertainment. The only thing you will have to do is decide where we are going. Quite possibly, you have a destination in mind. You may even have good reasons why we should go there. Where would you choose to go?

In reality, we *are* taking a trip. Our Heavenly Father has planned a magnificent journey for us. We choose our traveling companions in friendship and marriage. The cost of the trip is covered. The hardest decision we have to make is where we want to go.

What now? Just to make our trip more interesting, suppose we had to leave in an hour. Could you get ready? If your clothes are already organized, you would have an easier time. One hour probably is not enough time to both find and pack your clothes. Wouldn't it be a shame to miss the trip because you couldn't find the clothes you wanted?

Hour by hour we make decisions that bring us closer to or drive us farther from Heavenly Father. A lack of preparation can result in hasty and poor choices. Spiritual preparation allows us to be properly clothed. In preparing for our journey we would not want to forget the "armour of God" (Ephesians 6:11–17), our "robe of righteousness" (2 Nephi 4:33), or to clothe ourselves with the "bond of charity" (D&C 88:125). We should be so excited about our trip that we can't wait to tell our friends. Like Martin Harris was instructed to do, we should rejoice in our journey and "declare glad tidings" (D&C 19:29).

What now? Imagine that we arrive at the airport terminal only to discover that our flight is already in "final boarding." There would be no time to check baggage. We would only be able to take our "carry-ons" or miss the flight. Luckily, we already have our seat assignments and our boarding passes. Our preparation would become critical. Would you rather stay home or leave some baggage behind? Quickly you make your decision, you abandon your excess baggage, and we run through the terminal together.

"Terminal" is an interesting name. Terminal means final or to the end. "Terminally" affixed to each decision is a consequence. We cannot choose without choosing a consequence. We must leave behind our excess baggage. Moroni taught "Strip yourselves of all uncleanness" (Mormon 9:28).

And now what? No matter how late we might be, we would still have to stand in the security line. Hurriedly, we would place our bags on the conveyor belt, empty our pockets, and walk through the metal detector. Since we wouldn't have brought any dangerous weapons or hazardous materials, the security officers would wave us through the checkpoint. On the other side, we'd grab our things, run down the concourse, and search for our gate.

In our life's journey, each of us needs to periodically undergo a spiritual "security check." Latter-day Saint youth can be spiritually checked by loving parents, faithful leaders, and inspired teachers. Alma recorded that even in his day, the church was "a great check" for the people (Alma 15:17).

Yes, that's right . . . what now? As we approach the gate, hope would increase. Fumbling through our belongings we would have that momentary surge of adrenaline thinking we had lost our tickets. Relieved to find them in our carry-ons, we would hand them to the flight attendant and would be welcomed aboard. Breathing much easier, we would proceed down the jetway, into the cabin, squeeze our carry-ons into the overhead compartment, and settle into our seats. In your mind's eye, take a panoramic look around at your fellow passengers. Surely you would see professional people, families, vacationers, and maybe even honeymooners. Since you and I had to leave our "extra baggage" and run down the concourse, we might assume that everyone else was slightly more prepared. You and I, however, would be most grateful to be on board.

As spiritual brothers and sisters we have many different roles. Whether we choose to be a teacher, an engineer, a nurse, a contractor, or a mechanic, the most important decision we make is to be righteous. When we travel with righteous companions, we can have the same blessing Lehi gave Zoram. "Thou art a true friend unto my son Nephi, forever. Wherefore, because thou hast been faithful thy seed shall be blessed with his seed, that they dwell in prosperity" (2

Nephi 1:30–31). Even our children can be blessed when we choose the right friends.

That's right, what now? The next minutes would quickly pass with normal preflight activities: putting on seat belts, stowing things under our seats, checking the movie, and adjusting the air conditioner. Minutes later we would taxi down the runway and take off. Only then would we realize that all of our efforts had been worth it. Because of our decisions and effort, we would be on our way to a great destination.

One day we will discover that our decisions have indeed plotted a course for us that will terminate in a destination. We will hardly be able to avoid the destination that will be determined by our decisions. If our choices have been righteous, we will be enroute to eternal life. If our choices have been wicked, our destination will be "captivity and death" (see 2 Nephi 2:27–29). Why would we ever choose anything but happiness? Why would anyone ever choose "captivity and death" rather than "eternal life?" The Book of Mormon frequently talks about those who choose the flight to misery. To his misguided son, Corianton, Alma suggested, "These shall be cast out into outer darkness; there shall be weeping, and wailing, and gnashing of teeth, and this because of their own iniquity, being led captive by the will of the devil" (Alma 40:13).

When we choose iniquity, we choose suffering; indeed, we cannot choose iniquity without choosing suffering. Alma explains that once we enter a pattern of iniquity, we run the risk of being caught in a cycle that is difficult to escape. In other words, when we sin, we are more likely to continue choosing sin. Alma continues, "And if their works are evil they shall be restored unto them for evil. . . . The one raised to happiness according to his desires of happiness . . . and the other to evil according to his desires of evil" (Alma 41:4–5).

While not impossible, changing flights once we have

begun our journey is very difficult. Similarly, changing our desires may not be impossible, but that too is very difficult. Where we earnestly want to alter our direction of flight and change our desires, we can draw upon the powers of Jesus Christ and his atonement.

What if, while settling into the expected eight-hour flight, the captain were to announce over the intercom that our destination was a nearby city? Instead of the expected eight-hour flight to an exotic destination, we would be flying only forty minutes to a city we have visited frequently. We might look around frantically to see the response of the other passengers. Anticipating a longer flight to an exciting destination, we would doubtless be disappointed if we only traveled as far as an adjacent city. Just think of the opportunities we would miss, the places we would not see. Trying to make the best of our situation would be little comfort. Assigning blame would not help. We couldn't blame security guards, flight attendants, or the captain. You might want to blame me because I hurried you. Usually you are smart enough to get on the right plane. We would, however, still land in the next city, despite blame, mistakes, and disappointment. We need to make certain we board the flight that will take us where we intend to go.

Like choosing the destination of a trip, we daily choose our master. Apparently, there are only two choices, and we can't serve both. In the Sermon on the Mount, the Savior taught: "No man can serve two masters: for either he will hate the one, and love the other; or else he will hold to the one, and despise the other. Ye cannot serve God and mammon" (Matthew 6:24). The word mammon refers to "riches" (see Bible Dictionary, p. 728) and by inference means "the world." We cannot serve God and the world.

Some of Heavenly Father's children may choose misery instead of happiness because they don't think they will suffer. You would never board a plane destined for Africa and expect to land in the Bahamas. Yet frequently we choose to serve the world or our selfish desires and naively expect to be happy. The advice given by Alma to Corianton might be more applicable today than ever. This loving father told his wayward son that "wickedness never was happiness" (Alma 41:10). To this timely warning we might also add: laziness, mediocrity, contention, indecision, anger, hatred, blame, and pettiness never led to happiness either.

Some travelers choose misery because they don't really believe that righteous choices terminate in happiness. Hundreds of planes from dozens of origins bring thousands of passengers to the same place. When we find eternal happiness, we will be amazed that thousands of our brothers and sisters have traveled to the same spot from hundreds of different points of origin. Then we will agree that righteousness is the only way to arrive at happiness.

Some of Heavenly Father's children may choose misery because they don't listen to the security guards. I have had personal experience that taught me the importance of heeding security guards. A few years ago I used a garment bag to carry my clothes to a speaking engagement in a nearby town. For one of the talks I was asked to give, I used a starting pistol to teach an object lesson. The gun was designed only to fire blanks. I gave the talk, put the gun in my bag, and returned home. Three weeks later, I was late for a flight to another speaking engagement. Knowing I was nearly missing my plane, I rushed to the security check at the airport. Unsuspecting, I put my garment bag on the X-ray machine conveyor belt and walked through the metal detector. Somewhat baffled, I was asked to step away from the conveyor belt. To my horror, I saw the obvious outline of my gun on the screen. That careless mistake meant that I would miss my flight.

The next several hours were spent explaining the presence of the pistol in my luggage to the airport authorities, the district attorney, the county sheriff, the FAA, and the FBI. After my interrogation, they were all finally convinced that the gun was only intended to be used as a teaching tool. The FBI agent, however, had me recite my whole talk before he was ready to believe that I was not planning to do any harm. I've never taught an audience of one with so much conviction!

Aren't we glad security guards are careful? Shouldn't we be happy too that our parents, teachers, and youth leaders are careful about checking the contents of the baggage with which we choose to travel? Aren't we glad that the adults around us are concerned about such things as curfews, music, movies, friends, and fashion? I will be eternally grateful for the "officers" that have helped me "secure" my future. Because of one incident with the security guards, I can't walk past the checkpoint without doing a mental check to see if I am carrying any dangerous things with me. As Latter-day Saints we should frequently check to see if we are traveling with hazardous contraband—things like immoral music, immodest clothing, indecent movies, improper friends, or inappropriate language. For those of you who need to be reminded what exactly is on the list of "hazardous materials," it may be found in the pamphlet *For the Strength of Youth*. I recommend you read it and eliminate any of the items from your luggage that may put your boarding pass in jeopardy.

Finally, some choose misery because they don't know how to choose happiness. The first decision we made is still the most critical: where do we really want to go? We are accustomed to stories whose endings are predictable. If I tell you a young man had been drinking at a party and that he had tried to drive home while under the influence, you might expect the horrible death of the boy, his friends, or innocent victims. Sadly enough, most of us know true stories that have ended in this way. What a mistake it would be for a young person to decide that as long as he or she doesn't drive after drinking, that it is acceptable to drink. What a tragic mistake for a young woman to assume that as long as she doesn't get pregnant, it is okay to be immoral. How sad it would be if we condoned drug usage as long as no one besides the user was hurt.

Paul teaches us that sin brings death (see Romans 6:23). Because every sin does not result in physical death, the death of which Paul is speaking must be spiritual. In order to understand spiritual death, it might be useful to understand the following definitions:

Physical	Spiritual
Birth: Uniting our spirit with our body.	Birth: Uniting ourselves with Heavenly Father (Mosiah 27:25).
Death: Separation of our spirit from our body.	Death: Separation of our spirit from Heavenly Father (Helaman 14:16).
Immortality: Uniting our spirit and our body for eternity (Alma 11:43–45).	Eternal Life: Being united with Heavenly Father for eternity (D&C 76:58–62).

What now? What a question! Every single decision we make has a consequence that follows. If we drink alcohol, there is a consequence. If we are immoral, there is a consequence. If we lie, hate, or steal there are consequences. Some of the consequences are not obvious; but all consequences are real. If we sin and ask "what now?" we are lying to ourselves. We know what happens next—we lose the Spirit. Mosiah taught: "After ye have known and have been taught all these things, if ye should transgress and go contrary to that which has been spoken, . . . ye do withdraw yourselves from the Spirit of the Lord, that it may have no place in you to guide you in wisdom's paths that ye may be blessed, prospered, and preserved" (Mosiah 2:36).

The natural result of sin is that we lose the Spirit. If we

knew where the "loss of the Spirit" trip terminated, we would never travel without the Spirit. The only way to have the Spirit as a companion is to keep the commandments. Some say that keeping the commandments is hard. If we realize how wonderful the destination is, we will gladly be obedient: "And, if you keep my commandments and endure to the end you shall have eternal life, which gift is the greatest of all the gifts of God" (D&C 14:7).

Keeping the commandments is worth it! Eternal life is a much better destination than we can possibly imagine. Choose now to maintain gospel standards, to pursue an education and prepare for employment in something you enjoy. Choose now to prepare for missionary service. Choose now to marry for time and eternity in the temple.

What now? Choose! Choose life and happiness. Choose righteousness. There are some great destinations in this world. You may never have visited Africa, the Bahamas, or India; but surely, you believe these places exist. None of these earthly places can compare with eternal life. We have not yet visited eternal life, but we have been provided with some great descriptions of how it will be there (see 1 Nephi 8–15; D&C 76; Abraham 1–3; and D&C 138). I haven't been there, yet I know it exists, and I want to go. I hope you want to go also. Let's go together. Let's abandon our sins, pass the judgment, choose to live, and end up living with Christ in the kingdom of our Father.

Kim Peterson is the principal of the Cherry Creek, Colorado, seminary. He attended both the University of Utah, where he obtained a bachelor's degree in psychology and sociology, and Brigham Young University, where he earned a master's degree in communications. He has worked as a seminary instructor and as a teacher in the BYU continuing education department. Kim is a certified ski instructor who also enjoys photography, oriental cooking, and rock climbing. He is married to Terri Metcalf, and they have two children.

23

GET A CLUE!

MATT RICHARDSON

One beautiful winter day, a group of my friends and I went skiing at a local resort. We built some jumps and were doing different types of tricks. By the fourth or fifth run, I watched my friends do their "tricks" and then came my turn. I was the last one to hit the jump on this particular run. My friends waited below, yelling encouragement, daring me to try something new or impossible. As soon as I went off the jump I knew that something was wrong. I over-rotated and landed on the backs of my skis which resulted in a complete wipe-out. I felt like one of those snowballs rolling down the mountain—picking up speed and size with my arms poking out of the sides! When I finally came to a stop, my gear was strewn across the mountainside. A glove here, my hat there, a pole and a ski way up there, and so forth.

I found the sunglasses that I had borrowed from my friend, half buried in the snow. When I picked them up, to my horror, I found one of the lenses was missing. I saw tiny pieces of dark glass scattered in the snow. I felt sick. My friends, who were waiting for me about fifty yards down the mountainside, wanted to know if I was all right. "I'm fine . . ." I yelled, "but I broke your sunglasses, Cory. I'm *really* sorry!" He tried to relieve my anxiety by saying that it was no problem. "Don't worry," he yelled back, "they're not mine anyway . . . they're my dad's!" Suddenly I felt even more sick.

I had picked up the rest of my clothing and gear and started to put my skis back on when I noticed a few bright red spots on the snow. Another spot quickly appeared, and then another. They appeared faster and faster. I soon realized it was blood that was spotting the snow, and it was dripping off *my* chin! With my gloves on, I felt my face to find the source of the blood. I held my glove up for closer examination after swiping under my nose and found my glove covered with blood. "Humph, bloody nose," I said to myself, "Of all the rotten timing." Then I tilted my head back and pinched the bridge of my nose. I yelled to my friends that I had a bloody nose and I would be there in a minute. Every time I checked my face, it was still bleeding. Impatiently, I shoved two wads of Kleenex up my nose in the hope they would stop the bleeding. Desperate measures for desperate times! I finally got my skis on and started to ski down the mountain to rejoin my friends. As soon as I started skiing towards them, however, they started skiing down as well. I tried to ski faster and catch them.

I passed other skiers who stared at me wide-eyed. "Bloody nose," I said to them, holding up my glove so they could see the blood as I skied past. I finally caught up to my friends at the bottom of the run. "Sorry it took me so long," I apologized, "but I have a bloody nose that just won't stop!" I noticed that their eyes were practically bulging out of their heads, and they were staring at me as if I were clueless. "Matt," one of my friends said solemnly, "you don't have a bloody nose."

"What are you talking about?" I said as I wiped blood from my face and showed him my glove. I even pulled out the tissue logs as evidence. Again my friends looked at me as if to say, "you haven't a clue about what's really going on, do you?"

"You need help, Matt," another friend said.

"I don't need help, I'm not crazy," I retorted defensively.

"You need *medical* help. It's not your nose, it's your eye!"

I took off my glove and felt under my eye. I was shocked to find a wide cut under my eye. The gash was bleeding quite badly and would require stitches. Even worse than the cut, however, was the embarrassment that I felt over having tried to convince myself, my friends, and even complete strangers that I only had a bloody nose. I couldn't believe I was pinching and tissuing my nose all that time . . . and it was my eye! I guess my friends were right in thinking that I was clueless!

To this day, I carry a scar under my eye that reminds me of that clueless adventure. I can think of many other experiences in my life where I didn't have the slightest idea of what was going on or what I should do. I didn't have a clue. In fact, I have heard that phrase, *Get a Clue!* more times than I care to remember. I'm sure that you have probably heard that phrase yourself. We all know what it means. One dictionary of slang usage (yes, there really *are* dictionaries of slang!), states that to be clueless is "to be ignorant; without information; not knowing what is happening."

Being occasionally clueless is part of life. Fortunately, there have been times when I really didn't mind being clueless. For example, my wife and I were in a foreign country where we didn't speak the language. Most of the locals were not very helpful, so we wandered around lost, got on the wrong subways, asked many questions, and received only blank stares for answers. We couldn't even figure out the money! As you can see, we were clueless. Although it was frustrating, we were loving it! Deep down I knew that someday I would be back home; in control of my language, money, and sense of direction. I knew that my present state of cluelessness was only temporary. "Clueless and Loving It!" became our motto while we were in Europe.

Most of the time, however, life's "clueless" episodes aren't so fun. They can be embarrassing, painful, and discouraging. Consider those times when you feel completely alone, and no one seems to understand; or when your confidence is lacking and you're unsure of your future. Another of life's most difficult times is when you have made some mistakes and then feel so overwhelmed that you can't possibly see a way out. These are definite states of cluelessness. Since we all experience a clueless time or two, what can we do about it?

Perhaps we should start at the beginning. Let's start with the phrase we've been talking about. "Get a clue" is actually a phrase coined in Greek mythology. There is a story about Minos, the wicked King of Crete. Because one of his sons was killed in Athens, Minos required a sacrifice of young Athenian men and women every nine years. Naturally, this was extremely distressing to the Athenians. A daring young man by the name of Theseus, the son of the King of Athens, volunteered to be one of the seven young men and seven young maidens to be offered as a sacrifice to Minos's other son, the Minotar. The Minotar was a creature—half human and half bull—that was kept in a cavernous labyrinth—a difficult maze from which no one had ever escaped. Theseus was determined to find and kill the Minotar.

Upon his arrival on the isle, Theseus was spotted by Minos's daughter, Ariadne. In that single glimpse, Ariadne fell madly in love with Theseus. She didn't want Theseus to die as a sacrificial offering so she secretly gave him a sword and a "clue." It is obvious why Ariadne gave Theseus the sword. But the clue? Did she give him some "hints" on how to kill her half-brother, the Minotar? Or did she give him some knowledge about how to escape the maddening maze? Actually, Ariadne gave Theseus a *Kliuwe* which is a ball of string. That's right, a ball of string. Theseus was told that the ball of string would help him find the Minotar and then show him the way out of the maze. He tied his "clue" to the door post at the entrance of the maze and let the ball unwind as he made his way through the maze. Turning this way and that, he became dizzy, yet he held fast to his string as he followed the unwinding ball. The string led Theseus directly to the Minotar. During a ferocious battle, Theseus fought bravely with the sword in one hand and the clue firmly clutched in the other. After the exhausting battle, the dreaded Minotar lay dead. The victory was won, not just because of Theseus' courage and skill, but because of his "clue"; which led the way to victory and then the way out of the mind-boggling maze.

I love that story. Although it is only a myth, it has taught me some important lessons—vital, *real-life* lessons. I think back to all those times that I heard someone say: "get a clue," "he is clueless," or "he is without a clue." I never really understood what that meant. I know that when we use the world *clueless* or the phrase *get a clue* that we aren't really meaning to say, "You're stringless," or "Hey, buddy, get a ball of string!" It doesn't sound quite right, does it? But perhaps, it is more *right* than we realize.

As I think back on how many times I have literally been clueless, I can see that those were the times when I really didn't know where I was going and I couldn't seem to find a way out of the problem at hand. Remember, Theseus learned that the clue did *two* important things. First, it led the way to his objective; and second, it led him out of the labyrinth. We know that Theseus was smart, brave, and filled with courage even without the clue. It was the clue, however, that provided the direction and means of escape for Theseus. Without the clue, Theseus would still be

wandering around in that maze, either looking for the
Minotar or for the exit to his freedom. As funny as it may
sound, it is appropriate, even helpful, to tell someone
trapped in a difficulty to literally "get a clue." Aren't you
really telling them to figure out how to get out of the mess
and then find the way they should be going? Isn't that
really what they need?

Life is filled with discouraging moments; times when
there is little or no hope for peace, happiness, and meaning.
That's right—those clueless times. If, however, we could
somehow get a clue, a sense of where we should be going
and of how to escape or get out of problems as they arise,
wouldn't doubt and fear be replaced by hope and freedom?
Yes . . . but only partly! Having a clue is not enough.
Granted, Theseus had a clue, which did indeed save the day
(not to mention Theseus and the thirteen others). If Theseus
had kept his clue in his pocket or set it down when it was
inconvenient, how different would the story have been?
Before the clue could lead Theseus to the Minotar, it had to
be tied to something. Long before Theseus needed the clue
to find freedom from the dark pits of the maze, he needed
to secure it (the clue) to something. If Theseus hadn't tied
his string to the door post of the exit or even if he had tied
his string to the wrong portal, he could never have found
the Minotar or secured his freedom from the maze. He
would have spent his remaining days in confusion, roaming from one portal to the next, without ever finding the
right path. If tying the string to the right foundation is necessary for the clue to give direction, perhaps the essential
question we must ask ourselves is this: "To what are we
tying our life right now?"

Just as Theseus was led by the clue, so will you be led . . .
but where? It all depends on where you tie your life's clue.
I am intrigued by a scenario in *Alice in Wonderland*. Alice is
lost and finds the Cheshire Cat in the forest. The scene, as

written by Lewis Carroll, goes like this: "Alice, confused and befuddled over her precarious adventure, asked the Cheshire Cat: 'Would you tell me, please, which way I ought to walk from here?' 'That depends a good deal on where you want to get to,' said the Cat. 'I don't much care where—' said Alice. 'Then it doesn't matter which way you walk,' said the Cat. '—so long as I get somewhere,' Alice added as an explanation. 'Oh, you're sure to do that,' said the Cat, 'if you only walk long enough'" (*Alice's Adventures in Wonderland* [New York: William Morrow & Co., 1991], pp. 89–90).

It seems that a lot of us are like Alice. We walk this way and that, without knowing where we are headed and often not really even caring. This could be considered a true state of *cluelessness*. If your string dangles in open air, without any connection whatsoever, you will spend your life roaming from one interest to the other; always looking for happiness, but never able to find it. Perhaps that is what Paul was referring to when he talked about people who are ever learning but unable to come to the knowledge of the truth (see 2 Timothy 3:7).

Others, instead of keeping their clue in their pocket or allowing it to dangle unattached, will tie it to some*thing*, a purpose, a goal, or an object . Maybe it's grades, a boyfriend or girlfriend, sports, a car, a club, a gang, the Church, clothes, money, or ourselves. Whenever we tie our life to something, we pour our attention, time, efforts, and emotions into that thing. We begin to cherish those things and they become our treasures. This is what Christ meant as he was delivering his Sermon on the Mount and said, "For where your treasure is, there will your heart be also" (Matthew 6:21).

I am convinced that wherever you tie your life is where you will end up . . . if you follow it long enough. If you tie your life to money, you will eventually get money. If you are solely interested in becoming popular, I am sure that you will eventually achieve that as well. I have a box filled with my "clueless treasures." These treasures include a letter jacket, trophies, graduation tassels, certificates, photographs taken on prom nights, ticket stubs, etc. These are the items that I tied my life to at one time or another. These are the treasures that I *thought* would bring me happiness. I thought, at one time, that this was *the* item that would put me over the top, make me feel better about myself, and give me ultimate happiness. Granted, that box is filled with wonderful memories and valuable experiences, but it is not filled with life. Those achievements or things didn't fill my empty heart or comfort me when I was discouraged or feeling lost. Sadly, many times I have tied my life to temporary moments of success. When the times are stormy, however, we need a lifeline that is tied to something that can give life.

After participating in the miracle of loaves and fishes, many people couldn't see past the physical *things* in Christ's message, and they abandoned the Savior. Christ turned to the Twelve and asked, "Will ye also go away?" Peter answered for himself and for the others: "Lord, to whom shall we go? thou hast the words of eternal life. And we believe and are sure that thou art that Christ, the Son of the living God" (John 6:67–69). Can you see where Peter was tying his life? To something different than most people of the world. He left behind whatever else might have come into his life—his fishing business, friends, popularity, money, and power. Doctrine and Covenants 25:10 tells us, "And verily I say unto thee that thou shalt lay aside the things of this world, and seek for the things of a better."

I hope that you will not only seek for things of a better world, but that you will tie your life to something that is enduring, filled with hope and meaning, and able to provide you with fulfillment. That has to be only one thing— tie your life to Christ. He is "the way, the truth, and the life"

(John 14:6). It is only through him that we might be saved. When we tie our clue to Jesus Christ, we are building a foundation for a meaningful, peaceful life. Just as Theseus tied his clue to the right doorway and then followed the correct path, a life tied directly to Christ provides the hope of direction and deliverance.

If you live your life in accordance with the principles of the gospel of Jesus Christ, you can be assured of divine guidance. Wasn't Joseph's humble prayer answered in a grove of trees because a young man followed his clue to God for direction? Think of Nephi—a young man who tied his heart to Christ. Remember when Nephi and his brothers were assigned to obtain the brass plates? After failing twice, an angel appeared to the brothers and told them to go back to Jerusalem and try again. This time, however, they would obtain the plates according to the *Lord's* plan. Laman and Lemuel, whose hearts were tied not to Christ but to the pride of man, murmured and asked, "How is it possible that the Lord will deliver Laban into our hands?" (1 Nephi 3:31). They then gave all the supporting reasons why it wouldn't work. It was the younger brother, Nephi, tied to a greater source, who followed the Lord's string into Jerusalem that night. Just as Theseus never let go of his clue in the maze or in battle, Nephi clung to his clue, being "led by the Spirit, not knowing beforehand the things which I should do" (1 Nephi 4:6). We all know the outcome.

Think also of the trying times Jacob had as a young man. Jacob and his brother Esau had difficulty getting along. It is obvious that their lives were tied to different things. Esau was a worldly man, whereas Jacob was a devoted man of Christ. As Jacob was seeking to find a wife, the Lord promised him a great blessing: "I am with thee, and will keep thee in all places whither thou goest, . . . for I will not leave thee" (Genesis 28:15). This same promise is available to all those who tie their clue to Christ. If we will but trust in the Lord, he will not only direct our paths (see Proverbs 3:5–7), but he will light the way as well (see John 8:12).

Since all of us have our moments of doubt and despair, do you really think that our Father in Heaven would ever send us to earth without a clue? If our Heavenly Father's work and glory is to bring to pass the immortality and eternal life of each one of us (see Moses 1:39), it is hard for me to imagine that he would leave us alone. It is my belief that he does *not* leave us alone. He points the direction we should go and helps us find solutions to our problems.

Some of my most difficult times are when I can't find a way out. When life seems to be just like Minos's maze. Something new around every corner, but usually something that I didn't expect or desire. It is easy to give up hope when all you do is go around in circles. These are the times when we need to depend on the Lord and hold on to his clue for direction. But what about when we are already in the mess? How do we get out? Our Father in Heaven and brother, Jesus Christ, have given us a distinct way back. As a matter of fact, didn't Paul tell us that we would never be tempted beyond our strength to resist? He said: "But God is faithful, who will not suffer you to be tempted above that ye are able; but will with the temptation also make a way to escape, that ye may be able to bear it" (1 Corinthians 10:13).

Young Nephi also bore testimony of getting a clue. Remember his powerful and familiar declaration of faith in which he said, "I will go and do the things which the Lord hath commanded, for I know that the Lord giveth no commandments unto the children of men, *save he shall prepare a way* for them that they may accomplish the thing which he commandeth them" (1 Nephi 3:7; emphasis added). Sounds like getting a clue to me! You have been promised that regardless of how bad it may seem, there is a way out.

One of my favorite scriptural stories is about a group of

young men who tied their clue to Christ at a very early age. These young men were deeply dedicated to their country, their family, their liberty, and their God. These young men were courageous, valiant, strong, trustworthy, and they respected their mothers. But this was not all. They knew the commandments of God, and they lived them. Sounds like the type of young men I hope my son will be like and that my daughters will marry.

These young men, two thousand in all, carried their clues into a fierce battle. Clearly all the odds were against them. Most warriors, even those seasoned in battle, would have likely given up and lost hope for victory. Not this group of young men. They fought with a sword in one hand and their clue, firmly tied to God, in the other. Just before that great battle they boldly proclaimed, "God is with us, and he will not suffer that we should fall; then let us go forth" (Alma 56:46). During the battle, Helaman described them as fighting "with the strength of God; yea, never were men known to have fought with such miraculous strength" (Alma 56:56). Even in the heat of the battle they held tightly to that clue. They knew the source of their deliverance in the labyrinth of battle.

During trying times, the world weighs heavily down upon those who attempt to stand tall and firm. I'm sure that you have, at one time or another, sung "Shall the youth of Zion falter, in defending truth and right?" I have thought a lot about that lately. Shall the youth of Zion falter? I honestly believe the answer depends on you. Get a clue! We are living in a time of persecution, debate, and high emotions. You will see many things happen in your lifetime that some people might say are evidence enough to destroy your faith. Yet together we stand, tall and firm, tied to Christ. When we hold that line, it brings us hope. It doesn't really matter what the world says. Hold tight. Remember the words of Helaman: "And now, my sons, remember, remember that it is upon the rock of our Redeemer, who is Christ, the Son of God, that ye must build your foundation; that when the devil shall send forth his mighty winds, yea, his shafts in the whirlwind, yea, when all his hail and his mighty storm shall beat upon you, it shall have no power over you to drag you down to the gulf of misery and endless wo, because of the rock upon which ye are built, which is a sure foundation, a foundation whereon if men build they cannot fall" (Helaman 5:12).

President Ezra Taft Benson has said: "Men and women who turn their lives over to God will discover that He can make a lot more out of their lives than they can. He will deepen their joys, expand their vision, quicken their minds, strengthen their muscles, lift their spirits, multiply their blessings, increase their opportunities, comfort their souls, raise up friends, and pour out peace" ("Jesus Christ—Gifts and Expectations," Christmas Devotional, Salt Lake City, Dec. 7, 1986). It is my prayer that we may stand tied to Christ. During times of little hope, I pray that we will never let go of the lifeline that leads to hope, salvation, and deliverance. Get a Clue!

Matt Richardson is a doctoral candidate in education and a part-time instructor of ancient scripture at Brigham Young University. A former seminary instructor, he has taught Danish at the Missionary Training Center and worked on national Drug-Free Youth programs. His hobbies include cartooning, studying advertising strategies, participating in all kinds of sports, and watching old movies. Disneyland is his favorite place on earth. He and his wife, Lisa Jeanne Jackson, have three children.

24

"COME UNTO ME"

SCOTT SIMMONS

I love teaching seminary. However, one challenging aspect of the job is helping students to "experience" the scriptures. One day, while preparing a lesson on Matthew 11:28–30, I was having just such a challenge. I wanted my students to do more than read the passage. I wanted them to truly experience what the Savior meant when he said, "Come unto me." Then inspiration struck. I quickly gathered objects I would need for the lesson and headed to class.

Following the devotional, I walked to the front of the room and placed a chair so that it was facing the class. I noticed that my class members were almost as nervous as I was. (I'm known for my—sometimes—interesting teaching techniques.) The class waited in silence as I carefully dusted off the chair. Then, without warning, I said, "Matt, come up here." At that point the class relaxed. Now, Matt was the only one who needed to worry. Slowly he made his way to the front. Casually, I asked him to sit down. After carefully checking the chair for anything out of the ordinary, he did. I then asked Matt to take off his shoes and socks. Three girls sitting off to the right screamed, "No!!!" You see, Matt was a basketball player, and I guess, strange as it may seem, they had somehow smelled Matt's feet before. However, at that point , Matt began to relax and enjoy the situation. He took each shoe off with the flair of a performer, much to the aversion of the three girls.

When he had finished taking off his shoes, I reminded him, "Matt, the socks too." Again the girls screamed. So Matt did what any true senior boy in that situation would do, he threw one of his socks at the lead girl. It wouldn't have been that big of a deal, except this young lady had what I call "bangs to heaven." Her bangs went straight up for a good five inches. This effect is achieved by sculpting them into place with massive amounts of hair spray while riding a motor scooter at a high rate of speed. Because of the combination of hair spray and the height of her bangs, the sock stuck.

After finally getting the class under control and convincing the young lady who had been hit by the sock that she wasn't melting (the result of watching the "Wizard of Oz" too many times), I turned my attention back to Matt. I interrupted his enjoyment of his sock toss by pulling out a blindfold. The class once again focused on the situation at hand.

At this point, I blindfolded Matt, spun him around ten times and asked him to find his way to the back of the room. The class was silent as Matt teetered his way to the chalkboard. Once he found the chalkboard, he oriented himself and headed toward the back of the room. At that point everything got exciting.

My first period students were all kind, loving, and charitable. NOT! They did everything in their power to keep Matt from reaching the back of the room. Students started sliding desks toward him. They rearranged the furniture. Two boys got the piano and began moving it back and forth in front of him. (Matt must have thought this was the longest piano he had ever felt.) Finally, Matt got fed up. He climbed over the piano as well as three students and made it to the back of the room. As he went to take his blindfold off I stopped him and said, "Matt, before you take off your blindfold I want to ask you a few questions. First of all, what was it like trying to find the back of the room, blindfolded?" He said it was hard.

"Why?" I asked.

He replied, "Because this class is a bunch of jerks."

"Okay, other than that, why was it hard?"

"Well, mostly because I couldn't see."

I said, "Matt, you made it to the back of the room. Do you think you could now make it back to the front of the room?"

"No problem, Brother Simmons. This time I know what to watch out for and which direction to go."

"Okay, Matt. Find the front of the room." As Matt went to step forward I stopped him.

"Wait just a minute." While Matt paused, I reached in my coat pocket, pulled out a huge box of thumb tacks, and shook them for all to hear. In unison, the whole class took a deep breath. With my class not breathing, I scattered the tacks all over the floor in front of Matt. Everyone leaned forward in their seats as I said, "Matt, go ahead." Now, I had picked Matt on purpose. He had big feet. That meant more tacks per foot. He didn't move. I repeated, "Matt, go ahead."

He slowly backed up so that he was flat against the door and said, "Nope. No way. I'm not movin'."

I said, "Matt, what's the matter? Why not?" (Teachers sometimes ask dumb questions to make a point.)

Matt simply replied, "There are tacks all over the floor." The class sat motionless. I wondered if they were still breathing. I hadn't heard them breathe out since sucking all the oxygen out of the room.

With the tension mounting, I said, "Matt, you're blindfolded. You can't see. How do you know there are tacks on the floor?"

He said, "I heard you shake the box, I heard the tacks hit the floor, and I heard the class suck all the oxygen out of the room. I'm not movin'." Wanting my class to breathe again, I said, "Okay, I'll tell you what. You pick someone in the room you trust."

It was interesting to watch the class as Matt began to contemplate who he would pick. His friends began to point to themselves, gesturing like, "He's going to pick me."

Finally, after several seconds, he said, "I want Amy." I realize that doesn't mean much to the reader because you don't know Amy. Amy was the most quiet girl in the class. I was honestly surprised that he even knew her name. She was not someone Matt would date or even hang out with, but he trusted her. Why? Because Amy was good. She was righteous. Matt knew it. Everyone knew it. You should have seen the shocked look on Matt's friend's faces when he choose Amy. (Isn't it sad more people in tough situations don't put their trust in someone righteous?)

I said, "Amy, please come here." Amy made her way slowly to the back of the class. I then asked Amy to lead Matt through the tacks. I placed no restrictions on how she did it. I simply told her to lead him through the tacks. That's what makes this object lesson interesting. I've staged this demonstration a hundred times since, and I've probably seen a hundred ways to lead people through the tacks. Some people simply sweep the tacks out of the way. Others try to talk them through. One young man pulled a magnet out of his pocket and picked up all the tacks with it. (I still haven't figured out what he was doing with a magnet that big in his pocket.) My favorite experience came when one rather muscular girl grabbed the poor boy that was blindfolded and carried him bodily through the maze of tacks.

In the many times I've used this object lesson, only once

have I seen what I'm about to tell you. Again, I said, "Amy, lead Matt through the tacks." As we all waited and watched to see what Amy would do, Matt caught us off guard. He reached out. He extended his hand toward Amy. Matt is the only student that ever reached out. Everyone else has just stood there waiting for the person to come to them. Matt reached out.

Recently, I've been amazed at how many of my students are in the same situation Matt was. They are figuratively up against a wall, afraid to move because of the tacks they fear. The only difference is, their tacks are spiritual instead of physical. In every case, the real problem is not the tacks or even the blindfold. The problem is, they are unwilling to reach out. They are waiting for someone to come and get them, rather than reaching out to someone they can trust.

When the Savior said, "Come unto me," he was inviting us to reach out and trust him (see 2 Nephi 26:23–24). Are there tacks in your life? Are you up against a wall, spiritually, and afraid to move for fear of getting hurt? Reach out. The Savior is ever ready to lead you through your tacks if you just trust and reach out (see D&C 78:18). The real question is, how do we reach out? Let me share with you three ways.

Prayer

First, pray. Pray morning and night. Pray during the day. Pray always in your heart. Pray. In one scripture alone (3 Nephi 18:15–23) the Savior mentions prayer eight times. Now when I say pray, I mean *really* pray. Not the old "Now I lay me down to sleep . . ." prayer. Let me illustrate.

The other day, I asked my students to show me how they pray. I was amazed at what I saw. Some were lying on the floor. Others were draped over their desks, like they do to their bed. One young man remarked, "I always pray while lying in my bed. That way, if I fall asleep during my prayer, when I wake up in the morning I just have to say amen. Then I count that as my morning prayer, too." As I said, I was amazed. Try something; the next time you say your prayers, kneel in the middle of your room where you can't lean on anything. Some of you may have to clear a spot, but do it (see Enos 1:4). I promise you, if you will do this thing, it will make a difference in your prayers.

Once you're kneeling, and not leaning or lying down, talk to your Father in Heaven out loud (see D&C 19:28). Tell him what's in your heart and on your mind (see Alma 34:27). Tell him what your "tacks" are and how you feel about them. Be open and honest. Some of you may be thinking that there are some things you could never tell your Father in Heaven. I have news for you, he already knows. So why doesn't he just help you? He loves you enough not to infringe on your agency. Because of this sacred gift of agency, you and I need to reach out—to him. We can tell him everything.

When you finish your prayer, don't jump up and rush into your day or into your bed. Pause a minute. You may not get an answer, but you will know your Father has heard your prayer (see Philippians 4:6–7). You will find the promise found in Doctrine and Covenants 88:63 is true. "Draw near unto me and I will draw near unto you; seek me diligently and ye shall find me; ask, and ye shall receive; knock, and it shall be opened unto you."

Scripture Study

Second, study your scriptures. Someone once wisely said, "If you want to talk to God, pray. If you want God to talk to you, read your scriptures." The scriptures are the words of Christ. When "likened" (1 Nephi 19:23) to ourselves, they will "tell you all things what ye should do" (2 Nephi 32:3).

One major road block to studying the scriptures comes from the idea that we always need to start at the beginning. Perhaps this is the reason so many members of the Church have 1 Nephi 1:1 memorized. "I Nephi, having been born . . ." I'll bet you finished the sentence didn't you? Instead of always starting at the beginning, try opening the book to wherever it opens, or look up specific topics in the Topical Guide. As you read, think about your tacks. Ask yourself, how can what I'm reading help me through my tacks? Ponder what you need or what you have read. As you do, the scriptures will come alive (see D&C 30:33).

Young people often share experiences with me of how the scriptures have answered their prayers. For example, one young lady told me she had really been trying to live the gospel. Yet, she still felt spiritually empty. One day she opened her scriptures to Alma 34 and read verses 17–27, which are about praying. As she read, she thought, "I'm doing all that, so why do I feel so spiritually empty?" Then she read the next verse. "Do not suppose that this is all; for after ye have done all these things, if ye turn away the needy, and the naked, and visit not the sick and afflicted, and impart of your substance, [to the poor] . . . your prayer is vain." The scriptures came alive! She realized she had been forgetting the second great commandment, to love others (see Matthew 28:39). She wasn't serving others! The next day she volunteered to feed the homeless. As she served, she found the spirituality she had been missing. She walked through the "tacks" unharmed, because she reached out.

Service

Third, serve other people. In Matthew 11:29 the Savior invites us to take his yoke upon us. What does that mean?

A yoke is used to attach two animals together for the purpose of increasing the amount they can carry or pull. Notice the Savior doesn't say, "Let me take your yoke." Rather, he tells us to take his. He's inviting us to join him in his work. And what is his work? "To bring to pass the immortality and eternal life of man" (Moses 1:39). He desires to help our brothers and sisters make it home. So how do we help the Savior? We do so by serving other people. We must look for opportunities to help others. In my seminary classes, I assign two people to be what I call "secret service agents." Their assignment is to secretly do nice things for members of the class. It is amazing what this will do for the morale and spirituality of a class. Not to mention what it does for the people who perform the service.

Each morning I make it a point to kneel down and ask Heavenly Father who I can help that day. Each day, he tells me. (You know, it's funny, but I've never asked who I could help and had him say, "Thanks for the offer, but we've got it covered.") There is always someone who needs help.

One day while working at the seminary, I got a strong impression to telephone a close friend. I stopped what I was doing and made the call. We talked for over an hour. It seems he was really having a hard time making some difficult decisions and just needed someone to talk to. As we concluded our conversation, he thanked me, and then almost as an afterthought added, "You must have been inspired." I had no sooner hung up the phone when I felt impressed to call my mom and tell her I loved her. I know it sounds like I watch too many of those Mormon commercials, but I called. We visited for a minute, and then I simply said, "Mom, I just called to say I love you."

Mom asked, "How did you know?"

I said, "Know what?" She told me it had been a hard day, and that she really needed someone to let her know she was loved. Sometimes service can be as simple as a phone call. Don't always wait to be prompted. Remember to be "anxiously engaged in a good cause, and do many things of [your] own free will" (D&C 58:27).

Reach out. Pray. Study your scriptures. And serve. As you do so, the Savior will "lead [you] by the hand" through your personal maze of "tacks" and "give [you] answers to [your] prayers" (D&C 112:10).

Scott Simmons is a seminary instructor and principal who is noted for his sometimes zany but effective approach to teaching. He earned his bachelor's degree from Brigham Young University and has served as a counselor in a bishopric, labored as an elders quorum president, and enjoyed teaching Sunday School. Scott lists riding motorcycles, riding and caring for horses, and kissing his wife as his favorite hobbies. He is married to Nancy Wright.

25

SPIRITUAL DETERIORATION: FLIES IN OUR EYES

KATHRYN S. SMITH

The outdoor marketplace was a splash of color. The stalls were hand-hewn boxes, each about four feet square, where the merchant sat among his (or more often, her) wares. There were vegetables whose shape and color were entirely unfamiliar to me—big black eggplant, huge twisted roots, thick bunches of leaves, all edible, all for sale. There were beads, and dried meats; there were strips of cloth and stacks of articles, the use of which was known only to the natives who bought and sold them. Our group of tourists stood watching on the sidelines, almost as if the marketplace were a stage. Trees surrounded us, sun spattered through the thick foliage to brighten the scene, and I was fascinated. We were in Africa, although I no longer remember which country, and the day was one in early July, a mild but cool winter day below the equator.

We listened with interest to the sound of words that we did not understand. The bartering was keen, and the natives were obviously well-practiced in the rhythms of market interaction. No one was upset, and merchandise changed hands smoothly. The native dress was both colorful and drab. Some of the people were fully dressed in blankets and layers of cloth while others wore only loincloths or leather shorts. We were all mesmerized by the scene.

My eyes were drawn to a young mother who was bartering with a merchant. She was only a stone's throw off, and I studied her dark hair, her beaded necklace, and her colorful skirt. She held a nursing infant in her arms. To see her so was completely natural in that setting, and I was again reminded of the sense of stage and audience.

Then my eyes focused on the face of her infant, and my curiosity and fascination suddenly changed to revulsion. There were flies drinking from the corners of the eyes of the infant! My eyes flew to the mother's face again. "Look at your baby!" I wanted to scream at her. "Brush the flies away!" But she didn't notice. Then the horrible realization hit me—she had flies drinking from the corners of *her* eyes, and she took no notice of them either. Suddenly I rescanned the entire scene. Every merchant, every client, everyone, had flies in their eyes! No one waved at them. No one seemed to be aware of or feel the infectious germ-carriers. I couldn't believe it.

Those people did not know that the flies carried blindness. They were so used to them, that they no longer felt them or saw them or rejected them as pests. I wanted to join the peace corps and come to Africa as the great Han Solo of the fly-destroyers—landing in my space ship and blasting out ignorance while importing fierce pesticides that would rescue the native peoples from devastation. It seemed unthinkable that there wasn't *something* we could *do* to rescue those poor innocents from the danger they didn't even sense.

It has been several years since that experience. I have come to realize that we are all "innocents" or "ignorants" who do not fully sense the danger around us. Flies drink at our spiritual eyes, too, and the pests threaten us with spiritual devastation. There are evil voices that whisper to us,

trying to entice us to partake of the sins of the world. These
voices are as dangerous to our spiritual well-being as the
flies are to the physical health of the native shoppers in the
market place in Africa.

Consider a typical evening spent in front of the television. There we see men and women, teenagers, and children prancing humorously on our TV screens, many of
them mocking the values we know to be true. They lie,
deceive, swear, kiss, pet, and more, and it is all packaged in
a way to make it look innocent, fun, and acceptable. Repeat-
edly, show by show, we watch as Satan's teachings are dis-
played in our living rooms. Our eyes drink in *his* values, *his*
attitudes, and *his* promotion of laziness, of promiscuity, and
of dishonesty. A steady diet of this kind of "nourishment"
saps our spiritual strength and weakens our commitment to
our Heavenly Father's kingdom and His work. In time, we
can lose our spiritual bearings and succumb to the temptation to mimic the behavior we see portrayed on the screen.

Many pop groups convey the same message. So, too, the
movies. Even the "okay ones" all seem to agree: families
fight; it's okay for adults to have casual and frequent love
relationships; and teens have better things to do than study.
Life is for generating sensations and excitement! Youth are
justified in ignoring stuffy parents and teachers because
kids need to find themselves through self-expression and
freedom. Now, there is nothing wrong with finding oneself,
as long as we don't lose our salvation in the process. We
need to brush the flies away.

Even Disney's Little Mermaid and Aladdin's Jasmine
are only half-clothed. They are portrayed as innocent, beautiful heroines, but the media undresses them. Seeing that
example modeled from our earliest years, we can come to
feel that there is nothing wrong with immodest dress. And
in today's world, anyone who tries to teach modesty might
as well be selling lima beans and liver.

I traveled completely around the world during the summer of my nineteenth birthday. I had previously never been out of California, except to go to school at Brigham Young University. It was the 60s, and the university campus riots were in full swing. The war in Vietnam and the protests against it were both raging. Our young men were being called upon to risk their lives and die in a dubious cause. The age of "we deserve more" was awakening.

On that trip around the world, we visited India. It was July, and the sun bore down on us in red anger, and there was no relief from the heat. The stench in the streets in Calcutta attacked our noses as we stepped off the plane, and it did not let up until we flew away eleven days later. Factories belched their pollutions into the air. Discarded waste rotted in the alleys and streets. The constant stench sickened me, and I felt claustrophobic, as if I were being suffocated with no hope of escape.

We drove around in buses and observed the Indian people as they worked and milled about in the crowded, foul-smelling streets. I have never felt such pity. I felt so sad that these people had never experienced a backyard barbeque on a fresh-scented summer afternoon. They didn't know anything about beaches, or mountain trails, or horseback riding on the family farm. They didn't know about soda pop or popcorn or gabbing on the telephone.

I am certain they have their own pleasures, but everything I saw seemed pitiful and desperate. Children ran alongside our tour bus with hands outstretched, calling out, "Pennies. Nickels. Dimes." Mothers with babies sat on street corners, begging. Empty-eyed men with their bed frames strapped to their backs walked forlornly along the streets. At night these homeless ones would simply let down their bamboo beds and lie on them along the streets until morning.

We did our touring in the morning in order to avoid

the horrible heat of the afternoon. We watched these homeless people arise from their beds and prepare for the day. A
stream of foul liquid ran down the gutters, and the people
relieved themselves into the flow, in full view of any
passers-by. A short distance farther down the road another
homeless person would dip his homemade toothbrush into
that same stream of water and scrub his teeth. I was continually appalled by their ignorance of the fact that disease
flowed in those gutters. They trustingly used the water as if
it were fresh and pure. They were so accustomed to their
deplorable circumstances that they did not suspect the danger of their actions.

We are in similar danger of being overwhelmed by the
subtle influences that are attacking the moral values that
would steady us and keep us safe. Parents, Church leaders,
bishops, and advisers all warn us of the dangers. Because
they can see "up and down the road," they can often see the
perils we may not perceive. Their wisdom is based on the
experiences they have accumulated in a lifetime of living
and in the things they have both suffered and enjoyed.

One lie that Satan tries to feed us is that when women
become moms, they needn't stay at home to raise their children. There is a growing number of capable, brilliant
women in the working world. Of course women can run
business and law firms and professional offices. Of course
they can dress in suits and carry planners and wheel and
deal in the corporate world. Women make fine doctors, den-
tists, police officers, and attorneys. But what about their
children? Who will cuddle the little ones when they scrape
their knees? Who will teach the child to tie his shoe, to pick
a flower, to make a cookie? Perhaps those pursuits seem
trivial next to making big money deals in company board
rooms, but it is daily nurturing that provides the growing
child with self-esteem and a sense of security. It is the mother's training that helps a child develop a sense of right and

wrong and that introduces the child to God and His plan for us. It is the stability of home and the sense of family and roots that builds character and strength in the youth and young adult. It is mothers who shape the next generation and who teach children to be selfless, to be careful in their choices, and to make wise decisions.

An LDS mother of twelve children writes stories on a computer in her home. She is a published author, and after she had achieved a certain level of fame, a New York magazine wanted to do a write-up on her. They sent a polished team of journalists to do the interview. As the professionals entered the home of the mother/author, there was the expected chaos that twelve children would create. The mother tried to hush everyone, to have the older children keep the little ones in the kitchen, and to create a quiet moment for the interview to take place.

What a joke! She may as well have tried to stop a river. The children kept coming in and asking Mom questions, and the phone kept ringing. The mother apologized to the professional woman writer who sat through all of this, trying to get her story written. Finally, the five year-old had had enough of being strapped to the kitchen table and came in and plopped down on her mother's lap.

We can all picture the scene. The journalist from New York finally put down her pen. She looked at the mother and said, "You know, they sold us a lie," She went on. In graduate school they had told this woman and her peers that being a mother in the home, that being "only" a wife, was a waste of their wonderful minds and potential. So this woman—and many like her—had taken to the marketplace and made themselves rich by pursuing their careers. The journalists told this mother, "It was a lie. What you have is the only thing that is real. I would trade everything I have to become what you are."

Young women, don't drink from the waters of the

world. They are poisoned; they would mislead you. The prophets have instructed you to marry someone loving and righteous, someone who has decided, as you have, to serve the Lord first and who desires also to have a family and raise children up to the Lord.

Another lie that floats down the gutters of the world is that we should seek our own interests first. An attitude of "Me first, me best, and if I can yell the loudest, me wins" chokes the halls and classrooms of our schools, our quorums, and our classes at church. Competition motivates and can be productive, but the world has become cutthroat, and that mentality leads in the extreme to the drive-by shootings that are becoming so commonplace now. How did those vicious people ever get to that place? Did they fail to brush away the flies of hatred that have ended up blinding them?

Many of us try to make decisions without the benefit of the spiritual guidance that may be found through prayer. Is prayer a wall or a window for you? When you fail to get an answer to your prayers, do you blame the silence on the "mood" of Heavenly Father rather than on your own lack of preparation? The Spirit often whispers to us—it seldom shouts. By ignoring its whisperings too long, we can ultimately lose the ability to hear the whisperings at all.

Try an experiment with me. Tonight, when you kneel down to pray, ask Heavenly Father to tell you something specific that you can do to be a more loving son or daughter. Ask, how can I be a better son/daughter to my mom? To my dad? What can I do to be a better brother/sister to my brother or sister? Stick in their name. Then listen. Write down the words that come to your mind. Then follow your feelings. Demonstrate to Heavenly Father that you want to hear—that you want to practice listening to and obeying His voice.

As you open your heart to instruction from the Spirit, it

will flow more and more freely. Soon it will come unbidden, even in the middle of the day and moment by moment. If you pray every morning for instruction, and then at night you "report back in" with the result of your actions, and ask for further instruction, your partnership with God will build. Other questions you might want to ask could be: What sin is keeping me from being a better son/daughter to thee, Father? He will tell you. Fix it. Whom can I serve today? What can I do to lighten so and so's load? They seemed a little upset. Is there something I can do? Listen. Write it down. Do it. Report back. There is nothing irreverent about using paper and pencil to record impressions received during your prayers.

A much-respected young friend of our family came to visit us one weekend just after he had turned eighteen. One of my daughters had been struggling to get over a recurring bout of strep throat and was on her third bottle of antibiotics. It was not going away. She had also jammed her fourth finger playing basketball and thought it might be broken. Because it was the weekend, we simply taped the finger into a splint and waited for the doctor's office to open on Monday.

These problems were coincidental to Jeremy's visit. While he was in our home, however, this same daughter asked the missionaries to give her a blessing. She was tired of being sick, and the medicine wasn't doing much good. The elders happened to be in our home for dinner, and they were more than willing to use their priesthood in her behalf. The senior companion, aware that Jeremy had recently been ordained an elder, invited him to seal the anointing and to give the blessing.

This was a new opportunity for him, but he humbly agreed to do so. I think I have never heard so brief a blessing. Jeremy told her that she knew the things in her life that she needed to change; that Heavenly Father wanted her to work on those. Then he commanded her body to be whole in the name of the Savior and ended the blessing. Jeremy is a serene but powerful young man. When you look into his eyes there is power. He is not flashy; not particularly delicious to look at, although his righteousness is like a magnet. I feel completely at peace when I am in his presence. That night I came to understand more specifically, why.

The next morning Jeremy left very early, before any of the children were up. When Becca came into the kitchen she had removed the splint from her finger. "Look, Mom," she said, wiggling it easily and painlessly. The soreness in her throat was also gone. Perhaps it is coincidental, but five years have passed, and she has never had strep throat since.

I called Jeremy on the telephone and asked a very humble question. "How did you know what to say in your blessing?" He replied quietly, "I always [notice that this was not the first time this young man had prayed] clear my mind of all thoughts and wait for the first thing to enter. That is what I say." He and his Father in Heaven had a practiced partnership. Flies did not land in this young man's eyes. He kept himself clean, prayed, read his scriptures, and tried to be good. That is the prescription for spiritual health.

If we become accustomed to them, the flies in our eyes that blind us become easy to ignore. May I plead with you to brush them away—to focus on the steps required to live with the Spirit and be guided by the Light. Read the scriptures every day—more than just a random verse or two. Start at the beginning of a book, preferably the Book of Mormon, and keep going until you finish it; then start over. do this every day until you die. If you don't like to read, there are inexpensive tapes of the entire Book of Mormon. The reader has a great voice, and you can stick a tape into the stereo in your car and have a great companion on your roadtrips.

My first awareness of the truth of the gospel was based

on the Book of Mormon. I love it. I love Joseph Smith and am in awe of the price he paid that we might have the precious book. I am grateful for those friends along the path in my life who have reached out to me and lifted me when I was struggling. This is a beautiful life we have been given. Reach out. Listen to the Spirit. Seek to keep yourself unspotted from the world. That is how you brush those flies away.

Kathryn Smith is the single mother of four children and a middle school teacher of English and French. She has been an early-morning seminary instructor and has had such diverse experiences as studying at the University of Grenoble in France and teaching Chinese cooking at the University of New Mexico. A world traveler, who once toured around the world in ninety days, Kathryn is interested in the theater, writing, horseback riding, and raising dachshunds.

26

"FROG KISSIN'"
LIFTING THE HANDS THAT HANG DOWN
AND STRENGTHENING THE FEEBLE KNEES

A . D A V I D   T H O M A S

Well if you've never been a Frog Kissin'—
Then you don't know what you've been missin'—
There's a world of opportunity under each and every
    log.
If you've never been a charm breaker
And if you've never been a handsome prince maker
Just slow down, turn around, bend down, and kiss
    you a frog.
        —*from* Frog Kissin' *by Chet Atkins*

We all know the classic story. A young princess has the courage to plant a kiss on the warty face of a big green frog and thereby magically transforms him into a handsome prince. A fairy tale for sure, but it has a major thread of truth running through it—we can transform people through kindness. It happens all the time.

One of my children, my son Michael, is a gentle man. In the world of rough and tumble boys, as an artist and a musician, he didn't always fit in. He could play a good game of basketball and always had lots of guy friends, but he was a gentle, not a "macho" man. There is something needlessly mean about little boys growing up. For some boys, this results in a lot of pushing and bruising. Some boys like it. They even seem to need it, but Michael didn't. He had his art and his music. Now, lots of guys don't have music and art. In fact, pushing and shoving is all some boys have. It was such a group of boys who singled out Michael.

Every day (while growing up) Mike would have a bout with these artless little boys, and he would quietly "take it." Some thought he was chicken, but he just wasn't into pushing and hurting. Michael had gentility. He also had music and art.

Now, Michael had friends who recognized his talents. His friends encouraged him to practice, and when the time came, they encouraged him to display what he could do. He entered art contests and won. He tried out for plays and got parts. And then he went for the ultimate test of his courage—he would display his talent to the kids at junior high. Michael would sing and dance.

He practiced for weeks. He would be the first to perform in the talent show. The curtain went up. A whaling Chuck Berry guitar put down the opening licks, and the spotlight hit Mike:

> *Way down in Louisiana, close to New Orleans*
> *Way back up in the woods among the evergreens*
> *There stood a log cabin made of earth and wood*
> *Where lived a country boy, name of Johnny B.*
> *   Goode.*
> *Never ever learned to read or write so well*
> *But he could play a guitar just like ringin' a bell*
> *Go, Go, Go, Johnny Go!*
> *   —from* Johnny B. Goode *by Chuck Berry*

The room exploded. Only a few people knew this Michael. Most of the kids knew him as the guy who let the little boys pound on him. Everyone was clapping their hands and swaying. Some were on their feet dancing. Mike was all over the stage—a dancing and singing machine. He finished. The audience gasped for air and then exploded again. A standing ovation. Even the kids who had picked on him were yelling and screaming. Now they had seen, and now they knew what Michael had known for a long time. Michael was into art and music and he was good at it. And because there were some few of his friends and family who had encouraged him—frog kissers all—he hadn't given up.

Everyone has to follow the path that Michael courageously took, but a good frog kiss here or there can help. How many people miss their spotlighted mark because no one happens along with the courage to kiss a frog.

"That's Frog Kissin'." Everyone can do it. And God wants us to. Consider these scriptures: "Members should have the same care one for another. And whether one member suffer, all the members suffer with it" (1 Corinthians 12:25–26). "And be ye kind one to another, tenderhearted, forgiving one another, even as God for Christ's sake hath forgiven you" (Ephesians 4:32). "That which does not edify is not of God, and is darkness" (D&C 50:23). To edify means to lift, improve, or enlighten—to help others see the good in the gospel, in life, and in themselves.

"Succor [help] the weak, lift up the hands which hang down, and strengthen the feeble knees" (D&C 81:5).

Have you ever felt unsteady or been a little limp, or felt a little weak at the knees? People who encourage you at those times or who say kind things help, don't they? You could too. Heavenly Father wants us to look out for each other. We are commanded to be kind and speak the words that reveal and heal.

Do you see? We're all in this together. Each of us has a part to give and receive, but if we don't frog kiss, if we don't edify and lift each other, we don't do it the way the Lord has planned it.

Walt Disney was a genius. Once a young visitor to the Disney studios marvelled at all the people Walt had gathered around to help him, and she asked "Well, what do *you* do?" Walt explained that he was like a bumblebee. He would move from one part of the process to another like a bee visiting flowers. He would brush off a little of his visionary pollen at one artist's station while picking up some of that artist's creative input to carry to another artist. Walt buzzed and fussed about until the studio's output would match the vision in his head. You see, Walt Disney was the studio's heart and vision, but the staff was its body, its arms and legs. They drew and colored in the pictures that originated in Walt's mind.

Lots of talented people began their careers with Walt and then left. Walt Kelly (who draws the Pogo comic strip), Hank Ketchum (Dennis the Menace), and Chuck Jones (Bugs Bunny and Daffy Duck), just to name a few. Walt had difficulty sharing the stage. Many talented artists would come and glean from the Disney approach and then leave. But some stayed. And all of them agreed on one thing: "Walt's a genius." But so was Ub Iwerks.

Who was Ub Iwerks? Listen and I'll tell you, and in the story we will see the hazard of failing to be as kind as we should.

Walt Disney loved to draw, and his brother Roy knew of Walt's dream to be a cartoonist. Out of love, Roy began looking for opportunities. An outfit by the name of Pesmen-Ruben was looking for an apprentice illustrator to give a little life and color to their farming equipment catalogues. Walt got the job and in the process met another eighteen-year-old cartoonist—Ub Iwerks.

Honest, that's his name. Ub was an artistic craftsman, a brilliant technician. He could take a simple idea and make it come to life. If the idea was brilliant, he would make it soar. And Walt had lots of brilliant ideas. As the two young artists' relationship developed, Walt was dazzled by Ub's skill and became his eager student. Ub could take a simple illustration of plows and other farming equipment and vitalize it with crowing roosters, sunrises, and barns full of energetic animals. The mundane came to life under Ub's skill, and he could do it so quickly. The Disney flash and the Iwerks brilliance made for an effective and productive partnership, so, when they both lost their jobs, they went into business together—Iwerks and Disney. Two brash but highly talented kids had stepped into their destiny together. Walt was the creative thinker and the boss, and the crew of what was originally only Ub eventually grew into a room full of artists and inkers. Walt would continue to be the idea man, and Ub, with the help of his staff, would take Walt's sketches and turn them into remarkably smooth, moving pictures. Walt stopped drawing altogether in 1928.

With Disney's vision and flair and Iwerks's draftsmanship and expertise, the world of animation was just inches away from some of its finest hours. The phantasma of Disney began to produce. Oswald, and Mickey, the Silly Symphonies, Snow White, and more. And Ub was right there putting flesh on Walt's spirit creations. In their partnership, Ub was always recognized as a significant force, but Walt was the star. It would be a strange but creative marriage. And every aspect of what would one day be labeled "Walt Disney" had Ub Iwerks's signature written all over it. Walt had the vision—Ub gave the vision its fluid form. Walt envisioned Mickey Mouse, but Ub Iwerks actually brought him to life.

And there was a third force—Roy, Walt's brother. He was the money man, waiting just off stage in case they needed some help. This was the genesis of Disney Magic.

Walt was flamboyant and confident, but, being shy and

somewhat tongue-tied, Ub's genius could only be seen in his drawings. His quiet, withdrawn personality stood in total contrast to Walt's cocky, loud, and arrogant style. Their business had its ups and downs. There were some truly dark days. But Walt kept hustling, and whatever Walt could get, he'd share it with Ub. Ub never forgot this, and he was both a loyal employee and friend. Walt knew it and loved him for it. And Walt protected Ub from everything, everything that is, but Walt's jokes.

Walt loved a tall tale, and Ub believed all of Walt's stories. The man never smelled a rat. Jokes and pranks came thick and fast and Ub fell for them every time. Walt never sensed or saw the hurt. Ub just kept his feelings to himself. He was a tender soul and needed far more kindness than Walt was giving. Oh, Walt was never deliberately cruel, but he loved a good joke and Ub was so easy to set up. Walt would lock him in the bathroom, and then ignore his quiet pleading for help. Painfully shy, Ub would finally be forced to scream for help. Everyone seemed to take pleasure in his humiliation.

A favorite joke of Walt's was to send racy postcards with suggestive messages to Ub from women named Lulu or Fifi. Of course, the letters were sent and then intercepted by Walt before they could be delivered and then read for everyone's enjoyment. But for Ub, there was only hurt and shame.

Walt never saw or sensed Ub's pain. After all, these jokes were intended only to poke a little fun and get a laugh. But one joke went way too far. One of the staff, a woman named Margaret, really liked Walt. Ub had revealed to Walt how much he cared for Margaret. Sensing an opportunity for a "great" joke, Walt invited Margaret to spend the evening with him. Then he told Ub that Margaret had agreed to a date with Ub. When his two friends realized they had been tricked, a hidden camera set up by Walt caught Margaret's rage and Ub's humiliation on film. Of course, the practical joke was too good for Walt not to share it. The next day, as the entire staff gathered for lunch, Walt turned the film on. Margaret, still angry, reacted by splashing ink on Walt's sport jacket, but Ub characteristically kept his feelings to himself. One day, there would be a payback. One day, Walt would pay for his insensitivity.

Now, Walt Disney was not a bad guy. He was just possessed by his vision of how things could be. He was looking to set a new standard of excellence and he wanted his name on that standard. As he explained to one young animator, "I'm impressed with what you've been doing, but I want you to understand one thing—there is just one thing we are selling here and that's the name—'Walt Disney.' If you have any plans of selling your name you best leave right now." Walt was the last word and the sun around which the entire creative planetary system rotated, even for Ub.

This approach got Walt what he wanted in animated perfection, but it cost him a lot of friends. One of them was Ub. Someone gave Ub a chance to put his name on the product and he "jumped ship." Sadly, he failed at his only attempt to be independent of Walt. He had the talent and brilliance but not the aggressiveness that was so much a part of Walt's personality. Ub came back and continued to be a major force behind the Disney name. Of the thirty-two-plus Academy Awards and a multitude of other recognitions Disney Enterprises received, Ub earned his share. He'd learned to play it Walt's way, but the friendship was never the same. This fracture cost them both. When Ub left Disney, he sold his twenty percent share in Walt Disney Productions for $1500.00. Today, that stock would be valued at $750,000,000.00. The shock of losing Ub caused Walt to lose his confidence in the loyalty of people. If Ub would turn on him, he figured, he couldn't trust anybody. A bit more give and take and a whole lot more frog kissin' and it might never of happened.

We've got to frog kiss. Heavenly Father wants us to frog kiss. Frog kissing can help each of us discover the best that's inside us. We all mutually benefit when we all get our fair share of praise and credit.

David Thomas is a seminary principal and instructor in Park City, Utah, and an instructor of business at the University of Phoenix in Salt Lake City. Holding a doctorate in education, Brother Thomas has taught in youth and family programs at Brigham Young University. He is the author of There Are No Dragons Out There. *Besides writing, his interests include reading, running, swimming, and traveling. He and his wife, Paula, have six children.*

27

HE HEARD ME!
VERIFYING THAT GOD HEARS OUR PRAYERS

PAULA THOMAS

I was almost six years old when, for the first time in my life, I was led through the big white doors of a newly built church house. Holding on to my hand was my grandmother, whom I would also come to know as an angel in my life. As I have grown older, I have come to realize that a loving Father in Heaven sent her, not only to be my "grandma," but to be a guide for me as I worked to discover that God lives and that there is a pathway back to him.

The first thing I noticed, upon entering the large, impressive building, was the smell. It smelled so fresh and clean—so new. The second thing I noticed was the people. Happiness seemed to surround them. They all seemed so alive and so grateful to be there with one another. As I was led to a large room down the hall, I saw, to my amazement, little tiny chairs just the right size for my short legs. I had never seen such a sight. Without another thought as to what my grandmother was going to do, I broke free from her hand and ran to secure a chair for myself.

As I sat in that Junior Sunday School room I could hardly believe what I was hearing and seeing. I watched and listened as children sang some of the most beautiful songs I had ever heard. I didn't know that children could sing. Then, once again, I was amazed as children wold stand and give a talk, or say a prayer. I found myself desiring to do what they were doing. I wanted to be like them.

As I sat and studied what was going on around me, I felt a new but wonderful sensation. I felt all warm and safe inside (safety being something I hadn't felt very often). The warmth seemed to grow so large it surrounded me. Into my mind came a thought. The thought was, "Listen to what is going on here today because it will become a very important part of your life." While my mind was registering this very large thought for a six-year-old, a miraculous thing happened. My mind answered the thought back, and in my mind I said, "That was my Heavenly Father. He was talking to me." What made this little experience with my thoughts such a miracle to me was the simple fact that I had never heard the name "Heavenly Father," and yet somewhere planted in a tiny part of my brain was a memory. The memory was of a life before this earth life where I must have felt that warm, safe feeling regularly. That feeling is what had prompted the memory, "That was my Heavenly Father."

In my forty-eight years of life I have come to know a couple of things for certain: God is alive and is involved with the lives of his children on earth (you and me). Also, he has not left us alone to blindly find our way. He has carefully chosen people who care about us to help guide us, and he has given us, or made available to us, heavenly gifts to help us find our way back home. If we use these gifts they will help keep us on the path and clarify what it is God would have us do. These gifts, if used, will help us be receptive and open to the messages a loving Father may be trying to send.

In Alma 25:17, the four sons of King Mosiah are rejoicing with their brethren, the Lamanites, who have just experienced a miraculous conversion. "The Lord has granted unto them according to their prayers, and that he also verified his word unto them in every particular." God promised King Mosiah that their sons would be protected, and they were (see Mosiah 28:7). The Lord also led them to people and circumstances where conversions could take place, and people's hearts were softened and changed (see Alma 17:7–12).

Webster's dictionary says that to verify something you prove it to be true or confirm it. It also suggests that when you verify anything, you check on or test the accuracy of whatever the question or circumstance may be. Our Heavenly Father uses this process in our lives to communicate with us. He uses it in different ways and it always comes through the gift and power of the Holy Ghost. "God . . . knowest thy thoughts and the intents of thy heart" (D&C 6:16). Because of this knowledge, God will speak to us in words and circumstances that are unique to us personally and individually.

My first experience with this kind of communication took place when my grandmother took me to church for the first time. As I sat in that classroom on that little chair and watched what I perceived to be miracles take place, my heart was softened. The experience prepared me enough to hear with my spirit a message that would be remembered and used all the rest of my life. The need was there, the desire was there, my heart was where it needed to be, and God used that moment.

In section 6 of the Doctrine and Covenants, Joseph Smith and Oliver Cowdery received a revelation. In this revelation, the Lord expressed his love for Oliver. He told Oliver that He had blessings in store for Oliver and admonished him to be diligent and faithful. Just in case there remained any doubt in Oliver's mind about the reality of this revelation, the Lord then said to Oliver "If you desire a further witness, cast your mind upon the night that you cried unto me in your heart, that you might know concerning the truth of these things. Did I not speak peace to your mind concerning the matter? What greater witness can you have than from God?" (vs. 22–23).

The Lord took an experience (a simple one) that only Oliver would know about and used it to verify that he had heard Oliver "cry in the night." I can't help but feel that as these words were spoken by the Lord to Oliver Cowdery, he might not have heard the rest of the revelation because in his mind were ringing the words, "He heard me! He heard me!"

As I was growing up, I was troubled deeply by the fact that my mother always seemed to me to be very anxious and unhappy. My greatest desire was to be able to bring her happiness. I would write poems. I would create and sing songs that talked about her beauty and my love for her, and it never seemed to be enough in my eyes. I didn't feel that I had the power to give her the great and wonderful gift of happiness.

Not long after I had turned eight years of age and had been baptized, my Primary teacher taught a lesson on prayer. She told us stories of how prayer worked and explained why it was a very important practice that we should add to our lives. She explained to us that we needed to pray to our Heavenly Father in the morning to start the day and in the evening to close the day. I had one dilemma, I didn't know how to pray. I had never seen anyone in the act of saying a personal prayer. So I hung around after class, and I asked the simple question, "How do you pray?" My teacher suggested some things I might want to say and explained how to begin and end a prayer. That very night I began to say my daily prayers.

One of the desires that I incorporated into each prayer

was the statement, "Please help me find a way to make my mother happy." That sentence was repeated every night and morning in my prayers during all of my growing-up years.

When I was sixteen years old I had the exciting and wonderful opportunity of getting a patriarchal blessing. Our patriarch was out of town so I was sent to a neighboring stake to receive my blessing at the hands of another stake's patriarch. I had never seen this man before and have not seen him since. He knew nothing about me or my family. He laid his hands on my head and began my blessing. In the second paragraph he said, "I have heard the prayers of your heart. You have been blessed with an angel mother who has loved and cared for you all the days of your life. You will have the opportunity, when the time is right, to give your mother the great gift of happiness. You will return with a deep feeling of love this gift that your mother has graciously given to you."

My thoughts locked on this statement. I heard very little of the rest of the blessing. God had verified to me he had listened to my prayers. Over and over in my mind, as the hands of the patriarch lay heavily on my head, rang the words, "He heard me! He heard me!"

As I listened to the verification that the Lord knew me and was aware of my needs, I experienced the same feeling I had felt in church so many years before.

Three years ago, on a cold January evening, I went out my back door to walk to the mail box and get the mail. As I stepped down off my porch, I felt prompted not to walk down my driveway in the shoes I was wearing because the soles were too slick. Until I felt the prompting, I had taken no notice of the shoes I had on. I looked down to see that they were leather shoes with wooden soles. (They used to make skis out of wood!) I then surveyed the driveway. The cement looked wet but not icy. Just in case the prompting was real, I picked up the snow shovel leaning next to the back door to use as a crutch. And I started my trek down my driveway. I took three steps, then I began to slide. The wet-looking cement was coated with black ice. I slid down the entire length of the driveway without having to take another step. I was able to stop only because the driveway met the road. I caught myself and remained standing. I thought "I am woman, hear me roar!" I had skied down my own slope, and I couldn't even ski.

I retrieved my mail and started back up my slope— snow shovel in hand. I had taken only two or three steps when my feet slipped out from under me. I fell face-first onto the pavement. I had been holding onto the shovel for security, but when I fell my mouth landed on the handle of the shovel. I was knocked out for several seconds. When I began to regain my faculties I discovered I was in pain. I also discovered that my front teeth had been knocked out. And I discovered I couldn't get up because of the ice on the driveway. I also discovered something far more important. God, once again, had tried to get involved in the life of Paula Thomas and I hadn't listened. His word was verified quite effectively that evening. I kept saying, "Why didn't I listen!" He had tried to save me from a great deal of pain and from months of inconvenience.

If you have been baptized and confirmed by someone who holds the proper authority, you have heard the words "receive the Holy Ghost." In that ordinance we are given the gift of the Holy Ghost, but it remains for us to do what is necessary to actually obtain this great and wonderful gift. We must soften our hearts and put ourselves in harmony with the Spirit if we are to enjoy its companionship. We need to ask the Holy Ghost to abide with us. The more often we follow the prompting, the sooner we will come to recognize the source.

As you have been reading this article, perhaps you have

been saying to yourself, "I have never had any experiences with the Holy Ghost." Maybe you feel like you have never felt the hand of God in your life at all. I testify to you, even if you haven't recognized him, he has been and is still involved in your life.

The Lord told Oliver Cowdery "Thou hast received instruction of my Spirit. If it had not been so, thou wouldst not have come to the place where thou art at this time" (D&C 6:14). Many times in our lives we have been wrapped in the arms of God's love and yet been unaware that he is even mindful of us.

It is my prayer that you will have God's involvement in your life so verified that you too will gratefully cry, "He heard me! He heard me!"

Paula Thomas has worked for Brigham Young University youth and family programs for ten years. A mother and homemaker, she is completing a degree in family science at BYU. Sister Thomas has served as a ward Young Women president and with the Governor's Conference on Drug-Free Youth and Families. Her interests include reading, writing, and caring for her family and home. She and her husband, David, both wrote a chapter for this book. They are the parents of six children.

28

THE BOOK OF MORMON
AS A TESTIMONY OF JESUS CHRIST

THOMAS R. VALLETTA

Although I have long been converted to the Book of Mormon as an authentic ancient record, I have not always felt its profound power to convince "Jew and Gentile that Jesus is the CHRIST, the ETERNAL GOD" (see the title page of the Book of Mormon). This was something I learned the hard way. Years ago, when my call came to serve a mission for the Lord, I had to formally drop my classes at the school I was attending. The process of getting my various teachers to sign the drop slip went smoothly until the meeting with my history teacher. After expressing surprise that I would drop her class, she inquired concerning my plans. When I proudly exclaimed that I was leaving on a two-year mission for my church, she lit up with excitement. Assuming correctly that I was a Mormon, she gave me some line to the effect that "Mormonism is the American religion." She then cornered me with the proposition that I should speak to her class. To close the deal, she suggested that as a missionary for the Church, I would likely know all about it. How could I refuse?

A few days later, I found myself standing fearfully before my former classmates, being introduced as an authority on Mormonism. As a required survey course in American history, it was a large class of well over a hundred students. I began the presentation by reciting the First Vision account from the missionary discussions. Since that was about all I had memorized, I embellished the story dramatically. I told of the vision occurring on a beautiful spring day, with birds chirping and flowers blossoming. The teacher interrupted with questions that revealed her intense hostility toward the Church. I began to feel very uncomfortable.

I shifted gears to my testimony of the Book of Mormon. I began with Joseph Smith's statement that "the Book of Mormon was the most correct of any book on the earth, and the keystone of our religion, and a man would get nearer to God by abiding by its precepts, than by any other book" (see the "Introduction" to current editions of the Book of Mormon).

My teacher jumped in again, this time shouting: "Most correct! How can you say that?"

Not quite getting it, I simply checked the quote for accuracy and confirmed it.

The teacher, frustrated with my ignorance at this point, exclaimed, "How could the book be the 'most correct' when there have been many editorial changes from the first edition?"

Not realizing that the Prophet Joseph Smith had in mind the teachings, doctrines, precepts, and testimony rather than spelling, punctuation, and typesetting when he described the Book of Mormon as "the most correct book" (see Monte S. Nyman, *The Most Correct Book* [Salt Lake City: Bookcraft, 1991]), I moronically replied: "Gosh, I don't know."

She handed me a facsimile of the original 1830 edition of the Book of Mormon. I examined it and naively blurted out: "Wow, this really is different."

Recognizing that I was getting hammered, I lamely tried to move on to other topics in Church history. The teacher viciously attacked every subject I approached. Even when I attempted to bear my testimony, she mocked it as the emotional last resort of all Mormons. Finally, and way too late, the bell rang. I crawled back to my seat in embarrassment. The students filed by to the exit just staring at me, some with pity and others with scorn.

Soon the teacher approached my seat. Seeing my humiliation, she patted me on the head sympathetically saying: "I hope I wasn't too rough on you."

"Who are you," I sarcastically asked, "Mrs. Korihor?"

She scoffed and indicated that she was sure I was familiar with her writings. She then proudly proceeded to tell me the name of her popular anti-Mormon book. Her feelings were hurt when it became obvious that I did not have a clue as to who she was or what she had written. Finally, she handed me a copy of her highly acclaimed anti-Mormon book and mockingly told me to read it and pray about it.

My testimony was not destroyed, nor for that matter, much damaged. Obviously, my conversion was based upon an answer to prayer, not on some sophisticated intellectual arguments. My teacher's attacks did bother me though. I knew that the Book of Mormon and the restored gospel of Jesus Christ were true, but I sure did not know much about them. My zealous ignorance was humiliating. Unwittingly, I fell right into my teacher's trap by reading her book, over and over. I responded to her attacks in the book. Diligently searching for responses, I consumed as much pro- and anti-Mormon literature as I could lay my hands upon. I became an anti-anti-Mormon (see Carlos Asay, "Don't Be An Anti-anti-Mormon," *Ensign,* November 1981, p. 67). In this misguided zeal, I discovered a couple of important principles: 1) There are answers for every anti-Mormon criticism. In fact, most of the criticisms turn out to be, upon closer examination, evidences in support of the Church. 2) I also discovered that my search was in vain. I was spinning spiritual wheels and going nowhere fast. Satisfaction was not to be found in being anti-anti-Mormon. Although I was spending considerable time in the Book of Mormon, my focus was to thwart my enemies rather than to draw closer to the Savior.

Tools Have Their Proper Uses

While there are many positive uses of the Book of Mormon, it is possible to make the mistake of trying to use it to perform functions it cannot. For example, have you ever been forced to use the handle of a screwdriver in the place of a lost hammer? While it may suffice for a time or two, there is no question that a hammer would work better. If that is the most common way you use your screwdriver then you are likely not getting all you possibly could out of it. The same is true with the Book of Mormon. To use the Book of Mormon for reasons other than its intended purposes is to lessen its effectiveness, power, and impact.

To study and ponder the Book of Mormon in accordance with its purpose is an exciting, spiritual adventure. The Book of Mormon fulfills its purpose on virtually every page. References to, from, or about Jesus Christ and his gospel permeate the book. Research by Susan Easton Black, a professor at Brigham Young University, reveals that there are at least 3,925 references to Jesus Christ in the Book of Mormon in the 6,607 verses into which the book is divided. In other words, the Book of Mormon prophets made reference to Christ's name an average of once every 1.7 verses. By comparison, according to Professor Black, New Testament writers "mention a form of his name on an average of once every 2.1 verses" (*Finding Christ through the Book of Mormon* [Salt Lake City: Deseret Book, 1987], pp. 15–16).

This should not be surprising considering the fact that the Book of Mormon is "Another Testament of Jesus Christ."

The Convincing Power of the Book of Mormon

The number of references to Jesus Christ in the Book of Mormon is impressive, but the real gold mine is in the quality and directness of many of these verses. One of my favorite examples is Nephi's lucid explanation of why he wrote what he wrote: "For we labor diligently to write, to persuade our children, and also our brethren, to believe in Christ, and to be reconciled to God; for we know that it is by grace that we are saved, after all we can do. . . . And we are made alive in Christ because of our faith; . . . we talk of Christ, we rejoice in Christ, we preach of Christ, we prophesy of Christ, and we write according to our prophecies, that our children may know to what source they may look for a remission of their sins" (2 Nephi 25:23–26).

Years ago, I had the opportunity to actually observe the convincing power of Nephi's testimony of the Lord. A major Protestant faith received considerable media attention when they sent missionaries to Utah to help bring the Mormons to an understanding of Christ. They came through my neighborhood early one Saturday morning. While on my way out to the car to head for work, I noticed these gentlemen walking my way. Their appearance gave them away as religious representatives of some sort. They kind of looked like fifty-year-old Mormon missionaries. Anxious to chat with them, I waited by my car. As they approached, I greeted them cheerfully and vigorously shook their hands. Indicating they were doing a brief survey in the area concerning people's beliefs in Christ, they inquired if they could ask me a few questions. I readily agreed.

The first question was, "Do you believe in Christ?"

"Yes," I responded.

Then they asked, "Do you accept him as your personal Savior?"

Again, I answered in the affirmative.

Finally they asked, "Do you believe that it is by grace that you are saved?"

"Yes," I declared.

They looked relieved and relaxed somewhat. "Well, how do you feel living here amongst all of these Mormons?" one inquired.

"Great!" I exclaimed. "I am a member of The Church of Jesus Christ of Latter-day Saints."

Surprised, one responded, "You couldn't be too 'church-going.'"

"Well, I teach seminary, work at Deseret Book Company, go to Brigham Young University, and I am on the high council. Is that 'active' enough?"

They were puzzled. Finally one said, "You sure don't believe what your church does. Mormons don't even believe in Jesus as the Christ, let alone salvation by his grace. They only count him amongst their prophets. Their scripture teaches them about Mormonism, not Christianity. That's why it is called the Book of Mormon."

Now I was the surprised one. To show them that my answers were consistent with the teachings of the Church, I grabbed my Book of Mormon from the back seat of my car and showed them the passage in 2 Nephi 25:23–26. Both of my guests expressed amazement. Excitedly, I showed them other verses to support this jarring new idea—members of The Church of Jesus Christ of Latter-day Saints really *do* worship Jesus Christ. Several points of contention were raised by them during our discussion, but they had clearly lost their fire. Both seemed genuinely surprised to learn that we truly believe in and follow Jesus Christ and that for our temporal and eternal salvation, we rely upon his grace after all we can do.

The doctrine, atonement, and resurrection of Jesus Christ are central to the teachings of the Book of Mormon. There are few, if any, more profound and uplifting writings on the birth of the Lamb of God, on his exemplary life, his merciful and infinite atonement, or on the significance of his resurrection than in the Book of Mormon (see, for example, 1 Nephi 11; 2 Nephi 31; 2 Nephi 9; Alma 40–42). There is no more powerful sermon on the Savior's power to change lives than King Benjamin's address in Mosiah 2–5 or Alma's "born again" discourse in Alma 5. Jacob, the brother of Nephi, summarized the efforts of the Book of Mormon writers when he declared that "for this intent have we written these things, that they may know that we knew of Christ, and we had a hope of his glory many hundred years before his coming" (Jacob 4:4).

Patterns within the Book of Mormon

It is not only through the obvious and direct statements, teachings, and doctrines or even by the incredible number of references to the Lord that the Book of Mormon teaches of Christ. This book takes its readers to Jesus Christ in myriad ways. Often these ways are not readily apparent to the casual reader. To illustrate this point, take a close look at 1 Nephi 1. Jot down a brief outline. Your outline should probably include at least the following: "a prophet prays, has a vision, sees heavenly messengers (apparently including Jesus), receives a book, and is rejected by most of the people" (Jeffrey Holland, "Daddy, Donna, and Nephi," *Ensign*, Sept. 1976, pp. 8–10). The events of this chapter should seem familiar. Compare it with Joseph Smith's experience, or for that matter, many of the ancient prophets. 1 Nephi 1 fits the pattern of the call of a prophet.

Another example is the persistent pattern in the Book of Mormon of what Hugh Nibley has labeled the "Nephite disease" (*Since Cumorah* [Salt Lake City: F.A.R.M.S./Deseret Book, 1988] p. 354). The current Book of Mormon institute manual states: "An ever-recurring theme of the Book of Mormon is a tragic cycle: When the people of God are righteous, they prosper. When they prosper, they become proud and forget God, the source of their blessings. When they become proud and forget the Lord, they fight, quarrel, make war, and commit all manner of wickedness. This wickedness in turn leads to a disintegration and destruction of nations. These calamities bring the people to repentance, they turn to the Lord in righteousness, and the cycle begins again" (*Book of Mormon Student Manual 121–122* [Salt Lake City: Corporation of the President of The Church of Jesus Christ of Latter-day Saints, 1989], p. 107). There are powerful examples of this cycle sprinkled throughout the pages of the Book of Mormon. Early in this dispensation the Lord declared that he gives "a pattern in all things, that ye may not be deceived" (D&C 52:14).

Types in the Book of Mormon

"Types and shadows" which testify of Jesus Christ and the eternal plan of salvation are found throughout the book's pages. A type is defined as "a person, event, or ritual with likeness to another person, event, or ritual of greater importance. . . . True types will have noticeable points of resemblance, show evidence of divine appointment, and be prophetic of future events" (Joseph Fielding McConkie, *Gospel Symbolism* [Salt Lake City: Bookcraft, 1985], p. 274).

An excellent example of a "type" appears in 1 Nephi 16:10. One morning, as Lehi's family arose to continue their journey to the land of promise, Lehi discovered at his tent door a "round ball of curious workmanship; and it was of fine brass. And within the ball were two spindles; and the one pointed the way whither we should go into the wilderness." This spiritual compass worked "according to the faith and diligence which [Lehi's family] gave unto it" (1 Nephi 16:29). They "called it Liahona, which is, being interpreted, a compass" (Alma 37:38). Now, if you think about it, this is an odd story. Why does God work with them this way? Although some readers may dismiss the Liahona as just an interesting physical phenomenon, the Book of Mormon prophets explain its real significance as a type of the words of Christ.

In Alma 37, Alma brings up the Liahona while teaching his son, Helaman. After reminding Helaman that it functioned according to their faith in God, he noted "that these things are not without a shadow; for as our fathers were slothful to give heed to this compass (now these things were temporal) they did not prosper; even so it is with things which are spiritual" (Alma 37:43). Alma then assured his son, "It is as easy to give heed to the word of Christ, which will point to you a straight course to eternal bliss, as it was for our fathers to give heed to this compass, which would point unto them a straight course to the promised land" (Alma 37:44). Finally, he declares: "Is there not a type in this thing? For just as surely as this director did bring our fathers, by following its course, to the promised land, shall the words of Christ, if we follow their course, carry us beyond this vale of sorrow into a far better land of promise" (Alma 37:45). So, the Liahona was not only significant as a part of Nephite history, it actually typified the "word of Christ." Numerous examples of types fill the Book of Mormon (see, for example, 2 Nephi 10:4; Mosiah 3:15; Alma 13:16; Helaman 8:14–15). Conforming with the purpose of the book, they teach and point our minds towards Jesus Christ and the plan of redemption.

Gain a Testimony of Jesus Christ
by the Power of the Holy Ghost

There are many other ways and examples of how the Book of Mormon fulfills its purpose to lead us unto Jesus Christ. But the most crucial testimony of Jesus Christ must come by the power of the Holy Ghost. That point is established very early in the Book of Mormon. Nephi quoted his father, Lehi, as declaring prophetically that after the Messiah was slain, "he should rise from the dead, and should make himself manifest, by the Holy Ghost, unto the Gentiles" (1 Nephi 10:11). Nephi, himself, was informed by a vision that the Holy Ghost has borne record of "the Messiah who is the Lamb of God" from the beginning of the world and that he would bear record of him forever (1 Nephi 12:18).

A testimony based on any other thing can only be temporary. To believe in Christ because of parental guidance and trust can only be considered a positive step toward gaining the strength and desire to receive one's own testimony. To believe because of men's logic or reason is dangerous. Nephi warns that "Cursed is he that putteth his trust in man, or maketh flesh his arm, or shall hearken unto the precepts of men, save their precepts shall be given by the power of the Holy Ghost" (2 Nephi 28:31). Only by the Spirit can we gain a valiant and lasting testimony of Jesus Christ. And then by that same Spirit and by faith in Jesus Christ we can know the truth of all things. This is the message of the Book of Mormon. It is, as Moroni declares, the test given whereby one can know that the Book of Mormon is true. "And when ye shall receive these things, I would exhort you that ye would ask God, the Eternal Father, in the name of Christ, if these things are not true; and if ye shall ask with a sincere heart, with real intent, having faith in

Christ, he will manifest the truth of it unto you, by the power of the Holy Ghost" (Moroni 10:4).

I testify to you that the Book of Mormon is true as a record and true as a witness of Jesus Christ. I know this, not by any logic or evidence manufactured by man, but by an outright and profound answer to my prayers. The Book of Mormon is the "most correct book" in its testimony of Jesus Christ. The closer I live in accordance with the teachings of the Book of Mormon, the nearer I feel to my Redeemer and the more I love him.

Thomas Valletta is an instructor at the LDS Institute of Religion at Weber State University in Ogden, Utah. He earned his doctorate from Northern Illinois University after receiving his bachelor's and master's degrees from Brigham Young University. Brother Valletta serves as a counselor in a bishopric in a university ward. He enjoys books, baseball, and computers. He is married to Charlene Bordonaro, and they have five children.

29

FILLING YOUR TESTIMONY TANK

BRAD WILCOX

I'm trying to prepare for my mission but I have found myself doubting, questioning, and worrying," one young man told me. "I don't even know exactly what I am feeling. It's like there is this huge black hole in my heart. I don't know what's wrong, and I'm scared. Everything I hold dear is slipping through my fingers and everything I used to know for sure, I don't know anymore. Where did my testimony go? Or did I just never have one in the first place?"

Many young people feel like this young man, at one time or another. They question and struggle. They speak about testimonies in light switch terminology—on or off—you have one, or you don't. Perhaps a better analogy would be that of a gas tank. It doesn't sound all that spiritual, but it applies because, besides having marks where the tank is clearly empty or full, a gas tank also registers varying levels in between.

Young people, like my future-missionary friend, usually have stronger testimonies than they realize. The needle on their gauge may not be pointing to full, but it's not on empty either. Just as gas gauges usually have three marks between empty and full, there are also three levels of testimony between faithlessness and a perfect knowledge (see Alma 32). A testimony based on experience could be called the quarter-tank mark. A testimony gained through study might be compared to the half-tank mark. And a testimony received through revelation would be the equivalent of the three-quarter mark.

Testimony of Experience

A testimony of experience is gained as we participate in the Church and interact with other members. We attend Primary, Mutual, and social activities. We go to sacrament meeting where we partake of the sacrament. We worship the Savior and learn of him. We shake hands, sing hymns, give talks, and are surrounded week in and week out by family, friends, and wonderful experiences. We know what it is like to be Latter-day Saints because we have experienced it firsthand.

Even the youngest Primary children can legitimately bear a strong testimony based on experience. Those little ones know better what really goes on in the Church than some adults in the world who publish books, give seminars, and make movies about the subject. Christ taught, "If any man will *do* his will, he shall *know* . . ." (John 7:17; emphasis added). Young people who "do" Church, know much more than they give themselves credit for. Even if they have not yet received an intense spiritual witness, they can still stand and, with President Heber J. Grant, declare in all honesty, "I can bear testimony, *from my own experience* . . ." (Conference Report, April 1944, p. 7; emphasis added).

One year at Education Week, there were several European, non-LDS exchange students who had come with their friends. When I was introduced to them, I asked if they planned to attend the youth dance that evening. One of the boys, a young man from England, said, "I thought Mormons didn't dance."

I assured him that he was mistaken and that if he would

attend the dance with his friends he would have the time of his life. The next morning, the young man from England came running up to me with his report, "I had so much fun! It was the greatest dance ever." His enthusiasm bubbled. He said, "Now I *know* Mormons dance—can they ever dance! What's even better is that everyone was having fun without any alcohol. When I get back to England, I'm going to straighten out all my friends who told me Mormons don't dance because now I know they do."

This young man, not even a member of the Church, possessed a certain level of testimony—though very limited—based on experience. After Education Week was over, I took the liberty of sending in a referral card on this young Englishman. Not long thereafter, I received a letter from the young man: "Dear Brad, I would like to thank you for sending the missionaries out to my home. They have visited three times and I am becoming very good friends with them. It is really good to have them visit. I have attended one of the activities that they have arranged and will be attending another this weekend. I know it might sound a bit weird, but after a visit with the elders, I feel really good, but at the same time I just want to cry. It is a really strange feeling but . . . [also] a warm feeling. Do you know what I mean?" This young man's testimony, based on experience, was growing.

On another occasion, Barbara Jones and I met a Spanish-speaking young man in Texas who had recently joined the Church. Barbara asked him, "What is the first thing you noticed about the Church?"

He said, "There are basketball hoops right in the center of the building—they even decorated them for parties." Then he added more seriously, "It was the special feeling I had the minute I walked through the front doors. I hadn't even met the missionaries or had the discussions, but I knew that there was something unique about this church."

Another young man from the Northwest had only been

baptized a few weeks when he was selected to represent his school in an All-State band and orchestra. He traveled to another city and was housed in a motel room with other young men from across the state.

Late one night the boys were talking. This newly baptized young man told me, "I didn't like what they were saying, so I pretended to be asleep, but I heard them bragging about the drugs that they were taking. One guy was even selling drugs in an elementary school. They spoke of the shoplifting they had gotten away with and the young women they had defiled. Suddenly, one of the guys threw a pillow at me and said, 'Hey, I heard you just joined the Mormon Church.' I said, 'Yeah, what of it?' He said, 'My minister says that you are going to Hell.'"

This wonderful young man said to me, "I don't know a lot about the Church—I mean, I don't know the scriptures or the doctrine very well. But one thing I know for sure is that there is no way that those guys can be talking about selling drugs to little kids and sleeping around with different girls and then tell *me* that I'm going to Hell for joining a church!" This young man's testimony, based on experience, had carried him through.

Most young people who claim their testimonies are on empty are usually sitting on at least a quarter tank and they don't even realize it. They need to open their eyes and see that when it comes to their experiences in the Church, they are already expert witnesses of the truth.

Testimony of Study

One young man from Laramie, Wyoming, told me, "I've always heard people talk about the Book of Mormon and quote from it, and I've read parts for Sunday School. But it wasn't until I really started to read it straight through in seminary that I began to understand what was going on and

how deep it is. There is so much there that I had just overlooked. When I used the cross references with the Bible, I
saw for myself how the books go hand in hand and how
either one, without the other, is incomplete. The more I read,
the more convinced I was that the book could never have
been written by one man alone, especially not Joseph Smith
who was a young man with very little formal education."

A testimony obtained through study is gained as we
learn the revealed word of God and find answers to our
questions. Missionaries know the excitement felt by many
upon hearing the plan of salvation for the first time. Such
investigators sense that all the puzzle pieces are finally fit-
ting together for them. They see things confirmed that they
have always felt to be true. They discover new truths concerning what they had previously thought to be mysteries.

While serving as a missionary in Chile, my companion
and I were walking down a street in the city of Los Andes.
From across the way, a lady leaned out of her window to
shake a blanket and said, "Good morning, elders." She then
disappeared into her house. I was surprised by her greeting. I
walked up to the front door, knocked, and when the woman
answered, I asked, "How did you know our names?"

"I read your tags," she responded.

"We were too far away for you to see our tags. How did
you know who we are?"

She invited us in and explained that she and her husband had been two of the first members baptized in that
community many years earlier. They loved the Church until
other members offended them, and they had begun attending another church. "Now we have been going there for
many years, and we know that the Mormon Church is not
true," she said, concluding her story.

I prodded, "How do you know that for sure?"

"We have a book that proves it," she said, producing a
thick volume, printed in Spanish, that was titled something

like, *Everything You Want to Know about the Mormons.* The book was written of course, as such books usually are, by a non-Mormon.

I glanced through the first few pages. I don't pretend to be a scholar of Church history, but I knew that Joseph Smith did *not* see two angels named Urim and Thummim. "Not all this stuff is true," I said to the woman, "Look, if you want to know everything about the Mormons, talk to us. We'll help you."

That was the beginning. In the weeks that followed, my companion and I watched the members of this family fill their testimony tanks. They became reactivated in the Church. When this mother stood in testimony meeting in the small branch, she said, "I know this is the true Church." And everyone felt sure that, at last, she really did.

Relying on experiences alone was not enough to see this sister and her family through when the going got rough. But now, because she had studied hard and found answers on her own, she could say with President Joseph Fielding Smith, "Do I believe that the Prophet [Joseph Smith] saw the Father and the Son? I certainly do. I know it. I do not need a vision. *Reason teaches that to me*" (Conference Report, Apr. 1960, pp. 70–72; emphasis added).

Although experience and study can be the basis of a testimony, young people must understand that these alone are not sufficient. We can't make it all the way to the celestial kingdom on half a tank of gas. We need to continue filling the tank. Elder Boyd K. Packer said, "No one of us can survive in the world of today, much less in what it soon will become, without personal inspiration" ("Reverence Invites Revelation," *Ensign*, Nov. 1991, p. 23).

We all remember the story of the three little pigs. Each built a house for himself, but the two pigs who chose to build with straw and sticks were sorry in the long run. The wise pig, who built his house of bricks, not only provided for his own security but also was able to offer shelter to the other two. When it comes to testimonies, those who build with the straw of experience or the sticks of study alone will not be as safe and happy in the end as those who build with the bricks of revelation (see Matthew 7:25; 16:18).

Testimony of Revelation

One young woman wrote me the following letter, "In the scriptures it says, 'Ask, and it shall be given you' but I didn't know how literally I could take that. . . . Now, I have asked and an answer was given to me. I have come to know through the Spirit that God really is there and that the Church is true. It wasn't anything dramatic or big. It was more like a good feeling, lots of good feelings put together, like all the Christmases you remember rolled into one. It felt warm. I knew I was in the right place."

The third level of testimony is based on revelation—when *the* Spirit bears witness to *our* spirits. President Joseph Fielding Smith said, "When a man has the manifestation from the Holy Ghost, it leaves an indelible impression on his soul, one that is not easily erased. It is Spirit speaking to spirit, and it comes with convincing force. A manifestation of an angel, or even the Son of God himself, would impress the eye and mind, and eventually become dimmed, but the impressions of the Holy Ghost sink deeper into the soul and are more difficult to erase" (*Answers to Gospel Questions* [Salt Lake City: Deseret Book Company, 1979], 2:151).

One evening, after a testimony meeting for youth held on the BYU campus, I was standing in the doorway of one of the dorms. A handsome young man from California came in, tears streaming down his face, and told me, "I know. I know. I have learned for myself."

I was struck by what he said because it was almost exactly what Joseph Smith said when he walked out of the grove and into his home in 1820. As Joseph leaned against the fireplace, his mother inquired what the matter was. He replied, "Never mind, all is well—I am well enough off." He then said to his mother, "I have learned for myself . . ." (Joseph Smith–History 1:20).

Joseph had received a beautiful testimony by revelation. Yet, even his powerful and world-changing testimony came by degrees. Before the grove, there was the groundwork. Before the pillar, there was the prayer. Before the revelation, there was the reading. Joseph's experiences and study had built the faith, humility, and obedience necessary for him to receive a perfect knowledge of God's existence.

There are no shortcuts. No one gets to a full tank of gas without passing each measured mark along the way, and cars don't run forever on a single tank of gas. Testimonies, like gas tanks, must be filled and refilled regularly. It's up to you. Others may polish the pumps, hang some flags, and even advertise the benefits and blessings of filling your tank. But, when it comes right down to it, the salvation station is strictly "self-service." Without exception, each of us puts gas in his own tank—or, should I say, puts oil in his own lamp? (See Matthew 25:1–13.)

When you feel as though you do not have a testimony, remember that testimonies come in levels. You may already have much more gas in your tank than you realize. Now, it's up to you to do all you can to "fill 'er up!"

Brad Wilcox holds a Ph.D. in education from the University of Wyoming and is on the faculty of the Department of Elementary Education at Brigham Young University. He works extensively with CES in youth and family programs. A frequent speaker at EFY, Brad has written several books and also published his talk "Sex Is Like an Apple" on audiocassette. Brother Wilcox enjoys reading bedtime stories to his four children, and he and his wife, Deborah Gunnell Wilcox, serve together as ward nursery leaders.

30

TO KNOW JOSEPH AND TO FOLLOW HIS EXAMPLE

RANDAL A. WRIGHT

He looked very nervous as he stood at the pulpit to give his first sacrament meeting talk. Nathan, my oldest son, had just turned twelve but he had not asked for help with this assignment. He spoke of Joseph Smith and the trials he endured, including the ultimate sacrifice of his life for the gospel. Several times during his talk, his lip quivered and his voice cracked with emotion. When he sat down, tears were in his eyes. I assumed that the reason he was so emotional was because he was afraid of speaking. After the meeting, we talked about his experience. I asked if he had been afraid. He indicated that he had been a little scared. I then asked if that was the reason that he cried. He replied, "No Dad." He got emotional again and said, "I just knew that Joseph Smith was a prophet while I was talking about him."

Have you discovered the fact that Joseph Smith really was a prophet of God? Have you felt the peace that comes into your life by knowing that God has spoken again from heaven? When we know for a surety that Joseph is a prophet, then we also know that the Book of Mormon is true and that the Lord's church has been restored to the earth. Then we realize that God is our spiritual father and that we are his children.

Being a teenager in our day is not easy. Many of you are experiencing difficult times. Some are dealing with the death of a loved one. Others have felt the pain of divorce, physical handicaps, or perhaps even abuse. High school days can be filled with peer pressure, stress, and put-downs. Would you like help with the challenges that you face?

Let me briefly share with you a few events from the life of the Prophet Joseph Smith that will help all of us live happier and more rewarding lives. He showed us how to live life to its fullest, even under the most trying circumstances. Joseph described what it was like for him to live on earth with these words, "From my boyhood up to the present time I have been hunted like a roe upon the mountains. I have never been allowed to live like other men. I have been driven, chased, stoned, whipped, robbed, mobbed, imprisoned, persecuted, accused falsely of everything bad" (John Pulsipher Autobiography, typescript, BYU–S, p. 7).

How did Joseph Smith deal with the many trials he faced? By looking at a few incidents in his short life, we can see how he coped with difficulties and trials. Perhaps we can be better prepared to deal with the challenges we will have in our own lives by following the example he set.

Keep a Positive Attitude

No matter what difficulty he faced, Joseph Kept his "cheery temperament" and a positive attitude. He once said, "If I were sunk in the lowest pit of Nova Scotia, with the Rocky Mountains piled on me, I would hang on, exercise faith, and keep up good courage, and I would come out on top" (John Henry Evans, *Joseph Smith, an American Prophet* [Salt Lake City: Deseret Book Co., 1989], p. 9).

When you are down and discouraged and things look bleak, will you remember the Prophet Joseph's attitude and remain positive? If you will accept this challenge then you, like Joseph, will come out on top.

Share the Gospel

The Prophet Joseph Smith was a great missionary and seldom missed an opportunity to share the gospel with others. Even while in prison, he told the guards about the Book of Mormon. When he visited Washington, D.C., he told the president of the United States about the restoration of the gospel. Following are a few representative entries from the Prophet's journal:

"Saturday, 26.—Preached at Mount Pleasant; the people were very tender and inquiring.

"Sunday, 27.—Preached to a large congregation at Mount Pleasant, after which I baptized twelve, and others were deeply impressed, and desired another meeting, which I appointed for the day following" (*History of the Church*, 1:422).

Sharing the gospel with our friends brings great happiness into our lives. Most of you attend high schools where opportunities to share the message of the restoration arise. Be like Joseph. Be a missionary for the Lord. Tell those you feel comfortable with about the Book of Mormon and give them a copy. Invite your nonmember friends to your church activities. Many are searching for the truth and will be forever grateful to you if you share what you know.

Set a Good Example

Wilford Woodruff spoke often of the great example Joseph Smith was to him. He once said, "I have felt to rejoice exceedingly in what I saw of brother Joseph, for in his public and private career he carried with him the Spirit of the Almighty, and he manifested a greatness of soul which I had never seen in any other man" (*Journal of Discourses,* 7:101).

Brigham Young was also deeply impressed by Joseph's example. On one occasion he said, "Who can say aught against Joseph Smith? I do not think that a man lives on the earth that knew him any better than I did, and I am bold to say that, Jesus Christ excepted, not a better man ever lived or does live upon this earth. I feel like shouting Hallelujah all the time, when I think that I ever knew Joseph Smith, the Prophet" (*Millennial Star,* July, 11 1863, p. 439).

People inside and outside the Church are watching you. What will they think and say about you? Will they feel like "shouting Hallelujah" because they know you? By setting a good example as the Prophet did, many will look to you when they are searching for the truth.

Appreciate the Beauty around You

Joseph Smith had great admiration for the earth on which we live. He appreciated God's creations and took time during his busy life to notice the beauty around him. A simple journal entry demonstrates this fact. "In the afternoon I rode out with Emma. . . . The peach trees look beautiful" (*History of the Church,* 6:326).

There are many things in our world today that are not beautiful. Great pollution and wickedness cover the earth. The news is filled with reports of violence, prejudice, immorality, and crime. Sometimes, if we listen too closely to what is wrong with our world, we will fail to see the good. As you go through life, will you accept the challenge to notice the beauty around you like Joseph did? Will you learn to cherish the wonderful things that our Heavenly Father has created?

Have Fun with Your Family

The following journal entries give us insight into the Prophet's family activities:

"In the morning I took my children on a pleasure ride in the carriage" (*History of the Church*, 5:369).

"At four in the afternoon, I went out with my little Frederick, to exercise myself by sliding on the ice" (*History of the Church*, 5:265).

"Rode out in the afternoon . . . and afterwards played ball with the boys" (*History of the Church*, 5:307).

You are at a time of life when friends your own age are very important to you. Don't forget to enjoy the greatest people in your life—your parents. Sometimes teenagers and parents fail to realize how short the time is they have left together. A typical sixteen-year-old, for instance, has already spent approximately 85 percent of the time he or she will spend in the home. By age nineteen most young people are on missions or at college and never return home for any extended period. Time together is very short. Make it a point to have fun with your family now, before your time together is over.

Be Quick to Forgive

W. W. Phelps was a very dear friend of Joseph Smith's. Unfortunately, he apostatized while living in Missouri, turning against the Church and the Prophet. His actions resulted in the suffering of many of the Saints, including Joseph. Later he wrote to the Prophet to ask forgiveness and to request reinstatement into the Church. Brother Phelps's defection hurt Joseph deeply, but he wrote the following reply:

You may in some measure realize what my feelings, as well as Elder Rigdon's and Brother Hyrum's were, when we read your letter—truly our hearts were melted into tenderness and compassion when we ascertained your resolves. . . .

Believing your confession to be real, and your repentance genuine, I shall be happy once again to give you the right hand of fellowship, and rejoice over the returning prodigal.

Your letter was read to the Saints last Sunday, and an expression of their feeling was taken, when it was unanimously *Resolved*, That W. W. Phelps should be received into fellowship.

"Come on, dear brother, since the war is past,
For friends at first, are friends again at last."
Yours as ever,
Joseph Smith, Jun. (*History of the Church*, 4:162–164).

People may offend you sometime in your life. It could be that some will be rude and will do things that will hurt your feelings and try your patience. When forgiveness is sought by those who have offended you, be quick to forgive and forget, just as the Prophet did.

Serve Those in Need

Edwin Holden recorded the following incident. "In 1838, after the Church moved to Missouri, Joseph and some of the young men were playing various outdoor games, among which was a game of ball. By and by they began to get weary. He saw it, and calling them together he said: 'Let us build a log cabin.' So off they went, Joseph and the young men, to build a log cabin for a widow woman. Such was Joseph's way, always assisting in whatever he could" (*Juvenile Instructor*, March 1, 1892, p. 153).

Sometimes we get so busy with school and other activities that we forget the more important things in life. One of the most rewarding things we can do is help those in need. We can still play games and have fun, but when we get weary of these things, let's help the widow and others in need like Joseph and the young men did.

Love Your Parents and Show It

Joseph loved his parents dearly and often spoke of them in a kind, reverent manner. He was always close to his mother. He once said, "My mother . . . is one of the noblest and the best of all women. May God grant to prolong her days and mine, that we may live to enjoy each other's society long" (*History of the Church,* 5:126).

The following journal entry demonstrates the love he had for his father: "Waited on my father again, who was very sick. In secret prayer in the morning, the Lord said, 'My servant, thy father shall live.' I waited on him all this day with my heart raised to God in the name of Jesus Christ, that He would restore him to health, that I might be blessed with his company and advice, esteeming it one of the greatest earthly blessings to be blessed with the society of parents, whose mature years and experience render them capable of administering the most wholesome advice" (*History of the Church,* 2:289).

Sometimes youth hesitate to show love to their parents or listen to their counsel. Joseph was a great example of the relationship we should have with our parents.

Love Your Brothers and Sisters and Show It

William Taylor gave us insight into the relationship that Joseph had with his brother Hyrum. "Never in all my life have I seen anything more beautiful than the striking example of brotherly love and devotion felt for each other by Joseph and Hyrum. I witnessed this many times. No matter how often, or when or where they met, it was always with the same expression of supreme joy" (*Young Woman's Journal*, December 1906, pp. 547–48).

Joseph once said of his brother Hyrum, "I love him with that love that is stronger than death, for I never had occasion to rebuke him, nor he me" (*History of the Church*, 2:338).

When was the last time you told your brother or sister that you love them? When was the last time you acted glad to see them after an absence? Some of the greatest friends we can ever have are our own brothers and sisters.

Love Others and Show It

Margarette Burgess tells the following touching story about the love Joseph had for others. "Joseph's wife, Sister Emma, lost a young babe. My mother having twin baby girls, the Prophet came to see if she would let him have one of them. Of course it was rather against her feeling, but she finally consented for him to take one of them, providing he would bring it home each night. This he did punctually himself, and also came after it each morning. One evening he did not come with it at the usual time, and mother went down to the Mansion to see what was the matter, and there sat the Prophet with the baby wrapped up in a little silk quilt. He was trotting it on his knee, and singing to it to get it quiet before starting out, as it had been fretting. The child soon became quiet when my mother took it. . . .

"After his wife became better in health he did not take our baby any more, but often came in to caress her and play with her. When, after a time, the little one died, he grieved as if he had lost one of his own. I remember seeing him embrace the little cold form and say, 'Mary, oh my dear little Mary!'" (*Juvenile Instructor*, Jan. 1, 1892, pp. 66–67).

Life as a teenager is not easy in our day. Temptations are around every corner. It is easy to lose sight of the important things that are sources of living a happy life. By following the example the Prophet Joseph Smith set for us, we can gain strength and become more like the Father and the Son whom he represents. With this strength, we will be able to face the trials of life with courage and happiness.

Randal Wright is an instructor of religion at Brigham Young University. He has served as an area coordinator and director of seminaries and institutes. Randal is the author of Protecting Your Family in an X-Rated World, *and he was founder and editor of* Mormon Sport Magazine. *Brother Wright enjoys speaking to youth, going to waterparks, playing and watching basketball, reading autobiographies, and listening to country/western music. He and his wife, Wendy, have five children.*